How to Buy a Diamond and its National Diamond HelpLine are endorsed by the National Bureau of Fraud Prevention in Washington, D.C.

"Whenever anybody asks me about buying a diamond, I give them this book. It's filled with a lot of common sense, practical advice. Diamond buying can be difficult. This book can help." Rob Bates, Editor, *National Jeweler Magazine*

"This book helps make dreams come true." *Houston Chronicle*

"Get a diamond education!" *New Man Promise Keepers*

"Educate yourself before you make the big purchase." *Money's Worth*

"Inside information on purchasing a diamond." *Library Journal*

"If diamond buying figures into your future...*How to Buy a Diamond*...gets you your money's worth." *Tribune Media Services*

"Expert advice for diamond buyers." *Tribune Review*

"Spending even thirty minutes with *How to Buy a Diamond* can save anyone time, aggravation, and hard-earned money." *Black Elegance*

"A cut above." *Dallas Morning News*

"Takes the intimidation out of diamond shopping." *Mobile Register*

"*How to Buy a Diamond* offers consumers an easy-to-understand crash course in the basics of diamonds and diamond shopping." *Orlando Sentinel*

"The book enables a person to walk into a jeweler's store with confidence and to walk out with the right diamond at the right price." *Argus Press*

"*How to Buy a Diamond*—give this to him early!" *Complete Woman*

"If we didn't believe in the book we wouldn't sell it!" American Museum of Natural History, New York

"Pure genius!" Erno Rubik, inventor of the Rubik's Cube

"Simply fantastic!" Jim Harris, cofounder, Compaq Computers

"He's what people are talking about." *USA Today*

"He knows more about diamonds than I know about romance!" Greg J.P. Godek, author of *1001 Ways To Be Romantic*

"Saved me thousands on my diamond purchase!" Doug Brown, Hoboken, NJ

How to Buy a
Diamond

*Insider Secrets for Getting
Your Money's Worth*

Fred Cuellar

SOURCEBOOKS CASABLANCA™
AN IMPRINT OF SOURCEBOOKS, INC.®
NAPERVILLE, ILLINOIS

Published by Sourcebooks Casablanca, an imprint of Sourcebooks, Inc.
P.O. Box 4410, Naperville, Illinois 60567-4410
630-961-3900
FAX: 630-961-2168
www.sourcebooks.com

This publication is designed to provide accurate and authoritative
information in regard to the subject matter covered. It is sold with
the understanding that the publisher is not engaged in rendering
legal, accounting, or other professional service. If legal advice or
other expert assistance is required, the services of a competent professional person should be sought. From a Declaration of
Principles Jointly Adopted by a Committee of the American Bar
Association and a Committee of Publishers and Associations

Diamond Information Line: 800-275-4047
www.thediamondguy.com

Photograph of Fred Cuellar by Gittings Lorfing
Cover and inside photography by Leeming Studios • 401-941-9459
Media Relations & Marketing: LaTeace Towns-Cuellar

Cataloging-in-Publication Data is available from the Library of
Congress

Printed and bound in the United States of America
VP 10 9 8 7 6 5 4 3 2

Dedication

*This book is dedicated first to my mother and father.
This book would not have been possible without their love and support.*

*Second, I dedicate this book to every man in love and doing his best to
make the love of his life happy by buying the perfect diamond.*

*Third, and most of all, I dedicate this book to the love of my life,
LaTeace. She makes life worth living and I could not imagine a better
companion with whom to spend all the days of my life.*

*Fourth, a special thanks to O. Keith Owen IV for his invaluable
research and editorial assistance.*

Table of Contents

Acknowledgments

LaTeace
Hector & Elvira
Greg J.P. Godek
Alfonso & Delia Cuellar
Alfredo & Jovita Montalvo
George & Betty Woody
Elisa & Knox Wright
Maxine & Clayton Prawl
Sha Shane, Cytinya &
   Clayton Jr.
Rick & Kerry Antona
Neil & Rhonda Malhotra
Grayland Noah
Jose Garcia
Ricky Fernandez
O. Keith Owen IV
Ricardo Calderon
Barry Berg
Emil Jay Greenberg
Miriam Rosen
Houston Astros
Casablanca Press
Lou Lamoriello
Jim Harris

Arlene Ball
Dallas Cowboys
New Jersey Devils
Houston Rockets Players
Marti Boone
Nick Mills
Mr. and Mrs. Ricardo V.
   Antona Sr.
Pierre Lacroix
Colorado Avalanche
Detroit Redwings
Denver Broncos
Dallas Stars
Henry Grossbard
Stan Grossbard
Roula Christie and Ryan Chase
Maria Aramburuzabala
Mr. and Mrs. O. Keith Owen III
Jose Feliciano
Kimberly Johnston

Preface

Buying a diamond may be one of the most important purchases of your life. Think of it. If you are a man, you're probably selecting a diamond to present to your bride-to-be as a shining symbol of eternal love. Only a diamond can say it all: your love for her is clear, pure, brilliant, perfect, and indestructible. If you're a woman buying a diamond for the most important man in your life, the symbolism is much the same. The diamond says, "You are the one."

For most people, the engagement ring is the first—and surely the most important—diamond they will ever buy. Selecting the right diamond, therefore, is a big responsibility. Let's make sure you get it right!

Yes, diamonds are romance, the highest expression of love, glamour, elegance, wealth, and refinement. (No one ever sang, "cubic zirconias are a girl's best friend!") Some diamonds can be seen as a commodity. There are different grades of diamonds, and each grade has a different value. And—very importantly—dealers are trying to make as much money from you as they can. You know the old expression, "A fool and his money are soon parted." Nowhere is that more true than in the diamond market. Diamond dealers can fool you in a hundred ways. Don't be fooled! In this book, I'll teach you how to judge diamonds so that when you make that all-important purchase, you get your money's worth.

Charlie's Gift

One day a few years ago I boarded a jetliner in Houston, bound for New York. When I had stowed my carry-on bag and buckled myself in, I looked over to see who I had for a seatmate. I saw a small, elderly lady, sitting straight and prim in her seat, clutching her handbag and trying very hard not to appear concerned. I guessed this lady had not flown often in her life. I leaned over and reminded her gently that she would have to stow her handbag before takeoff.

"Oh, thank you," she said. "I'm a little nervous, to be quite frank. I've never flown before."

I asked her why she was travelling to New York.

"Well," she said with a sigh, "I'm going to live with my daughter. She's meeting me at the airport. You see, my husband of fifty-five years passed away recently and my daughter doesn't want me living alone."

I offered condolences and, trying to brighten her up, I said she was lucky to have enjoyed such a long marriage.

"Thank you. Yes, I was fortunate. We had a good marriage, and now it seems like the time went by so fast...seems like just yesterday we were saying our vows." She was quiet for a long moment, replaying some cherished moments of her married life, before she returned to our conversation.

"And what about you?" she asked. "Why are you going to New York?"

I told her I was in the diamond business and was going there to close a deal on some diamonds.

"Oooh, diamonds!" Her lined face brightened. "Charlie—that was my husband—always said I'd have a diamond one day. When we got married all we could afford were the wedding bands. Then came the children, and with one thing or another we never did have enough money for luxuries. Every anniversary Charlie would say, 'My dear, next year we'll get you that diamond!' But now there is no next year."

She bowed her head and tried not to let me see the tears, but eventually she had *to dab them away with a handkerchief tugged from the pocket of her old coat.*

In that moment, this sweet woman's tears revealed to me why I was on that plane, sitting beside her. I asked her name.

"Evelyn," she told me. "Evelyn Benson."

"Well, Evelyn," I said, "my name is Fred Cuellar and I just realized that Fate has brought us together. What is your ring size?"

"I—I don't know, really," she stammered. "Why?"

"Because I am here to give you your diamond ring. Charlie had something to do with seating us together. I'm sure of it." I guessed her ring size at about a six; I had a grin sized Extra Large at this point.

"But I can't afford it," she protested. "We never could."

"Evelyn," I told her, "I am not selling you a diamond ring. I'm giving it to you, at Charlie's request."

Well, that made her cry even more, but the tears were happier now, and she gave me a big hug when we parted company at JFK airport.

When I got back to Houston I put together a modest, but very nice, diamond engagement ring and mailed it to Evelyn at the address in upstate New York she'd given me. Putting that package in the mail made me feel like a million dollars. No, better than that.

Six months later I received a small package at my Houston office. When I opened it, I found the diamond ring I'd sent to Evelyn Benson. With the ring was a note from her daughter:

"Dear Mr. Cuellar, I'm returning the ring which you so graciously allowed my mother to wear for the last six months. Not a day went by that she didn't show it to someone, proud as can be. She told people it was a gift from her late husband Charlie (my Dad). I'd never seen her as happy with anything in my life. My mother passed away last week, so I am returning your ring with many thanks for the joy you brought my mother. Sincerely, Jane Adams."

Foreword

by Gregory J.P. Godek

I'm proud to introduce you to Fred Cuellar. He's not only a jeweler, he's an educator. He not only advises the Saudi royal family on their gemstone investments, he also advises guys buying their first diamond engagement ring. He not only runs a cutting house, he's an outrageous entrepreneur. He's not only the creator of the most expensive toy in the world (the $1.2 million 15th Anniversary Rubik's Cube), he's also the creator of simple yet elegant diamond engagement rings. He's not a typical, quiet jeweler. He's a frequent guest on radio and TV, including *The Today Show*. He not only creates jewelry for Harley Davidson, many professional sports teams, and lots of celebrities, he also creates jewelry for regular folks like you and me. He's not only a sought-after lecturer, he's also now a bestselling author. He's not only the creator of the 1996 Superbowl rings for the Dallas Cowboys, he's also the creator of diamond rings that grace the hands of thousands of men and women throughout the world. He's not just any jeweler; he's a maverick who imports his own diamonds. He's not only a creative genius when it comes to jewelry, he's also a sensitive advisor who understands people's feelings as they make a very emotional and meaningful purchase. And, he's not only recognized as one of the world's leading diamond experts, he's also a regular guy.

You'll learn all this as you read this awesome book. You'll also learn how to be a wise and discriminating diamond customer, a person who won't be intimidated by jewelers or diamond brokers—or by friends who think they know all about diamonds. You'll learn how to choose the perfect diamond: one that reflects your love (as well as your newfound knowledge of diamonds!). And you'll learn how to save money in the process. That's a lot to get out of one little book, isn't it?

Fred's book speaks for itself, but I'd like to add my personal guarantee. I guarantee you that the right diamond for your loved one will have a significant impact on your relationship. Diamonds really are the perfect gift of love.

Congratulations on acquiring this book. You will find that it is not only a great investment, but it is also fun to read, easy to understand, and at the same time wise and witty. Enjoy!

~ Gregory J.P. Godek
author, *1001 Ways To Be Romantic*

Introduction

My first experience with diamonds, long before I became a gemologist and diamond merchant, happened for the best of all reasons: I was a young man in love, with a burning desire to offer my bride-to-be a diamond ring and ask for her hand in marriage. It seemed simple enough. Between college classes I would stop by a jewelry store, select a diamond worthy of my beloved, and be on my way. I thought it would be easy—and it was, until I glanced at my first price tag.

After I was resuscitated by the jeweler, I realized this wasn't going to be as easy as I thought. The only "rock" I could afford then was one I could pick up off the ground.

That experience, however, led to a management trainee position with a major jewelry chain, followed by an opportunity to run a jewelry store. Then I became a wholesaler, and over time my business evolved into what it is today, where I can practice what I preach about buying and selling diamonds.

Keeping in mind my own first experience with diamond buying, I have always tried to teach my customers everything they should know before making their purchase. If you were planning to buy a new car or a washing machine, you'd probably read *Consumer Reports* to educate yourself before the purchase, and you'd at least want to kick the tires and look under the hood before putting your money down. That's what this book is all about. It puts you in charge of the transaction by showing you how to tell one diamond from another, what makes a diamond expensive, and what "investment grade" diamonds are. I'll also show you the tricks of the trade, how to avoid shysters—in short, how to get the most for your money.

When I first published *How to Buy a Diamond*, it created quite a stir. Honest diamond dealers—and there are many—loved the book. They said to me, "Fred, we've needed this for a long time, because it's hard to compete with dealers who cheat." The *dishonest* diamond dealers—and there are many of them, too, unfortunately—hated the idea of educating consumers, of revealing the "tricks of the trade." They were the ones who made threatening phone calls, who vowed to put me out of business. "You can't do this," they warned. "You can't let the suckers (that's *you*) see behind the curtain. You'll ruin us!" So of course they threatened to ruin *me* instead, and even went so far as to make attempts on my life! Things got so bad I had to hire a bodyguard to stay at my side for a couple of years. During that time, a lot of people saw me on TV, heard me on the radio, read about me in their newspapers—and bought my book. Becoming well-known made me harder to threaten. Now I'm the jeweler to the Super Bowl Champion Dallas Cowboys and Denver Broncos, and service the diamond needs of nineteen other pro sports franchises. I supply two hundred jewelers with their diamonds and colored stones, supply replacement diamonds for three major insurance companies, and I'm one of a few suppliers of diamonds to the Saudi royal family. But I also provide fine diamonds to private clients, individuals who may be just like you. And what matters most to me is that I've helped thousands of ordinary people get diamonds at fair prices. Helping you get a good deal on a diamond is just as important to me as creating a ring for baseball star Roger Clemens, because it takes me back to when I was a young man in love, shopping for an engagement ring.

Read my book. Call my HelpLine if you have questions. And walk through your jeweler's door with confidence that you'll walk out with the right diamond at the right price.

The Shortcut

Although this book has been written and designed for ease of use, I realize that some of you may be in a bit of a hurry. If you just need a crash course on what quality diamond to buy—or want a quick refresher course on the rest of the book before you head out the door to the jeweler—go directly to chapter 2 and read the section, "What Kind of Customer Are You?" Following the recommendations in that chapter:

- go to a reputable jewelry store
- request the quality you have selected
- get an independent appraisal guaranteeing your selection, and then you are done

Remember, if at any point in the buying process you feel overwhelmed, intimidated, or underinformed, you can always come home and read the chapters relating to your questions. In fact, you might just want to keep this book in the car!

B.E.S.T.

W hat are the four things all consumers need to do to get their B.E.S.T. start before buying the perfect diamond?

Budget—Figure out what you have to spend, and stick to it. One month's salary is a good guideline.

Expectations—Listen to her. Try to understand her expectations (her needs and wants) so you will have a feel for what to pick out.

Savvy—Become savvy! Know what any given diamond should cost and what the best qualities are to wear. Knowledge is power. You will never win the race without training.

Timetable—Figure out when you want to give it to her and do not rush. Haste makes waste. Give yourself enough time to study up, shop around, and plan the perfect proposal.

Chapter 1

The 4 Cs

Clarity, Color, Cut & Carat Size

Diamonds have been prized through the ages for their beauty and rarity. How beautiful—and how rare—they are is determined by the four Cs. First, let's define them.

The Four Cs			
Clarity	*Color*	*Cut*	*Carat Size*
This indicates how clear the diamond is, how free from blemishes and other imperfections.	Diamonds are found in a variety of colors, but in general, the whiter the better.	This refers to not only the shape of the stone, but its proportions, factors which determine the sparkle of the diamond.	This is actually the weight of the stone, not its dimensions.

The price you'll pay for a diamond depends on the four Cs. They determine what I call the fifth C: Cost.

What is a Diamond?

Diamonds are pure crystallized carbon, often containing minor traces of impurities. Diamonds are formed at very high pressure and very high temperatures deep in the earth, and diamond is the hardest natural substance on earth.

Before we learn how to grade the quality of a diamond and determine what it should cost, let me share some acquired wisdom about diamond buying. Don't ever lose sight of the fact that you're probably buying a diamond to make the love of your life happy. If you ask a woman what she'd like in a diamond, she's not going to say, "Honey, I want a one-and-a-half carat, VS1, F(1) in a Class II cut." (If she does, better rob a bank—this woman's going to be expensive!) What she will say is something like, "Honey, I want it to be big, clear, white, and sparkly." It's your job to take those general adjectives, translate them into diamond grades, decide on a stone, and get your money's worth.

Remember: Focusing on only one C will rarely satisfy anyone. You can buy a one-carat diamond for a few hundred dollars if you ignore color, cut, and clarity. The idea is to find a balance.

Also Remember: Never buy a diamond that's already in a setting. The setting makes it almost impossible to examine the stone carefully. Buy the diamond first, then decide what setting to put it into.

The Hope Diamond

*O*ne of the most famous diamonds in history, the Hope diamond, came from India and weighed *112 3/16* carats when it was acquired around *1642* by French merchant Jean Baptiste Tavernier, who was struck by its "beautiful violet" color. He sold it to the King of France, Louis XIV, who had it recut to a *67 1/8* carat stone. The blue diamond passed through ownership by French and British royalty, famed jeweler Pierre Cartier, and U.S. socialites before it was purchased by jeweler Harry Winston along with the *94.8* carat Star of the East diamond, in *1949*. In *1958*, Winston donated the Hope diamond to the Smithsonian Institution, where it quickly became a star attraction.

Resettings and recuttings over the centuries reduced the Hope diamond to its present *45.52* *carats,* *40%* *of its original size. Today, it is set in a spectacular pendant surrounded by sixteen white diamonds, and still attracts countless admirers at the Smithsonian.*

Carat Weight

When you ask someone what they want in a diamond, usually the first thing they'll say is "big." So let's talk first about carat weight.

What is a "carat"? We already know it's a measure of weight, not size, but it's also a word with a fascinating history. Carat is derived from carob, the bean that's often used as a chocolate substitute.

Carob trees grow in the Mediterranean region, and in ancient times a diamond of one carat, or carob, was equal in weight to a single bean, or seed, of the carob tree. In the Far East, rice was used—four grains equalled one carob bean. Eventually the carat was standardized at 200 milligrams (1/5 of a gram), and the grain was standardized at 50 milligrams. Sometimes you will hear a diamond dealer refer to a one-carat diamond as a "four-grainer."

Diamond Factoid

Seventy-six percent of all new brides in the United States will wear a diamond ring; 4.6 percent of these rings will be inherited.

Diamond weights are also referred to in points. One carat equals 100 points, so a 75-point diamond would weigh 3/4 of one carat. (It's not a diamond with 75 points on it, as some people think!)

The "Magical" One Carat

You've no doubt heard or seen the marketing slogans, "A diamond is forever"; "Say you'd marry her all over again with a diamond anniversary ring"; and, "A one-carat diamond is one in a million." These all come from ad campaigns by DeBeers, the world's largest diamond conglomerate. Through their clever marketing, they have established the one-carat diamond as the minimum size to buy.

---

20 Percent Rule

Question: If you're looking at two diamonds of the same shape and quality, how much larger does diamond B have to be than diamond A to look bigger?

Answer: When you have two diamonds of the same shape and quality and want one of them to look noticeably larger than the other one, it must have a minimum of 20 percent more in carat weight. This is known as the 20 Percent Rule.

That's one reason for the substantial price jump when a diamond reaches one carat. Another reason is that a good one-carat diamond is one in a million. But don't be swayed by advertising. There's no magic in size, and the average diamond purchased in the U.S. is 38 points—just over 1/3 of a carat.

Clarity

The clarity of a diamond depends on how clear or "clean" it is—how free it is of blemishes and inclusions, when viewed with the naked eye and with a 10X loupe, or magnifier. Let's define our terms.

Blemishes - Imperfections on the outside of a diamond.

Chip: A little piece missing, caused by wear or the cutting process.

Scratch: A line or abrasion.

Fracture: A crack on the diamond's surface.

Polishing lines: Fine lines on the stone's surface formed during the polishing stage.

Natural: An unpolished part of the diamond.

Extra facets: Additional polished surfaces that shouldn't be there and spoil the symmetry of a diamond.

Bearding: Very small fractures on an edge of the diamond.

Big Diamonds

The biggest diamond ever found in the world is the Cullinan diamond from South Africa: 3,106 carats.

The biggest diamond ever found in the United States is the Uncle Sam from Arkansas: 40 carats.

On May 17, 1995, a flawless 100.10 carat diamond was sold by Sotheby's in Geneva for $16.5 million, the highest price ever paid at auction for a diamond

---

Inclusions - Imperfections inside a diamond.

Carbon: Black spots inside a stone.

Feather: Internal cracking.

Crystal: White spots inside a stone.

Pinpoint: Tiny spots, smaller than a crystal.

Cloud: A group of pinpoints, which may give the impression of a single large inclusion.

Loupe - (pronounced "loop") A small magnifying glass used to view gemstones. Any good jeweler will let you use one, and show you how. They should be 10X, or 10-power magnification, and the housing around the lens should be black so as not to distort the color of the stone. The Federal Trade Commission requires diamond grading to be done with a 10X magnifier, and any flaw that can't be seen under 10X magnification is considered nonexistent.

Here are the clarity grades of diamonds, as established by the Gemological Institute of America (GIA):

Flawless
Free from inclusions and blemishes when viewed under 10X magnification. *Very rare and very expensive.*

Internally Flawless
Free from inclusions; may have slight blemishes when viewed under 10X magnification. *Also very rare and very expensive.*

VVS1 and VVS2 (Very, Very Slightly Included)

Has minute inclusions or blemishes the size of a pinpoint when viewed under 10X magnification. *Rare and expensive.*

VS1 and VS2 (Very Slightly Included)

Has inclusions or blemishes smaller than a grain of salt when viewed under 10X magnification. No carbon, fractures, or breaks. *High quality.*

SI1 (Slightly Included)

Has inclusions or blemishes larger than a grain of salt when viewed under 10X magnification, and these inclusions can be carbon or fractures. Almost all SI1 diamonds are "eye-clean," which means the flaws can't be seen with the naked eye. *Good quality.*

SI2 (Slightly Included)

Has inclusions or blemishes larger than a grain of salt when viewed under 10X magnification, and some of these flaws may be visible to the naked eye. *Borderline diamond.*

I1 (Imperfect)

Has inclusions and blemishes visible to the naked eye. Commercial grade. *Not my taste!*

I2 (Imperfect)

Has inclusions and blemishes visible to the naked eye that can make as much as one-fourth of the diamond appear cloudy and lifeless. *Same as above.*

I3 (Imperfect)

Has many, many inclusions and blemishes visible to the naked eye. Not a pretty diamond. Very little luster or sparkle. *Bottom of the barrel.*

Fred's Advice: Aim for an SI1 diamond. Many people unwittingly buy I1 and I2 stones, but if you shop carefully, you can buy an SI1 stone for the same price that most I2 stones are sold for.

How to Spot Clarity Grades

Note: All plottings that follow show what inclusions and blemishes look like in the different clarity grades when viewed under 10X magnification. **Actual color photographs of inclusions and blemishes can be found at the photo gallery online at my website www.thediamondguy.com.**

In the plotting of the **flawless** diamond, you will notice there are no marks, meaning the diamond has no inclusions or blemishes.

Flawless

In the plottings of the internally flawless diamond, there are no inclusions. But you will notice the slight markings representing slight blemishes.

IF (Internally Flawless)
Scratch

IF (Internally Flawless)
Polishing Lines

In the VVS plottings, you'll see some very minor inclusions and blemishes.

VVS1
(Very, Very Slightly Included)
Pinpoint

VVS1
(Very, Very Slightly Included)
Pinpoints, Extra Facet

VVS2
(Very, Very Slightly Included)
Pinpoints, Extra Facet

VVS2
(Very, Very Slightly Included)
Pinpoints, Scratch, Bearding

Important Note: An untrained person will have a very difficult or impossible time trying to find the inclusions or blemishes in a VVS1, or VVS2, internally flawless, or flawless diamond. Unless you're a gemologist, don't expect to. These top four grades will appear, to the average person, perfectly clean. You should only be purchasing one of these grades if you're buying the diamond for investment purposes. In my opinion, these grades are too high a quality to be worn. That would be like circulating a proof coin: it would ruin your investment.

Diamonds can get abrasions or even chips through normal wear and tear. Some people find this hard to believe. They say that since a diamond is the hardest thing in the world, that must mean it's very tough and cannot be damaged. The truth is that even though a diamond is hard (hardness being a stone's resistance to being scratched, and the only thing that can scratch a diamond is another diamond), that doesn't mean a diamond is tough (toughness being a stone's resistance to breakage). You see, a diamond can cleave in four directions, meaning it can be damaged.

A diamond is the hardest thing in the world, but not the toughest. I don't recommend wearing the highest clarity grade diamonds, because it is possible for someone to buy a VVS, or flawless diamond, and through normal wear lower the clarity grade to a VS or even SI grade.

In the VS plottings, the pinpoints become a little easier to see. Also, we start to see some of the other types of inclusions and blemishes.

VS1
(Very Slightly Included)
Pinpoints

VS1
(Very Slightly Included)
Pinpoints, Bearding, Small Feather

VS1
(Very Slightly Included)
Pinpoints, Extra Facet, Small Feather

VS2
(Very Slightly Included)
Pinpoints, Crystal

VS2
(Very Slightly Included)
Pinpoints, Crystal, Cloud, Scratch

VS2
(Very Slightly Included)
Pinpoints, Crystal, Feathers, Scratch

In the SI plottings, we start to see larger crystals, pinpoints, feathers, and the introduction of carbon.

SI1 (Slightly Included)

SI1 (Slightly Included)

SI1 (Slightly Included)

SI2 (Slightly Included)
Carbon, Crystals, Pinpoints, Feathers

SI2 (Slightly Included)
Pinpoints, Carbon, Feather, Crystals

SI2 (Slightly Included)
Chip, Carbon, Crystals

In the imperfect plottings, I get an opportunity to really do some drawing! You will see every type of inclusion and blemish in these grades.

I1 (Imperfect)

I1 (Imperfect)
Carbon, Pinpoints,
Fracture, Bearding

I1 (Imperfect)
Carbon, Crystals,
Bearding, Extra Facets

I2 (Imperfect)

Pinpoints, Major Feathers,
Carbon, Fractures

I2 (Imperfect)

Carbon, Major Feathers,
Chips, Clouds

I2 (Imperfect)

Crystals, Chips, Clouds,
Carbon, Fractures

I3 (Imperfect)

Chips, Carbon, Major Feathers,
Crystals, Pinpoints

I3 (Imperfect)

Major Feathers, Bearding,
Crystals, Clouds, Fracture Chips

I3 (Imperfect)

Clouds, Crystals, Pinpoints,
Carbon, Fracture Chips

Color

Diamonds come in virtually all colors of the rainbow, from the "beautiful violet" of the Hope diamond to shades of blue, brown, gray, orange, etc. But colored diamonds are very rare and precious. Chances are, all the diamonds you'll see in your diamond shopping will be white or yellow, and the whiter the better. The yellow color in diamonds comes from nitrogen, and as a rule, the more yellow the stone, the less value it has. There's a good reason for this. The yellower the stone, the less sharp and sparkly it appears. A whiter stone lets more light pass through it, making it sparkle and shine. The exception to the rule is the canary diamond, which is a beautiful bright yellow and very expensive.

Over the Rainbow

Yellow Diamonds—Also known as "canaries." Mother Nature's addition of nitrogen atoms sprinkled into the diamonds' lattice (approximately one hundred nitrogen atoms per one million carbon atoms) can cause the yellow color. That, combined with turning up the furnace to temperatures of over fourteen hundred degrees Celsius, agitates the nitrogen atoms in such a way that they dance around the interior of the crystal forming groups which alter the color from colorless to yellow. A top of the line canary yellow diamond can easily run $30,000 per carat.

Pink Diamonds—Pink diamonds have been around for hundreds of years, dating back before the fifteenth century. However, their presence seemed imperceptible due to their scarcity. It wasn't until the opening of the Argyle Diamond Mine in Australia in the 1980s that there was a sufficient supply to market them on a worldwide scale. The color of a pink diamond is due to a microscopic imperfection at the atomic level. No trace ingredient here, but rather an irregular growth pattern at a sub-molecular level. Fancy pink diamonds typically go for $100,000 per carat, with deep pinks easily running the gamut to over $250,000 per carat.

Blue Diamonds—The secret ingredient behind some of the world's most renowned diamonds, like the Hope Diamond in Washington DC's Smithsonian Institute, is boron. Just as nitrogen was stirred into the mix of the canary, boron gas turns a white diamond blue. Blue diamonds are one of the rarest colors of the rainbow, fetching prices from $100,000 per carat to $554,670 per carat, as was paid for a 13.49 carat fancy deep blue at auction in April, 1995.

Over the Rainbow

Green Diamonds—As we continue to climb the scale of the world's most valuable colored diamonds, we find green coming in second place. With prices that range from $500,000 per carat to $750,000 per carat, green diamonds owe their beautiful color to high-energy gamma or neutron radiation (not alpha or beta). The Ocean Dream, a 5.51 carat modified triangular brilliant by Cora Diamonds Corporation, is a classic example of the magnificence of Mother Nature on a good day.

Red Diamonds—Red diamonds are atop the food chain when it comes to the world's most expensive bauble. Ranging upwards to almost $1 million per carat (The Hancock Red set a world record of $926,316 per carat), these rocks aren't for the light of wallet or the impatient. Like the pinks, their atomic structure is imperfect. But if nature hadn't gone amok, we wouldn't have the handful of samples available to study. There are currently clients that have been waiting over fifteen years in line to get the next red when it hits the market.

Some people are more sensitive to the color of diamonds. What may appear slightly yellow to you may look clear to another person, so it will take a higher color grade to satisfy you.

The best way to judge the color of a diamond is to compare it to a master set or a colorimeter. (See "Color Typing" section for more information on colorimeters.) A master set of diamonds has been graded in a laboratory. A colorimeter is a device that grades the diamond automatically without the need of human eye participation.

Either ask the jeweler for a set and compare the diamonds you're thinking of buying with the diamonds in the master set, or have the jeweler place the diamond in the colorimeter to get an accurate grade.

Fred's Advice: Go for grades H or I. Once mounted they'll look just as good to the average person as the higher grades, without costing a bundle. The average diamond purchased in the U.S. is color grade M or N, but the customer is usually told it's higher.

Here's the GIA Color Grading Scale:

D, E, F	Colorless
G, H, I	Nearly colorless
J, K, L	Slightly yellow
M, N, O	Light yellow
P, Q, R, S, T,	
U, V, W , X	Darker yellow
Z	Fancy colors

Even though there are several grades in each category, there are slight differences between the letter grades. D is the whitest and most valuable, X is a dingy yellow and least expensive. Z grade and beyond—colored diamonds—are the rarest and most expensive.

Color Typing

Let's start this piece by asking what might, on the surface, seem like a very simple question: shouldn't two diamonds of the exact same weight, same clarity, same color, exact same proportions, non-fluorescent, same purchase date, same lab grading report date, both bonded with the exact same markup, cost the same? Well, if you ask the labs or check with any of the major price guides like Rapaport, the answer would be a resounding yes.

But pick up your phone, visit your local jeweler, or surf the web and I promise you that you'll find twins that are not the same price. In fact, not only are they not the exact same price but, in some cases, they're not even close. You'll even find two identical diamonds at the same location with totally different prices. Why? How can this be? It's true that not all SI1s are created equal. Some have centralized inclusions, while others have perimeter inclusions, making those SI1s more desirable and valuable. But what about the VSs? I can honestly tell you I've never met a VS diamond I didn't like. So where's the answer? The answer is in the color. What the industry has been aware of, but hasn't shared with the rest of the world, is "color typing."

In the spring of 1999, a wonderful gemological color-grading device hit the market. What I'm talking about is the Gran Fall Spectrum Colorimeter DC2000fs by Gem Instruments. For the first time, we can actually prove that not all Hs, Gs, or Fs are created equal. This new colorimeter is so precise that we can actually break down each color grade into five color types. For example, instead of asking someone what color a diamond is, we should ask what its color and type is. Example: an H can be an H(1), H(2), H(3), H(4), or H(5) (H(1) being the best borderline G, while H(5) is a borderline I color). When you combine colors and types with grade bumping (see page 165), two diamonds can have the perception of being the same, but be from different parts of the rainbow.

When will the labs start breaking down each color into types? Who knows! I know the price guides won't be the vanguard until at least one lab steps up to tell us that not all identical diamonds of the same color are created equal. Naturally an $F(1)$ should cost more than an $F(5)$. But if the labs won't tell you, how can you determine a diamond's color and type without their help? It's easy—have the store run a colorimeter tape and attach it to the appraisal so you will know if your G is a strong G or a weak one. Make the sale contingent on an independent appraisal that agrees with the colorimeter tape. I wish the labs did color typing since the technology is now available, but color typing is just not profitable for labs. Jewelers are naturally going to send their stones for evaluation where they get treated the nicest and the labs are the least critical. That's why there are five European Gemological Laboratory (EGL) or International Gemological Institute (IGI) lab grading reports out there for every one Gemological Institute of America (GIA) lab grading report. The labs may never recognize color typing, but that doesn't mean jewelers don't have access to colorimeters. Knowledge is power. As the buyer, you have every right to know a diamond's color and type. Just ask.

Quick and Easy Grading Tips

Clarity

1) If you can see any inclusions or blemishes with your own eyes, the diamond is no better than I1.

2) With a 10X loupe, if you see any black spots, cracks, or anything larger than a grain of salt, the diamond is no better than SI1.

3) With a 10X loupe, if you can see nothing wrong with the diamond, only then could it be a VS1 or VS2 or higher.

Color

Take a pure white business card. Fold it in half. Lay the diamond table down in the crease. If you pick up any yellow the diamond is no better than K.

More About Color: Fluorescence

Fluorescence is a diamond's reaction to ultraviolet (UV) light. Some diamonds glow in different colors under UV light, and the general rule is to avoid them. If you put a diamond under UV light and it glows strong blue, the diamond may look dull in sunlight. Diamonds with strong fluorescence may be worth up to 20 percent less than diamonds that do not fluoresce. Faint fluorescence that doesn't fog the diamond is okay.

Diamond Myth

"Yellow diamonds are worthless."

Yellow diamonds are worth less than white diamonds, but they still have value.

And if a diamond contains so much nitrogen that it's very bright yellow, it can be worth quite a bit. Bright yellow diamonds are known as "canary diamonds," and they're more valuable than light yellow diamonds.

Corresponding Grading

Corresponding grading means matching clarity grades with color grades. For every clarity grade, there's a color grade that *corresponds*, or makes the best match in determining value.

Diamonds that have corresponding grading sell for higher prices originally, and they also appreciate in value more than diamonds that don't, and therefore have higher resale value. Buying a diamond with non-corresponding clarity and color grades is like buying a pink Porsche: it's okay as long as you don't try to resell it. The market for pink Porsches just isn't as good as the market for, say, red Porsches.

Here's a list of clarity grades and their corresponding color grades. Notice that for each clarity grade there's a *perfect* match, and a high and low color that also works well.

Clarity Grade	Color Grade	Annual Increase in $ Value
Flawless and Internally Flawless	D (Perfect) E (Low)	10.00%
VVS1, VVS2	D (High) E (Perfect) F (Low)	9.25%
VS1, VS2	F (High) G (Perfect) H (Low)	8.50%
SI1, SI2	H (High) I (Perfect) J (Low)	6.50%
Lower	No corresponding color grades	

The value of a stone is always based on the *lowest* clarity or color grade and its highest corresponding grade. For example: let's say you purchased a stone with a clarity grade of SI1 and a color grade of G. You can see above that G is not a corresponding color for an SI1 stone. The SI1-G diamond will cost you more than the SI1-H, but will appreciate no more over time than the SI1-H.

When you *don't* correspond the grades—say, you buy high clarity and low color, or high color and low clarity—you'll never get your money back for the higher grade. For example, an SI1-F would resell no higher than the value of an SI1-H, and a VS1-I would resell no higher than the value of an SI1-I. A diamond that is *not* correspondingly graded could be expected to appreciate 2 percent to 4 percent per year.

Cut

Okay, we're three-fourths of the way to becoming diamond experts! We've learned to check the carat weight of a diamond. We know how diamonds are graded for clarity, and how to look for a diamond that's "clean." We also know that diamonds range from D to X, "colorless" to "darker yellow," on the color scale. Now we'll learn about the fourth C: Cut.

The first thing to know is that the cut of a diamond indicates more than its shape. The cut also determines how sparkly your diamond will be! It's not enough that a diamond is big and clear and white. No diamond can be truly attractive unless it sparkles, and it won't sparkle unless it's properly cut. You can buy a one-carat diamond, graded SI2 or higher for clarity, and rated J or better on the color scale, and it still won't sparkle unless the cut is good.

Diamond Myth

"Diamonds are indestructible."

False! Diamonds are the hardest natural substance known on earth, but they are

not the toughest. There's a difference between the hardness and the toughness of

materials. A sharp blow can certainly damage your diamond.

To understand what I mean, first let's look at some shapes. Diamonds can be cut into a wide variety of shapes. Shown on the following pages are some of the most popular.

Off-Makes

This is the No. 1 problem with diamonds! An "off-make" is a poorly propor-

tioned diamond, and no matter how white, how clean, or how big a diamond is,

it won't achieve maximum sparkle, fire, and brilliance unless it's cut correctly.

Always make sure a diamond is well-proportioned by following the Proportion

Questionnaire Sheet guidelines.

Modern Diamond Cuts

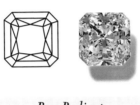

Box Radiant

Round

Marquise or Navette ✻

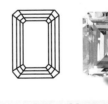

Emerald Cut ✻

Pear *

Quadrillion or Princess *

Standard Radiant

Oval *

* *Diamonds no longer fully bondable effective September 8, 2005.*
See page 116 for more information on fully bonded diamonds.

Old Era Diamond Cuts

The old era or non-modern cuts tend to be off-make, or poorly proportioned diamonds.

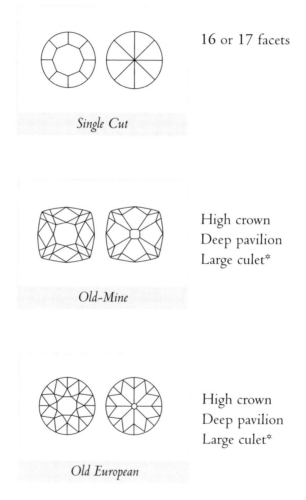

16 or 17 facets

Single Cut

High crown
Deep pavilion
Large culet*

Old-Mine

High crown
Deep pavilion
Large culet*

Old European

*Creates appearance of a hole in the center of the diamond when viewed from above.

Potato Chips and Rough Diamonds?

I know you are asking yourself what on earth could these things have in common. Surprisingly a lot. First, here are the five most common rough diamond shapes.

crystals

rounds,princess
box radiants
standard radiants

makeable

rounds

splittable

rounds and fancy shapes

macle

fancy shapes

flat

small stones,
trilliants and baguettes

Now to the potato chip analogy. Take any bag of potato chips. Firmly pinch both the left and right tops of the bag (right under the glued part). Now pull! See the chips? Smell the freshness (okay, freshness is not really a factor for this example but I'm trying to put you in the moment). Look in the bag. How many perfect chips do you see? Four? Five? One? An unopened bag of potato chips is like the earth before we started excavating diamonds. Now start pulling out the chips! Start with the perfect ones, then the next to perfect ones, then the half-broken ones, and so on and so forth. After you are done pulling, what do you have left? Crumbs! Potato microchip! That's where we are in the world of diamonds now. The bottom of the bag. Those first few perfect and less broken chips (in the diamond world) we call crystals, makables, and sawables. The chip crumbs are called macles and flats. The earth has been heavily excavated since the mid-1860s! The good stuff is gone and the world's miners are sitting on boatloads of macles and flats. They have no choice but to dump them on the market (which they have been doing now relentlessly for the last two years). Since marquise, pears, ovals, Asschers, and emerald cuts are all cut from the bottom of the barrel and since the bottom of the barrel is being dumped over our heads, there is now and will forever be an overabundance of these fancy shapes on the market! As any economist will tell you, if supply exceeds demand, the price falls! And diamonds that can't hold their value cannot be bondable. So, as of September 8, 2005, only box radiants, standard radiants, and rounds are bondable. As everyone knows, nobody wants what everyone can have.

Now that you've had a look at some diamond shapes, let's go over the parts of the cut diamond.

There are three basic parts to every cut diamond: the crown (top), the girdle (around the middle), and the pavilion (the bottom).

The crown consists of a large flat area on top called the table, and a number of facets. As the diamond catches the light, the job of the crown is to split the light entering the diamond into *white light*, which gives the stone its brilliance, and colored light, which gives it fire, or dispersion.

Crown

Table

Girdle

Pavilion

The Parts of a Diamond

The girdle is the thin band around the widest part of the diamond. The function of the girdle is to protect the edge of the stone from chipping (even though diamond is the hardest natural substance on earth, it can be chipped!).

The pavilion has the most important job, which is to reflect the light that passes through the crown back into your eyes. Think of it as a cone lined with mirrors. The light enters the diamond through the crown, splits into white and colored light, and bounces off the facets of the pavilion back up through the crown, where you see it as—*sparkle!*

But to achieve the maximum sparkle—that magic combination of brilliance and fire—the diamond must be well-cut and cut in the proper proportions. The size of the table, the symmetry of the facets, the thickness of the girdle, and the angle of the pavilion must all work together to give the diamond the sparkle you want. Let's take these areas one at a time to see how they affect the quality of the diamond.

Table

The size of the table, as a percentage of the crown, is important because it determines the amount of *brilliance*, or white light, the diamond will reflect. For example, if the table is 60 percent of the diameter of the crown, 60 percent of the light you see will be *brilliance* and 40 percent will be *fire*, or dispersion. *Avoid a diamond with a table area of 65 percent or higher.* It will give the diamond too much brilliance, and not enough fire—and the diamond will look fuzzy or foggy. (The only exception to this rule is square and rectangular cut diamonds that can have a 65 percent table. This includes all princess cuts, asschers, and radiants.)

Here's the formula:

Table area 53–60% = GREAT!

Table area 61–64% = GOOD!

Table area 65%+ = AVOID!*

*except square and rectangular cuts

So, how do you determine exactly what the table area is? It's obviously a measurement that's pretty difficult to make unless you have the right instruments. You may not be able to measure it, but from the given chart you know what it should be—*so, ask the dealer!* And tell the dealer you'll have his answer checked by an independent appraiser, so he might as well tell you the truth.

Sarin & Megascope

In previous editions of this book, from 1991 to 1998, I never made reference to the tools used to measure the angles and percentages in a diamond. Since as far back as I can remember, hand calipers and proportion comparators were all that were available. Most people refer to this type of measurement as H.E.M. (Human Eye Measurement) since good eyesight and a steady hand were required for accuracy. Well, the days of H.E.M. are over. Technology has brought us two wonderful computers that can measure all the proportions of a diamond in less than fifteen seconds and be thirty-five times more accurate. These two new mechanical marvels are the "Sarin" machine and the "Megascope." Literally all you have to do is drop a diamond into these devices' chambers and poof!, all the measurements are posted on a monitor.

Presidium Electronic Gemstone Gauge

The old standby gemstone guage has been thrust into the digital age. Enter the Presidium Electronic Gemstone Gauge. It has a digital display and is accurate to the hundredth of a millimeter.

Facets

The typical diamond is cut with fifty-eight facets, thirty-three on the crown and twenty-five on the pavilion. On a well-proportioned stone, these facets will be uniform and symmetrical. If they are not, the diamond's ability to refract and reflect light will suffer. Furthermore, a poorly cut diamond just won't look right to the eye. The sad fact is, *75 percent of all rounds and 88 percent of all other shapes on the market are poorly*

Diamonds in the Rough

An uncut diamond, as it is found in nature, is called "rough." As a rule of thumb, it takes a three-carat rough to produce a good quality one-carat cut stone.

Often, poorly proportioned diamonds are the result of a diamond cutter trying to make a one-carat stone from a two-carat rough.

---

proportioned! Poorly proportioned stones are more profitable for the dealer, because they retain more of the weight of the "rough" or uncut diamond. That allows the dealer to sell it as a bigger diamond than it should be, and get more money for it, even though it sparkles less. *Look closely! Choose a diamond that's well-cut, even if you have to search a while to find it.*

Girdle

This is a Goldilocks problem. You don't want a diamond with a girdle that's too thin, or one that's too thick—you want one that's just right! The whole purpose of the girdle is to protect the edge of the stone from chipping. A girdle that's too thin doesn't give enough protection. A girdle that's too thick *does* protect against chipping, but it doesn't look good. So you want a diamond with a medium girdle, neither too thin nor too thick. How do you tell? Look at the diamond from the side. If it looks like there's a white chalk line around the middle of the stone, the girdle is too thick. If you don't see any girdle at all with the naked eye, look at the same area of the stone with a 10X loupe. If you can't see a girdle with the loupe, it's too thin.

Shown here are diamonds with (in order) too large, perfect, and too small girdle.

Pavilion

The job of the pavilion is most important of all: to reflect light into your True Love's eyes. I think it's important to understand that when you look at a diamond and see it sparkle, you're not just seeing light reflected off the surface of the diamond. The light enters the diamond through the table and the facets of the crown, passes through the diamond, and is reflected back by the facets of the pavilion.

Here's the important part: The angle of the pavilion for a round diamond must be between 40–41.5 degrees. 40.75 degrees is perfect. For marquise, pear, and ovals, the perfect angle is 40 degrees, but an acceptable range is 39.25–40.75 degrees. For emerald and rectangular cuts, perfect is 45.05 degrees and an acceptable range is 43.3–46.8 degrees.

If the pavilion angle is not exactly right it will not reflect the light properly, and the diamond won't have the sparkle it should. In a round diamond, there's a dramatic loss of sparkle if the angle is even a tenth of a degree above 41.5 or below 40 degrees. In a marquise, pear, or oval, maximum sparkle is achieved with a 40 degree pavilion angle, but the angle can be increased or decreased by as much as three-fourths of a degree with only a 10 percent loss of sparkle. Emerald and rectangular cut diamonds have the widest allowable variance of 1.75 degrees. Each extreme will also cause a 10 percent loss of sparkle.

Buying Tip

If a diamond dealer can't (or won't) answer your questions, assume the worst!

For example, if the dealer can't tell you the girdle thickness, assume it's too thin or too thick. If the dealer can't tell you the crown angle, assume it's below 32 degrees and the diamond is spread-cut.

As I mentioned, 88 percent of fancy shapes are poorly cut. A great many people in the diamond industry believe that if that many are cut wrong, it must make it right. It doesn't! Some even argue that the angle can't be accurately measured on a fancy shape. Wrong! You simply measure the pavilion angle at the diamond's widest point. GIA has relaxed its guidelines for fancy shapes, but you and I have not! Insist on the correct angle, and if you don't get it, keep looking.

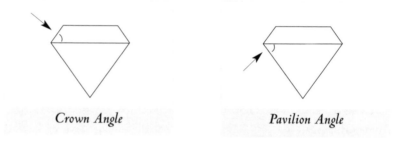

Crown Angle   *Pavilion Angle*

Crown Angle

The angle of the crown is also important, but it doesn't have to be quite as precise as the pavilion angle. *The angle of the crown should be 32–35 degrees.* If it's smaller than 32 degrees, the diamond is what we call "spread-cut." This makes the table area too large and the girdle too thin, and we already know what problems that causes.

If the angle of the crown is *above 35 degrees*, it makes the diamond "top heavy." This results in a smaller diameter, making the diamond look smaller than it really is. The last thing you want is a one-carat diamond that looks like a 3/4 carat!

Warping

Is it possible for a diamond to have more than one crown or pavilion angle? You bet! Now here is the million-dollar question: When a lab report or appraisal is done, which crown and pavilion angle are you given? Are you given the best one? Probably. In an ever-competitive race for your dollar, the cutter, jeweler, and even the appraiser can be caught up in "warping."

Warping is the placement of accurate pavilion and crown angles on a diamond, but solely in one location. The rest of the crown and pavilion angles are off. Warps can be very profitable for a cutter since most labs and appraisal services check for the best measurement, or at least an average, which allows a cutter to push through a Class III or IV (poorly proportioned) diamond as a Class I or II. In purchasing your diamond, ask to have the worst angles measured—if the worst are acceptable, then surely the rest will be as well. Or, ask for minimum and maximum pavilion and crown angles to see the extremes in both directions.

Culet

Finally, at the very bottom of the diamond—the base of the pavilion—there may be a small facet called the culet. If this facet is too large, when you look straight down through the table it will look like the diamond has a hole in the middle. *Make sure the stone has no culet or a very small culet.*

Two Other Important Diamond Measurements

Two other measurements to consider are total depth percentage and length-to-width ratio.

Total depth percentage is a simple, straightforward measurement: take the height of the stone and divide it by the diameter of the stone. For fancy-shaped diamonds, the diameter is measured at its widest part. The answer should be in the 56 percent to 61 percent range. If it's not, it means there's something wrong with the crown angle and/or the pavilion angle, or the girdle thickness. (The only exception to this rule is square or rectangular cut diamonds that can have a total depth of 65 percent.)

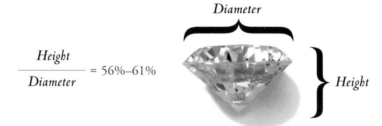

$$\frac{Height}{Diameter} = 56\%-61\%$$

How to Find the Total Depth

The *length-to-width ratio* is used to determine if a fancy-shaped diamond (anything other than round) is well-proportioned. For example, we don't want to buy a marquise that is so skinny it looks like a banana, or one that's so fat it looks like a football.

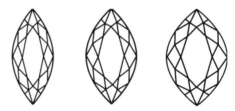

The length-to-width ratio: (from left to right) too long, well-shaped, too fat

42

Pleasing proportions aside, the length-to-width ratio also affects a phenomenon known as the bow-tie. Let me explain. *Fancy shapes are not symmetrical—only a round is.* And because fancy stones aren't symmetrical, they all have a bow-tie—two triangular shadows in the middle of the diamond where light leaks out the bottom.

The Bow-tie Effect

If the length-to-width ratio is off, it will intensify the bow-tie in the stone!

The 65/65 Rule

The 65/65 rule refers to all square- and rectangular-cut diamonds (princess, emerald, radiant, and asscher). A diamond that is square or rectangular cut is said to be well-proportioned if its table percentage and total depth percentage are each equal or less than 65 percent of the width.

For a marquise diamond, the length should be no less than 1.75 times the width, and no more than 2 times the width. For pear shapes, the length should be no less than 1.5 times the width, and no more than 1.75 times the width. For emerald and oval shapes, the length should be no less than approximately 1.3 times the width, and no more than 1.75 times the width.

The 65/68 Exception for Standard Radiants

My first preference in a standard radiant will always be a beautiful 65/65, 1.22 to 1 length to width ratio, 10 percent plus crown height and 45 degree pavilion angle. However, Stan Grossbard of The Original Radiant Diamond Company (his late father was one of my idols) showed me recently that by a slight adjustment of the lower mirror facets on the pavilion it was possible to use a 68 percent total depth percentage on standard radiants with an attractive outcome. The only drawback is that the higher the depth percentage, the more likely the diamond will appear smaller. I have yet to meet a woman who doesn't appreciate a bigger boat in her ocean regardless of the motion. But let's say you are in a tight squeeze and a 65/65 dream rock isn't available and the choice is a 65/68 or nothing. It has been my experience most women would rather have something over nothing.

Final note: 65/65 standard and box radiants are known as flagships.

Diamond Lore

Diamonds have been treasured throughout history for their special qualities, but for most of that time they have been very rare, and available only to the super-rich. Not until after the discovery of large diamond deposits in South Africa around 1865 did diamonds become plentiful enough to be affordable to people of more modest means. In fact, now diamonds are not rare at all! The market for diamonds is carefully controlled by the big diamond cartels to keep prices artificially high.

Proportions Made Easy

GIA originally made it easier to determine if a diamond is well-proportioned by dividing all cut diamonds into four classes. Here is GIA's original Classes of Cut system. Although they have abandoned it for their new cut-grade system, I still think it's the best.

Essentially, *Class I* and *Class II* diamonds are well-proportioned; *Class III* and *Class IV* diamonds are not.

Class I diamonds are investment-quality stones, beautifully proportioned and priced to match. For a stone to be rated Class I is like getting an A+ on a test. Class II diamonds get a straight A on the same test, and if your objective is to buy a beautiful diamond to wear, Class II is fine.

Fred's Advice: Don't go below Class II. And if the jeweler doesn't know what the GIA classes are—move on!

Proportion and Price

Here's an example of what proportion can mean to price: Let's say you go to two different jewelry stores, Joe's and Mike's. They are both offering a round, one-carat, VS1, G(1) diamond.

Joe's Price: $11,154

Mike's Price: $9,054

Immediately, you notice that Joe's price is $2,100 higher than Mike's. This could be because Joe is just trying to make more money on the same quality diamond. But you look more closely at the diamonds, and discover that Joe's diamond is well-proportioned, and Mike's is poorly proportioned. In this case you should buy at Joe's. You're getting your money's worth.

A poorly proportioned diamond is worth as much as 50 percent less than a well-proportioned stone.

One reason for the difference in worth is that it takes a three-carat "rough," which is a diamond as it's found in nature, to produce a well-proportioned one-carat cut stone. But it only takes a two-carat rough to produce a poorly proportioned one-carat stone.

But, you say, one carat is one carat! What's the big deal?

The big deal is that a poorly proportioned diamond will not sparkle nearly as much as a well-proportioned diamond. If a diamond is poorly proportioned, only 30 percent to 40 percent of the light that enters it will reflect back up into your True Love's eyes, while a well-proportioned diamond will reflect close to 90 percent of the light. A woman wants a diamond to be "big, clean, white, and sparkly," and it won't sparkle unless it's well-proportioned.

GIA Classes of Cuts

Class I	*American/Tolkowsky Cut (15% above cost)**
Table %	53–60% of diameter of stone for round, marquise, pear, and oval; 58–64% of diameter of stone for emerald, square, and rectangular
Total depth	59.3–61% of diameter of stone for round, marquise, pear, and oval; 58–64% of diameter of stone for emerald, square, and rectangular
Crown angle	34–35 degrees for round, marquise, pear, and oval; 33–35 degrees for emerald, square, and rectangular
Crown height	13.5–16.2% of diameter of stone for round, marquise, pear, and oval; 11.7–16.2% of diameter of stone for emerald, square, and rectangular
Girdle thickness	.7–2.7% of diameter of stone for all shapes (medium preferred)
Pavilion angle	40.20–41.20 degrees for rounds; 39.25–40.75 degrees for marquise, pear, and oval; 43.8–46.8 degrees for emerald, square, and rectangular
Pavilion depth	42.52–43.57% of diameter of stone for round, marquise, pear, and oval; 47.6–53.1% of diameter of stone for emerald, square, and rectangular

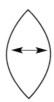 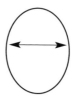

The diameter of any shaped diamond other than round is the diamond's maximum width.

Class II   (cost)*

Table %	53–64% for round, pear, marquise, and oval; 53–65% for emerald, square, and rectangular
Total depth	56–61% for round, marquise, pear, and oval; 56–65% for emerald, square, and rectangular
Crown angle	32–35 degrees for all shapes
Crown height	11.2–16.2% for all shapes
Girdle thickness	.7–2.7% of diameter of stone for all shapes (medium preferred)
Pavilion angle	40–41.5 degrees for rounds; 39.25–40.75 degrees for pear, marquise, and oval; 43.3–46.8 for emerald, square, and rectangular
Pavilion depth	42.31–43.89% for rounds; 41.51–43.1% for pear, marquise, and oval; 47.1–53.1% for emerald, square, and rectangular
Polish & symmetry	Good

Class III   *(15–25% below cost)**

Table %	65–70% for round, marquise, pear, and oval; 66–70% for emerald, square, and rectangular
Crown angle	30–32 degrees for all shapes
Girdle thickness	Very thin or very thick for all shapes
Pavilion angle	Any measurement other than 40–41.5 degrees for rounds or 39.25–40.75 degrees for marquise, pear, and oval; any measurement other than 43.3–46.8 degree
Polish & symmetry	Fair to Good

Class IV   *(50–60% below cost)**

Table %	70% and above for all shapes
Crown angle	30 degrees and below for all shapes
Girdle thickness	Extremely thin to very thin, or very thick to extremely thick for all shapes
Pavilion angle	Any measurement other than 40–41.5 degrees for rounds or 39.25–40.75 degrees for marquise, pear, and oval; any measurement other than 43.3–46.8 degrees
Polish & symmetry	Fair to Good

Cost refers to the price guide in this book.

The Box Radiant and Standard Radiant Exception

With the recent advancements made by radiant diamond company in lower mirror facet arrangements it is now acceptable for box radiants to have crown heights range from 9 percent to 16.2 percent and standard radiants to range from 10 percent to 16.2 percent.

"The 61 Percent Factor"

(In honor of Mark Osborne)

Question: Can a diamond whose crown angle is within tolerance of being a Class I or II, whose girdle thickness is neither very thin nor very thick, and whose pavilion angle is also within tolerance of being a Class II, actually be a Class III?

Answer: Yes, it is possible for the parts of a diamond to meet Class II tolerances but whose total exceeds the "61 Percent Factor." The 61 Percent Factor is when the crown height, girdle thickness, and pavilion depth exceed 61 percent. Mathematically, 61 percent is the magical total depth percentage that a round, pear, marquise, or oval must not exceed in order to remain a Class II (Class I and Class II diamonds are well-proportioned diamonds

---

and Class III and Class IV are not). Once the total depth percentage exceeds *61* percent, it can be proven very easily by taking the tangent of the crown and pavilion angles and their corresponding crown heights and pavilion depths to show how light enters critical angles in the pavilion of the diamond and leaks out to create a fish eye in round, and deep bow-tie shadows in pears, marquise, and ovals.

An avid reader of my book, How to Buy a Diamond, pointed out that I did not send this point home well enough to my readers and to visitors of my website. It is with his encouragement that I correct any omissions or explanations on this very point. With so many laboratories stating that total depths can exceed *61* percent my lack of emphasis on the importance of the "*61* Percent Factor" might have left too many question marks in the minds of some of the readers of my book, website, and columns. The importance of the "*61* Percent Factor" can now be placed in the limelight that it rightfully deserves.

In closing, someone once asked me how important not going over the 61 percent really was in terms of total depth percentage. My response was short and to the point. Imagine that you are 61 steps from the edge of a cliff; how big a deal is that 62nd step?
Note: Class I has an average of 91 percent light return

Class II, 88 percent light return

Class III, 38–39 percent light return

Class IV, approximately 32 percent

Artificial Lighting

In 1955, Gemological Institute of America's (GIA) Gem Trade Lab (GTL) began issuing Lab Grading Reports for diamonds. Concept: In order to assign a value to a diamond, you need to know its quality. GIA hit a home-run by creating a standardized system for grading diamonds (the four Cs; carat weight, clarity, color, and cut). Also, with GIA as an industry watch dog, misgrading or misrepresentation by unscrupulous jewelers might be avoided.

At first, it worked. Jewelers knew that if they had a good diamond, the ideal thing was to send it in for a Lab Grading Report. Then a funny thing happened; others realized there was money to be made in having the power to bless or condemn a diamond's quality, so they started their own labs (EGL, IGI, HRD, AGS, etc.).

The word certificate (see page 136) started being thrown around and it was implied that a diamond didn't have any value without its "papers." What the public wasn't aware of was that the labs do not discriminate as to which diamonds they issue reports on. Any diamond sent in, regardless of quality, got "papers" (a Lab Grading Report) so the jeweler could reference it during the sale.

Diamond Myth

"A fancy-shaped diamond is more difficult to cut and more valuable than a round diamond."

Actually, a fancy shape is no more difficult to cut than a round diamond, and a round diamond is generally the most expensive shape simply because of demand. Sixty-five percent of all diamonds sold are round. The emerald cut can be the least expensive because its shape is most like the natural shape of the rough—the uncut diamond.

While you'll read at great length about the current validity of lab grading reports in Chapter 4, I'd like to focus on a new aspect of Lab Grading Reports that will be incorporated into the reports in January of 2006 by GIA—a cut-grading system.

According to Tom Moses, GTL's vice president, computer-generated models were used to determine the most appropriate set of proportions (for round stones) to increase the amount of sparkle (brilliance plus dispersion) and scintillation of a diamond to the viewer's eyes. After the computer model calculations were done, Human Eye Measurement (HEM) was needed to solidify the predictions. It has been reported by GTL that over sixty-five thousand observations were made to quantify if human preferences matched what the computer light-tracing experiments predicted would be the most optimal way to cut a diamond. *Note: While sixty-five thousand observations sounds like sixty-five thousand people were used in the trial, in fact only three hundred fifty people were used. Every time they looked at a diamond, even if it was more than once, it was counted as an observation. (One million hits on a website doesn't mean one million unique visitors found the site.)* A reported two thousand diamonds were used for the calculations.

Regardless, after GTL's models suggested that the current cutting standards for "Ideal" or "Class 1" were too strict, the three hundred fifty participants couldn't agree with GTL's conclusions on which diamonds were more sparkly. Instead of going back to the drawing board, GTL blamed the disagreement on poor lighting. They then cranked up the lighting until the observations matched the predictions.

This leads me to an important point; the models appear to ignore mathematicians Tolkowsky and Ditchburn's work on proportions and light return in respect to their guidelines for maximum and minimum tolerances. If larger table percentages and larger depth percentages are acceptable, it will allow jewelers to sell what was previously considered a poorly proportioned diamond as a well-proportioned one, as was first reported in the May 16, 2004, article in *National Jeweler* by Victoria Gomelsky: "When the system is introduced, it will profoundly change the way that manufacturers cut diamonds and retailers sell them. The latter are among those who are concerned about the trade's lack of preparedness for such a development. They fear that consumers accustomed to the Ideal Cut will lose confidence in the industry's ability to agree on the issue of diamonds' appearance. But supporters say a third-party evaluation of cut will help people at all points of the supply chain sell diamonds previously considered unsalable."

In the article "Grading the Make" by Rob Bates, senior editor of *Jewelers Circular Keystone*, he writes that the only way GIA could get their numbers to jive was to choose a "standardized lighting environment!"

As you well know, you don't live in a standardized lighting environment! We live in cloudy days and fluorescent-lit offices; sunny days and candle-lit restaurants. Any test to determine a diamond's beauty must consist of multiple lighting environments. The diamond that averages the best under lighting conditions that range from the best to the worst should be declared the winner. That's how a decathlete is declared the world's greatest athlete: not because he's best in one event, but because his cumulative score in ten events ranks him the best.

Well, GIA is undeterred. The exact parameters of GIA's new cut-grading system are laid out in a twenty-six page article (Fall 2004) by Thomas M. Moses and colleagues, "A Foundation for Grading the Overall Cut Quality of Round Brilliant-Cut Diamonds."

One aspect of the new system changes "class" to "category" and adds a fifth category (category five, a.k.a. bottom of the barrel) by sub-dividing Class IV into two new categories.

I just can't sign up for the new far-reaching criteria. The laws of physics haven't been repealed. Reflection and refraction of light from a diamond does not differ today from over fifty years ago when R. W. Ditchburn, mathematician and author of *Light*, did his initial work on diffraction and resolution with noncoherent illumination.

To imply that a diamond can now be cut with crown angles between 27.0 degrees and 38.0 degrees and pavilion angles from 39.8 degrees and 42.4 degrees and still be a category two is misguided. It's true that with enough light and enough movement of the diamond, any rock will have some pop, but GIA's methods—standardized lighting, non-use of metrics for scintillation, equalization of polish and symmetry in classifying with fire and brilliance, over-reliance on subjective human observation, addition of star-facet length and lower-girdle-facet length measurements, and durability criteria—are not credible. While I understand that the jewelry industry will benefit from allowing more diamonds into a new category two, it gives the consumer a false sense of value. Even the new category one extends the acceptable crown angles to 36 degrees and increases the pavilion angle to a maximum 41.8 degrees! Of course the old Class Is and Class IIs will still get the highest marks on this new scale, yet it allows inferior grades to tout the same rankings.

If you accept this new cut-grading system, buying a well-proportioned diamond is going to get tougher, if not impossible.

Super Cuts?

EightStar

Founded by Richard Von Sternberg in 1990, EightStar's mission statement has always been to cut a diamond for maximum light return. This is the only one that probably deserves to be called a true super cut. Practically every single diamond faceted and proportioned from EightStar Diamond Company meets the standards for a Class I. It is important to note, however, that on June 10, 2004, it came to my attention that some lesser-quality diamonds have made it through the pipeline, so each stone must still be double-checked for accuracy.

A.G.S. 000

A.G.S. stands for American Gem Society. This society or club of jewelers got together decades ago to set higher standards for which jewelers should live by. Yada, yada, yada. Anyway, one of these standards is promoting "Ideal" made diamonds. But they have coined their own terminology. Instead of four classes of cut, they have a number scale ranging from 0 to 10. An A.G.S. 000 or 1 is sometimes equal to a Class I; an A.G.S. 2 or 3 is sometimes equal to a Class II. An A.G.S. 4, 5, 6, or 7 is sometimes equal to a Class III, and an A.G.S. 8, 9, or 10 is bottom of the barrel, equal to a Class IV.

Hearts on Fire

Hearts on Fire is a brand name for a type of cut diamond marketed by the company Di-Star Ltd. out of Boston. Their contention is if you cut a diamond to "Ideal" proportions, turn it upside down, and shoot a blue light through it, heart-shaped patterns will be visible through the pavilion, proving it is a well-cut diamond. Big deal! This is just a marketing ploy.

No matter what language you use, A.G.S. 000, Class I, "Ideal" make, Hearts on Fire, it just comes down to one thing: is it well-proportioned or not? I call all these cuts "Super Cuts" because they are perfection personified in cutting a diamond. But with their average 15 percent to 20 percent price premium for an increase in brilliance and dispersion of less than 4 percent, I would stick with a Class II and save the money.

High Definition Diamonds

Fact or Fiction?
Scene: (Also known as "The Set Up")
A young man walks into a jewelry store to buy a diamond. We'll call the young man Ralph, and the store salesperson Buddy.
Ralph: Hi there, I'm Ralph and I'm looking for a round diamond.
Buddy: Hi, I'm Buddy. What kind of round are you looking for?
Ralph: A shy 1ct, VS1, G, Class II, no fluorescence, natural, and bonded.
Buddy: No problem, what faceting arrangement would you like?
Ralph: Faceting arrangement?
Buddy: Well, are you looking for a Modern Era Cut? And if so, which one?
Ralph: Huh?
Buddy: A Modern Era Cut is not only well-proportioned, but

comes in 58–144 facet combinations. A Non-Modern Era Cut would be a single cut with 16–17 facets, or a full cut with 57–58 facets with Old Miners (squared round) or Old European (high crown, sawed off culet) for weight retention.

Ralph: I definitely want a Modern Era Cut, but I didn't know I could get a multi-facet arrangement to my liking. What's the theory behind adding more than fifty-eight facets?

Buddy: Oh sir, it's not a theory, but a proven fact! The more facets, the more brilliance.

Ralph: So a 144 faceted diamond has more brilliance than a 58 faceted diamond?

Buddy: You betcha!

Ralph: Well, if that's true, why would anyone buy less than 144 facets?

Buddy: Personal taste. Some people just can't handle too much brilliance so they pick the facet number that suits them best. Like picking out what wattage you want your bulb for a lamp.

Ralph: Do these multi-faceted diamonds cost more?

Buddy: Oh yes sir! They are very labor intensive and only the finest rough (what diamonds look like before they are cut) is chosen.

Ralph: So how do I refer to these diamonds?

Buddy: Well Ralph, they all have their own names. For example, The Zoe Diamond has one hundred facets and was invented by Gabi Tolkowsky, the grandson to Marcel Tolkowsky who invented the American Ideal. There's also the Leo Cut from Leo Schachter that has sixty-six facets for just a little extra zing! Try to think of these multi-faceted rounds as "High Definition Diamonds." You'll get a clearer, sharper, more brilliant picture.

Ralph: How many types of these "High Definition Diamonds" are out there?

Buddy: Tons, practically, a new one hits the market every day! Let me tell you about...

Ralph: No, that's okay. I'll get back with you; I've got a headache.

Fade to Black

The Facts:

1. The job of a facet with the exception of the table facet is like that of a prism, to break light into the color spectrum, not to increase its magnitude or intensity. Extra-faceted diamonds cannot, I repeat cannot, increase the brilliance or white light return to your eye.

2. All of these "High Definition Diamonds" are trademarked or branded, leaving only a few distributors able to sell them through a contract with the cutting company. (Translation: big cost, no secondary market value due to poor distribution.)

High Definition Diamonds are not bondable as of the publication of this book, leaving you with no guarantees.

High Definition Diamonds may be a fact (they do exist) but they are just slick marketing campaigns designed to get a bigger piece of an already shrinking diamond pie.

So what's the final word on these "High Definition Diamonds"? Leave them alone. The only thing high on these diamonds is their price and their definition is incomplete.

What's in a Name?

The Branding of Diamonds

Whether most people realize it or not, the diamond industry has been going through a revolution over the past few years—from baked diamonds¹, to bonded diamonds², to Color Typing³. And it isn't over yet. It won't be long before the slogan "A Diamond Is Forever" will be replaced with "A DeBeers Diamond Is Forever," or some other name brand or stamp. No longer will any large diamond conglomerate do generic advertising that will benefit the new competitors on the block. With DeBeers's stranglehold of the world's diamond market barely at 60 percent from their good old days of 85 percent, their long held monopoly is over.

Other players like Argyle Diamond Mines, Ekati from Canada, and the Russian United Syndicate are staking their claim to a piece of the polished diamond pie. What this means to the consumer is each diamond syndicate will be stating why its diamonds meet a higher level of excellence then its competitors. Soon you'll be doing the "Pepsi Challenge," but with diamonds. I can just see the ads now. Let me set the stage. A dark candle-lit restaurant; cherries jubilee has just been served; the Dom Pérignon has been poured; then you'll see a dark-haired man with chiseled good looks say, "Darling, you are the light that engulfs my life. Would you make me the happiest man in the world and be my wife?" At that moment he'll pop open a little black box and reveal a beautiful diamond engagement ring. The next thing you'll see is her closing the box and handing it back. "Listen baby, if I'm not good enough for an original DeBeers diamond, the King of Diamonds, then I'm going to have to say no!" At that moment the narrator will say "Why would you take a chance on a copycat when a DeBeers original is where it's at. A DeBeers diamond—when our one of a kind meets your one of a kind!" Oh, brother!!

The thought of this sickens me, but I know it's coming. With the breakup of the DeBeers monopoly, DeBeers has no choice but to start marketing their diamonds as the first, the best, and the original. DeBeers has opened stores using the DeBeers name. Through a massive media campaign, which has already started in the U.K., DeBeers will try to intimate that they choose only the purest, ripest, and most succulent diamonds in the world. (Maybe they'll team up with Sunkist.) They will say that their standard of excellence supercedes the Canadians', the Australians', or the Russians'. Listen folks, regardless of where you dig up a diamond or who mines it, a diamond is a diamond. Slick advertising campaigns may have convinced women from here to Japan that a diamond deserves to be on their wish list, but to say that one brand-name diamond, like the millennium diamond, is better than another of the same quality just because of who is selling it is ridiculous.

Every diamond syndicate will be selling great diamonds, good diamonds, and crappy ones. Don't let the new advertising onslaught that is to come convince you otherwise. Every consumer will still have to go over the four Cs and warranties *on any diamond they might consider buying regardless of what label is stuck on*

the rock. Is Coke better than Pepsi? You decide, but is a DeBeers diamond

better than an Argyle diamond? The answer is no!

1. A baked diamond is a diamond that has been heat treated to remove nitrogen or boron to improve its color. Baked diamonds are brittle and less valuable.

2. A bonded diamond is a natural diamond that is fully warranted by the jeweler and covers breakage, buy back, and exchange.

3. Color Typing is the divisioning of individual color grades into types to more accurately assess the diamond's nitrogen or boron content.

Proportion Questionnaire Sheet (P.Q.S): A worksheet

Now that you know what you're looking for, here's a quick questionnaire that will tell you if a stone measures up.

_____ 1. What is the table?
   53–60% (1 pt) 54
   61–64% (0 pt)
   65%+ (-1 pt)*
For square and rectangular cuts, deduct 1 point only if 66% or over.

_____ 2. What is the crown angle?
   32–35 degrees (1 pt)

Above 35 degrees (-1 pt)

Below 32 degrees (-1 pt)

_____ 3. What is the height of the crown?

11.2% to 16.2% of diameter (1 pt)   *15,6*

Above 16.2% (-1 pt)

Below 11.2% (-1 pt)*

croun Ang 32-35 = 34.5°

_____ 4. What is the pavilion angle?

40–41.5 degrees (round diamond) (1 pt)   *41.4°*

39.25–40.75 degrees (oval, marquise, pear) (1 pt)

43.3–46.8 degrees (square & rectangular) (1 pt)

Anything else (Disqualify)

_____ 5. What is the pavilion depth?

42.31–43.89% of diameter (round diamond) (1 pt)   *44 %*

41.51–43.1% of width (oval, marquise, pear) (1 pt)

47.1–53.1% of width (square & rectangular) (1 pt)

Anything else (Disqualify)

_____ 6. What is the total depth percentage?

56–61% (round, oval, marquise, pear) (1 pt)   *62.1%*

56–65% (square and rectangular cuts) (1 pt)   *62.2*

Above 61% (round, oval, marquise, pear) (Disqualify)

Above 65% (square and rectangular cuts) (Disqualify)

Below 56% (round, oval, marquise, pear) (Disqualify)

Below 56% (square and rectangular cuts) (Disqualify)

---

* *Please See Box Radiant and Standard Radian Exception on Page 50*

_____ 7. What is the girdle thickness?
Medium (1 pt)
Thick (0 pt)
Very thin to extremely thin (-1 pt)

_____ 8. What is the culet size?
None to small (1 pt)
Medium to large (-1 pt)

_____ 9. Is the cutting of the stone symmetrical?
Excellent to good (1 pt)
Fair to poor (-1 pt)

_____ 10. What GIA class of cut is the diamond?
I or II (1 pt)
III or IV (Disqualify)

_____ 11. How is the polish?
Excellent to good (1 pt)
Fair to poor (-1 pt)

For the diamond to pass proportionality it must not disqualify and must have a score of 6+ points.

Chapter 2

Cost

The Fifth "C"

Ok, time to talk real money. The prices listed here are the latest *wholesale* diamond prices at the time this book went to press. These are approximate prices, but because the supply of diamonds is so carefully controlled by the international diamond cartels, prices don't fluctuate very much. You can expect prices to rise no more than 5 percent a year on average.

How Much to Spend

I'm sure you have heard the rule of thumb that says you should spend two months' salary on a diamond engagement ring. Well, let's not forget whose thumb we're talking about here: the diamond cartel's. There is no magic in that guideline—it wasn't given to Moses on a tablet; it's not in the Bible or the Dead Sea Scrolls. It's a marketing gimmick aimed at getting you to spend as much money as possible for your diamond. Don't be bullied by the diamond industry into buying something you can't afford! You should examine your own budget carefully and decide what you can afford.

Even if you do use the two months' salary guideline, if you follow my advice and buy wisely, you'll only have to spend one month's salary to get what an uneducated buyer would pay double for.

Keep in mind as you look through the price chart that the *price per carat* increases with the size of the diamond. For example, a half-carat VS1-G(1) costs $2,788, or $5,576 per carat, while an actual one-carat VS1-G(1) costs $11,154. That's because the larger stones are rarer.

If you do your homework and shop around, you should be able to buy a diamond at these prices. If you have problems, call my HelpLine: 800-275-4047. The HelpLine is in operation 9 a.m.– 6 p.m. (Central Time) Monday through Friday, and 9 a.m.–Noon (Central Time) on Saturday.

Diamond Price Tables

1/3 carat (33 points)

CLARITY

Color		IF	VVS1	VVS2	VS1	VS2	SI1	SI2	I1	I2	I3
D	1	2170	1887	1651	1510	1368	1038	849	613	471	330
	2	2111	1851	1626	1484	1343	1026	837	602	460	319
	3	2052	1816	1603	1461	1320	1014	825	590	448	307
	4	1993	1781	1580	1438	1297	1002	813	578	436	295
	5	1934	1746	1557	1415	1274	990	802	566	424	283
E	1	1934	1746	1557	1415	1274	990	802	566	424	283
	2	1898	1723	1520	1390	1251	979	785	555	413	283

Color		IF	VVS1	VVS2	VS1	VS2	SI1	SI2	I1	I2	I3
	3	1863	1699	1485	1367	1227	967	775	543	401	283
	4	1828	1675	1450	1344	1203	955	765	531	389	283
	5	1793	1651	1415	1321	1179	943	755	519	377	283
F	1	1793	1651	1415	1321	1179	943	755	519	377	283
	2	1770	1615	1390	1284	1143	918	743	507	377	271
	3	1746	1580	1367	1249	1108	895	731	495	377	259
	4	1722	1545	1344	1214	1073	872	719	483	377	247
	5	1698	1510	1321	1179	1038	849	707	471	377	235
G	1	1698	1510	1321	1179	1038	849	707	471	377	235
	2	1639	1451	1262	1120	990	824	693	460	366	235
	3	1580	1392	1203	1061	943	801	682	448	354	235
	4	1521	1333	1144	1002	896	778	671	436	342	235
	5	1462	1274	1085	943	849	755	660	424	330	235
H	1	1462	1274	1085	943	849	755	660	424	330	235
	2	1378	1203	1052	918	824	743	649	424	330	235
	3	1296	1132	1015	895	801	731	637	424	330	235
	4	1214	1061	978	872	778	719	625	424	330	235
	5	1132	990	943	849	755	707	613	424	330	235
I	1	1132	990	943	849	755	707	613	424	330	235
	2	1073	954	907	812	732	685	602	413	330	224
	3	1014	919	872	777	708	661	590	401	330	212
	4	995	884	837	742	684	637	578	389	330	200
	5	896	849	802	707	660	613	566	377	330	188
J	1	896	849	802	707	660	613	566	377	330	188
	2	871	824	779	682	635	588	542	377	319	188
	3	848	801	755	659	612	565	518	377	307	188
	4	825	778	731	636	589	542	495	377	295	188
	5	802	755	707	613	566	519	471	377	283	188

Color	IF	VVS1	VVS2	VS1	VS2	SI1	SI2	I1	I2	I3
K 1	802	755	707	613	566	519	471	377	283	188
2	754	707	671	588	555	498	460	352	267	176
3	707	660	636	565	543	478	448	329	251	164
4	660	613	601	542	531	458	436	306	235	152
5	613	566	566	519	519	438	424	283	219	141
L 1	613	566	566	519	519	438	424	283	219	141
2	588	555	534	496	496	422	399	271	212	141
3	565	543	502	472	472	407	376	259	204	141
4	542	531	470	448	448	392	353	247	196	141
5	519	519	438	424	424	377	330	235	188	141
M 1	519	519	438	424	424	377	330	235	188	141
2	503	511	422	408	408	361	315	227	180	141
3	487	503	396	392	392	345	300	219	172	141
4	472	495	380	376	376	329	285	211	164	141
5	457	487	364	360	360	313	270	203	156	141

E.G. 1/3 carat SI-1 (clarity) H-3(color) = $731

1/2 carat (50 points)

CLARITY

Color	IF	VVS1	VVS2	VS1	VS2	SI1	SI2	I1	I2	I3
D 1	5434	4361	3932	3360	3074	2645	2145	1430	1072	715
2	5165	4253	3859	3325	3057	2610	2110	1412	1055	697
3	4897	4146	3788	3289	3039	2574	2074	1396	1037	679
4	4629	4039	3717	3253	3021	2538	2038	1376	1019	661
5	4361	3932	3646	3217	3003	2502	2002	1358	1001	643
E 1	4361	3932	3646	3217	3003	2502	2002	1358	1001	643
2	4253	3859	3531	3162	2930	2447	1967	1341	983	643

Color		IF	VVS1	VVS2	VS1	VS2	SI1	SI2	I1	I2	I3
E	3	4146	3788	3498	3109	2859	2394	1931	1323	965	643
	4	4039	3717	3465	3056	2788	2341	1895	1305	947	643
	5	3932	3646	3432	3003	2717	2288	1859	1287	929	643
F	1	3932	3646	3432	3003	2717	2288	1859	1287	929	643
	2	3859	3556	3341	2950	2644	2235	1806	1252	912	626
	3	3788	3467	3252	2896	2573	2181	1752	1216	894	608
	4	3717	3318	3163	2842	2502	2127	1698	1180	876	590
	5	3646	3289	3074	2788	2431	2073	1644	1144	858	572
G	1	3646	3289	3074	2788	2431	2073	1644	1144	858	572
	2	3538	3181	2949	2680	2340	2018	1609	1126	840	572
	3	3431	3074	2824	2573	2251	1965	1573	1108	822	572
	4	3324	2967	2699	2466	2162	1912	1537	1090	804	572
	5	3217	2860	2574	2359	2073	1859	1501	1072	786	572
H	1	3217	2860	2574	2359	2073	1859	1501	1072	786	572
	2	3074	2734	2466	2251	2000	1786	1484	1055	786	512
	3	2951	2609	2359	2144	1929	1715	1466	1037	786	572
	4	2788	2484	2252	2037	1858	1644	1448	1019	786	572
	5	2645	2359	2145	1930	1787	1573	1430	1001	786	572
I	1	2645	2359	2145	1930	1787	1573	1430	1001	786	572
	2	2502	2251	2072	1857	1732	1538	1412	983	786	554
	3	2359	2144	2001	1786	1679	1502	1394	965	786	536
	4	2216	2037	1930	1715	1626	1466	1376	947	786	518
	5	2073	1930	1859	1644	1573	1430	1358	929	786	500
J	1	2073	1930	1859	1644	1573	1430	1358	929	786	500
	2	2000	1875	1806	1589	1520	1376	1303	912	769	500
	3	1929	1822	1752	1536	1466	1323	1250	899	751	500
	4	1858	1769	1698	1483	1412	1269	1197	876	733	500
	5	1787	1716	1644	1430	1358	1215	1144	858	715	500

Color		IF	VVS1	VVS2	VS1	VS2	SI1	SI2	I1	I2	I3
K	1	1787	1716	1644	1430	1358	1215	1144	858	715	500
	2	1706	1663	1609	1412	1358	1215	1126	823	697	483
	3	1666	1609	1573	1399	1358	1215	1108	787	679	465
	4	1626	1555	1537	1376	1358	1215	1090	751	661	447
	5	1573	1501	1501	1358	1358	1215	1072	715	643	429
L	1	1573	1501	1501	1358	1358	1215	1072	715	643	429
	2	1520	1446	1446	1323	1323	1180	1055	697	626	429
	3	1466	1393	1393	1287	1287	1144	1037	679	608	429
	4	1412	1340	1340	1251	1251	1108	1019	661	590	429
	5	1358	1287	1287	1215	1215	1072	1001	643	572	429
M	1	1358	1287	1287	1215	1215	1072	1001	643	572	429
	2	1321	1241	1263	1191	1191	1048	984	631	566	417
	3	1284	1195	1239	1167	1167	1024	967	619	548	405
	4	1247	1149	1215	1143	1143	1000	950	607	536	393
	5	1220	1103	1191	1119	1119	976	933	595	524	381

E.G. 1/2 carat SI-2 (clarity) G-1 (color) = $1,644

3/4 carat (75 points)

CLARITY

Color		IF	VVS1	VVS2	VS1	VS2	SI1	SI2	I1	I2	I3
D	1	9652	7614	6971	6220	5791	5255	4719	3003	1930	1179
	2	9143	7480	6810	6113	5711	5201	4665	2976	1903	1179
	3	8634	7346	6649	6006	5631	5147	4611	2949	1876	1179
	4	8125	7212	6488	5899	5551	5093	4557	2922	1849	1179
	5	7614	7078	6327	5791	5469	5040	4504	2895	1823	1179
E	1	7614	7078	6327	5791	5469	5040	4504	2868	1823	1179
	2	7454	6944	6220	5711	5389	4960	4424	2848	1797	1153
	3	7294	6810	6113	5631	5309	4880	4344	2828	1771	1127
	4	7134	6676	6006	5551	5229	4800	4264	2808	1746	1101
	5	6971	6542	5898	5469	5148	4719	4182	2788	1716	1072
	1	6971	6542	5898	5469	5148	4719	4182	2788	1716	1072
	2	6837	6381	5818	5389	5068	4639	4102	2762	1716	1046
	3	6703	6220	5738	5309	4988	4559	4022	2736	1716	1020
	4	6569	6059	5658	5229	4908	4479	3942	2710	1716	994
	5	6435	5898	5577	5148	4826	4397	3861	2681	1716	965
G	1	6435	5898	5577	5148	4826	4397	3861	2681	1716	965
	2	6274	5738	5416	5014	4719	4317	3834	2628	1689	965
	3	6113	5578	5255	4880	4612	4237	3807	2575	1662	965
	4	5952	5418	5094	4746	4505	4157	3780	2522	1635	965
	5	5791	5255	4933	4611	4397	4075	3753	2466	1608	965
H	1	5791	5255	4933	4611	4397	4075	3753	2466	1608	965
	2	5550	5067	4772	4477	4263	3968	3619	2439	1581	965
	3	5309	4879	4611	4343	4129	3861	3485	2412	1554	965
	4	5068	4691	4450	4209	3995	3754	3351	2385	1527	965
	5	4826	4504	4290	4075	3861	3646	3217	2359	1501	965

Color		IF	VVS1	VVS2	VS1	VS2	SI1	SI2	I1	I2	I3
I	1	4826	4504	4290	4075	3861	3646	3217	2359	1501	965
	2	4558	4289	4102	3887	3700	3512	3136	2305	1474	938
	3	4290	4074	3914	3699	3539	3378	3055	2251	1447	911
	4	4022	3859	3726	3511	3378	3244	2974	2197	1420	884
	5	3753	3646	3539	3324	3217	3110	2895	2145	1394	858
J	1	3753	3646	3539	3324	3217	3110	2895	2145	1394	858
	2	3645	3539	3432	3217	3110	2981	2761	2038	1367	858
	3	3538	3432	3325	3110	3003	2852	2627	1931	1340	858
	4	3431	3325	3218	3003	2896	2723	2493	1824	1313	858
	5	3324	3217	3110	2895	2788	2574	2359	1716	1287	858
K	1	3324	3217	3110	2895	2788	2574	2359	1716	1287	858
	2	3163	3056	2949	2761	2681	2494	2279	1609	1233	831
	3	3002	2895	2788	2627	2574	2414	2199	1502	1178	804
	4	2841	2734	2627	2493	2467	2334	2119	1395	1125	777
	5	2681	2574	2466	2359	2359	2252	2037	1287	1072	750
L	1	2681	2574	2466	2359	2359	2252	2037	1287	1072	750
	2	2627	2520	2412	2305	2305	2198	2010	1260	1045	723
	3	2573	2466	2358	2251	2281	2144	1983	1233	1018	696
	4	2519	2412	2304	2197	2197	2090	1956	1206	991	669
	5	2466	2359	2252	2145	2145	2037	1930	1179	965	643
M	1	2466	2359	2252	2145	2145	2037	1930	1179	965	643
	2	2399	2294	2187	2082	2082	1977	1896	1159	948	632
	3	2332	2229	2122	2019	2019	1917	1862	1139	931	621
	4	2265	2164	2057	1956	1956	1857	1828	1119	914	610
	5	2198	2099	1992	1893	1893	1797	1794	1099	897	608

E.G. 3 /4 carat VS-2 (clarity) L-1(color) = $2,359

1 carat (100 points)

CLARITY

Color		IF	VVS1	VVS2	VS1	VS2	SI1	SI2	I1	I2	I3
D	1	25883	18304	16445	13299	12012	10010	8457	5863	3861	2145
	2	23881	17875	15915	13118	11869	9867	8329	5790	3823	2107
	3	21879	17446	15444	12940	11726	9724	8222	5719	3788	2072
	4	19877	17017	14944	12762	11583	9581	8215	5648	3753	2037
	5	17875	16588	14443	12584	11440	9438	8008	5577	3718	2002
E	1	17875	16588	14443	12584	11440	9438	8008	5577	3718	2002
	2	17570	16159	14262	12441	11332	9330	7900	5505	3680	1964
	3	17195	15730	14084	12298	11225	9223	7793	5433	3645	1929
	4	16820	15301	13906	12155	11118	9116	7686	5361	3610	1874
	5	16445	14872	13728	12012	11011	9009	7579	5291	3575	1859
F	1	16445	14872	13728	12012	11011	9009	7579	5291	3575	1859
	2	15800	14405	13442	11796	10832	8866	7507	5256	3539	1823
	3	15157	13941	13156	11582	10653	8723	7435	5221	3504	1787
	4	14514	13477	12870	11368	10474	8580	7363	5186	3469	1751
	5	13871	13013	12584	11154	10296	8437	7293	5148	3432	1716
G	1	13871	13013	12584	11154	10296	8437	7293	5148	3432	1716
	2	13121	12369	12090	10689	9938	8365	7257	5076	3396	1716
	3	12371	11725	11596	10224	9580	8293	7221	5004	3360	1716
	4	11621	11081	11102	9760	9222	8221	7185	4932	3324	1716
	5	10868	10439	10610	9295	8866	8151	7150	4862	3289	1716
H	1	10868	10439	10610	9295	8866	8151	7150	4862	3289	1716
	2	10475	10081	9652	8973	8544	7901	6971	4755	3218	1680
	3	10082	9723	9294	8651	8222	7651	6792	4648	3147	1644
	4	9689	9365	8936	8329	7900	7401	6613	4541	3076	1608
	5	9295	9009	8580	8008	7579	7150	6435	4433	3003	1573

Color		IF	VVS1	VVS2	VS1	VS2	SI1	SI2	I1	I2	I3
I	1	9295	9009	8580	8008	7579	7150	6435	4433	3003	1573
	2	8902	8651	8294	7758	7329	6935	6292	4290	2932	1573
	3	8509	8293	8008	7508	7079	6720	6149	4147	2861	1573
	4	8116	7935	7722	7258	6829	6505	6006	4004	2790	1573
	5	7722	7579	7436	7007	6578	6292	5863	3861	2717	1573
J	1	7722	7579	7436	7007	6578	6292	5863	3861	2717	1573
	2	7543	7400	7257	6828	6363	6077	5613	3840	2646	1537
	3	7364	7221	7078	6649	6148	5862	5363	3819	2575	1501
	4	7185	7042	6899	6470	5933	5647	5113	3798	2504	1465
	5	7007	6864	6721	6292	5720	5434	4862	3775	2431	1430
K	1	7007	6864	6721	6292	5720	5434	4862	3775	2431	1430
	2	6828	6685	6542	6149	5613	5327	4755	3653	2360	1394
	3	6649	6506	6363	6006	5506	5220	4648	3531	2289	1358
	4	6470	6327	6184	5863	5399	5113	4541	3409	2218	1322
	5	6292	6149	6006	5720	5291	5005	4433	3289	2145	1287
L	1	6292	6149	6006	5720	5291	5005	4433	3289	2145	1287
	2	6042	5899	5756	5470	5041	4755	4218	3146	2109	1287
	3	5792	5649	5506	5220	4791	4505	4003	3003	2073	1287
	4	5542	5399	5256	4970	4541	4255	3788	2860	2037	1287
	5	5291	5148	5005	4720	4290	4004	3575	2717	2002	1287
M	1	5291	5148	5005	4720	4290	4004	3575	2717	2002	1287
	2	5059	4916	4773	4487	4058	3772	3376	2584	1969	1287
	3	4827	4684	4541	4255	3826	3540	3177	2451	1936	1287
	4	4595	4452	4309	4023	3594	3308	2978	2319	1903	1287
	5	4363	4220	4077	3791	3362	3076	2779	2185	1870	1287

E.G. 1 carat, VS-1 (clarity), F-3 (color) = $11,582

1 1/2 carat (150 points)

CLARITY

Color		IF	VVS1	VVS2	VS1	VS2	SI1	SI2	I1	I2	I3
D	1	44616	32818	30673	26169	24238	20377	16731	10296	6220	3432
	2	41665	32334	29920	25900	23970	20214	16567	10188	6165	3376
	3	38716	31852	29170	25632	23702	20054	16407	10081	6112	3323
	4	35767	31370	28420	25364	23434	19894	16247	9974	6059	3270
	5	32818	30888	27670	25096	23166	19734	16087	9867	6006	3217
E	1	32818	30888	27670	25096	23166	19734	16087	9867	6006	3217
	2	32281	30190	27454	24828	22950	19465	15819	9759	5950	3162
	3	31745	29493	27240	24560	22736	19197	15551	9652	5897	3109
	4	31209	28796	27026	24292	22522	18929	15283	9545	5844	3056
	5	30673	28099	26812	24024	22308	18661	15015	9438	5791	3003
F	1	30673	28099	26812	24024	22308	18661	15015	9438	5791	3003
	2	29439	27186	25954	23539	21879	18232	14746	9330	5736	2947
	3	28206	26275	25096	23057	21450	17803	14478	9223	5683	2894
	4	26973	25364	24238	22575	21021	17374	14210	9116	5630	2841
	5	25740	24453	23380	22093	20592	16945	13942	9009	5577	2788
G	1	25740	24453	23380	22093	20592	16945	13942	9009	5577	2788
	2	24397	23218	22254	21072	19786	16671	13779	8901	5521	2737
	3	23057	21985	21128	20054	18982	16409	13619	8794	5468	2689
	4	21717	20752	20002	19036	18178	16141	13459	8687	5415	2641
	5	20377	19519	18876	18018	17374	15873	13299	8580	5362	2593
H	1	20377	19519	18876	18018	17374	15873	13299	8580	5362	2593
	2	19680	18927	18339	17533	16782	15388	12975	8472	5254	2586
	3	18983	18338	17803	17051	16193	14906	12654	8365	5147	2582
	4	18286	17749	17267	16569	15604	14424	12333	8258	5040	2578
	5	17589	17160	16731	16087	15015	13942	12012	8151	4933	2574

Color		IF	VVS1	VVS2	VS1	VS2	SI1	SI2	I1	I2	I3
I	1	17589	17160	16731	16087	15015	13942	12012	8151	4933	2574
	2	16892	16462	16033	15390	14317	13350	11583	7827	4825	2574
	3	16195	15765	15336	14693	13620	12761	11154	7506	4718	2576
	4	15498	15068	14639	13996	12923	12172	10725	7185	4611	2576
	5	14800	14371	13942	13299	12226	11583	10296	6864	4504	2574
J	1	14800	14371	13942	13299	12226	11583	10296	6864	4504	2574
	2	14211	13779	13350	12762	11742	11098	9907	6703	4396	2518
	3	13622	13190	12761	12226	11260	10616	9521	6542	4289	2465
	4	13033	12601	12172	11690	10778	10134	9135	6381	4182	2412
	5	12441	12012	11583	11154	10296	9652	8749	6220	4075	2359
K	1	12441	12012	11583	11154	10296	9652	8749	6220	4075	2359
	2	12012	11583	11154	10777	9972	9384	8490	6060	4020	2304
	3	11583	11154	10725	10402	9651	9116	8234	5900	3967	2251
	4	11154	10725	10296	10027	9330	8848	7978	5740	3914	2198
	5	10725	10296	9867	9652	9009	8580	7722	5577	3861	2145
L	1	10725	10296	9867	9652	9009	8580	7722	5577	3861	2145
	2	10348	9972	9598	9384	8685	8203	7398	5362	3753	2145
	3	9973	9651	9330	9116	8364	7828	7077	5147	3646	2145
	4	9598	9330	9062	8848	8043	7453	6756	4932	3539	2145
	5	9223	9009	8794	8580	7722	7078	6435	4719	3432	2145
M	1	9223	9009	8794	8580	7722	7078	6435	4719	3432	2145
	2	8879	8711	8545	8331	7423	6729	5937	4520	3333	2145
	3	8525	8413	8296	8082	7124	6380	5439	4321	3234	2145
	4	8176	8115	8047	7833	6825	6031	4941	4122	3135	2145
	5	7827	7817	7798	7584	6526	5682	4443	3923	3036	2145

E.G. 1 1 / 2 carat, VVS-1 (clarity), J-1 (color) = $14,371

2 carat (200 points)

CLARITY

Color		IF	VVS1	VVS2	VS1	VS2	SI1	SI2	I1	I2	I3
D	1	93236	74360	67782	56342	46046	36322	29744	16302	9152	4862
	2	88088	72714	65351	54982	45617	36106	29528	16159	9079	4789
	3	82940	71070	62920	53624	45188	35892	29314	16016	9008	4718
	4	77792	69426	60489	52266	44759	35678	29100	15873	8937	4647
	5	72644	67782	58058	50908	44330	35464	28886	15730	8866	4576
E	1	72644	67782	58058	50908	44330	35464	28886	15730	8866	4576
	2	71141	65421	56841	50050	44094	35178	28670	15587	8793	4503
	3	69640	63062	55626	49192	43758	34892	28456	15444	8722	4432
	4	68139	60703	54411	48334	43472	34606	28242	15301	8651	4361
	5	66638	58344	53196	47476	43186	34320	28028	15158	8580	4290
F	1	66638	58344	53196	47476	43186	34320	28028	15158	8580	4290
	2	63635	56269	51264	46545	42398	33818	27742	14942	8507	4290
	3	60632	54196	49334	45616	41612	33318	27456	14728	8436	4290
	4	57629	52123	47404	44687	40826	32818	27170	14514	8365	4290
	5	54626	50050	45474	43758	40040	32318	26884	14300	8294	4290
G	1	54626	50050	45474	43758	40040	32318	26884	14300	8294	4290
	2	51623	47190	43329	41683	38324	31460	26455	14084	8221	4217
	3	48620	44330	41184	39610	36608	30602	26026	13870	8150	4146
	4	45617	41470	39039	37537	34892	29744	25597	13656	8079	4075
	5	42614	38610	36894	35464	33176	28886	25168	13442	8008	4004
H	1	42614	38610	36894	35464	33176	28886	25168	13442	8008	4004
	2	40326	37107	35534	33961	31673	27955	24523	13299	7865	3931
	3	38038	35606	34176	32460	30172	27026	23880	13156	7722	3860
	4	35750	34105	32818	30959	28671	26097	23237	13013	7579	3789
	5	33462	32604	31460	29458	27170	25168	22594	12870	7436	3718

Color		IF	VVS1	VVS2	VS1	VS2	SI1	SI2	I1	I2	I3
I	1	33462	32604	31460	29458	27170	25168	22594	12870	7436	3718
	2	31816	30888	29887	27955	25810	23951	21663	12441	7220	3718
	3	30172	29172	28314	26454	24452	22736	20734	12012	7006	3718
	4	28528	27456	26741	24953	23094	21521	19805	11583	6792	3718
	5	26884	25740	25168	23452	21736	20306	18876	11154	6578	3718
J	1	26884	25740	25168	23452	21736	20306	18876	11154	6578	3718
	2	25810	24809	24237	22664	20948	19518	18161	10795	6505	3645
	3	24738	23880	23308	21878	20162	18732	17446	10438	6434	3574
	4	23666	22951	22379	21092	19376	17946	16731	10081	6363	3503
	5	22594	22022	21450	20306	18590	17160	16016	9724	6292	3432
K	1	22594	22022	21450	20306	18590	17160	16016	9724	6292	3432
	2	21450	20878	20306	19232	17446	16086	14942	9365	6219	3359
	3	20306	19734	19162	18160	16302	15014	13870	9008	6148	3288
	4	19162	18590	18018	17088	15158	13942	12798	8651	6077	3217
	5	18018	17446	16874	16016	14014	12870	11726	8294	6006	3146
L	1	18018	17446	16874	16016	14014	12870	11726	8294	6006	3146
	2	17303	16801	16302	15514	13369	12298	11224	7935	5863	3146
	3	16588	16158	15730	15014	12726	11726	10724	7578	5720	3146
	4	15873	15515	15158	14514	12083	11154	10224	7221	5577	3146
	5	15158	14872	14586	14014	11440	10582	9724	6864	5434	3146
M	1	15158	14872	14586	14014	11440	10582	9724	6864	5434	3146
	2	14560	14340	14121	13549	10812	10050	9259	6399	5301	3146
	3	13962	13808	13656	13084	10244	9578	8794	5934	5168	3146
	4	13364	13276	13191	12619	9779	8986	8329	5469	5035	3146
	5	12766	12744	12726	12154	9314	8454	7864	5004	4902	3146

E.G. 2 carat, SI-1 (clarity), I-2 (color) = $23,951

Buying Shy

"Buying shy" is a term I coined. It's one of my shrewdest and most valuable suggestions for buying diamonds. Buying shy can save you a lot of money!

Here's what I mean by buying shy: *shopping for diamonds that weigh just under half-carat and full-carat weights.*

For example, instead of a one-carat (100-point) diamond you'd buy a .90-carat diamond. Instead of a half-carat, you'd buy a .46-carat stone. It's as simple as that.

But Fred, you're saying—why should I buy a smaller diamond than I want?

The simple answer: to save a lot of money.
Because the price of a diamond jumps dramatically when it reaches a true half-carat or full-carat, the advantage of buying shy is also pretty dramatic!

And let's see how much "smaller" we're talking about. The diameter of a one-carat diamond is 6.5 millimeters. The diameter of a "shy" .90-carat stone is 6.3 millimeters. The difference is the thickness of a piece of ordinary paper! Looking at the stones side by side you'd be hard-pressed to tell the difference.

Look at the savings:
.50ct SI1-I $1,573
.46ct SI1-I $1,249   **You save $324!**

.75ct SI1-I $3,646
.65ct SI1-I $2,044   **You save $1,602!**
1.00ct SI1-I $7,150
.90ct SI1-I $5,534   **You save $1,616!**

You'll notice that buying shy sometimes means a difference of 1 point and sometimes a difference of 10 points. And you're thinking, "Why don't I buy the .99-carat stone instead of the .90 carat stone? Won't I still get the same price break and a slightly bigger stone?" Yes, but the problem is finding that 99-pointer. Diamond cutters, who are well aware that the full one-carat stone is worth quite a bit more than the 99-pointer, will cheat on the proportions a bit to get the stone up to the full carat. So don't be obsessed with trying to get closer than 10 points on full-carated stones, but you will find .90s and 1.90s, etc.

The one potential problem with buying shy is a psychological one. What sort of person is your True Love? If she's going to be upset that you didn't get the full carat, and will forever think of you as a cheapskate, then it may be worth the extra money.

Your fiancée may never ask how big her 90-point diamond is, but if she does, you might say, "About a carat," and leave it at that. I believe that happiness is a dream that becomes a reality—and if she sees a diamond that is just what she dreamed of, she'll be happy!

Of course, if you're a practical couple and you decide to shop for the diamond together, you should both read this book first and then decide what you're going to shop for.

Fred's Advice: Always buy shy! You'll pay a lot less for a diamond that looks just as good.

The Day My World Changed (September 6, 2005)

The Day Before
My father and I were going to New York to have a meeting with the manager of DCI New York to see why clients were experiencing unusual delays on the processing of their orders. The meeting should have lasted only thirty minutes…it lasted nine hours.

September 6, 2005
The meeting was at our offices at 579 Fifth Avenue scheduled for 9:00 a.m. We had the whole day for the meeting and whatever (shopping and eating) because we weren't flying back until Wednesday, September 7. I had no idea when I walked into the office my life was going to forever change!

The Meeting
We exchange pleasantries for a while and then I got to the point of the meeting.

Me: "Neil, as you know DCI New York is falling a little behind in filling all the orders, and we just want to see what's up." (I wanted to say "What's up?" like the Budweiser commercials but realized it was a little lame to use a seven-year-old bit regardless of how much

I personally loved to say "Wazzzzzup?").

Long dramatic pause…

Neil: "Fred, do you know how for twenty years you've been telling people to buy shy?"

Me: "Uh-huh."

Neil: "Well, they did. And now they're all gone—the good quality ones."

Me: "What do you mean they're all gone?"

Neil: "They are all gone! All the shy stones (.45–.49 ct, .65–.69 ct, 1.45–1.49 ct, 1.85–1.95 ct, 2.85 ct–2.95 ct) are gone, and it's not only those. All the full sizes over 3 carats are gone. The rough to cut 1.25 ct and 1.75 ct box radiants are gone. The rough-to-cut 65/65 princesses in any size are gone. The 65/65 asschers are gone! Fred, they're all gone!"

The conversation proceeded from there. For nine hours, we tackled many questions. What rough was still available to fill current and future orders? What type of rationing was needed to stretch the current supply of "fulls"? A full is a hard-weight diamond .50 ct, .75 ct, 1.0 ct, 1.50 ct, 2.0 ct, and rough-to-cut full sizes were still available. Important note: When I tell you, the reader, that the world is running out of diamonds, again, I am only referring to the good diamonds, not the commercial grade stuff that consolidators like

Costco, Sam's, Blue Nile, Zales, Bailey Banks & Biddle, Mondera, or Dirt Cheap Diamonds sell. There is no shortage, nor will there ever be a shortage of commercial grade diamonds.

Everyone defines a "good" diamond as a diamond that holds or appreciates in value over time when you try to sell it. Commercial grade diamonds, on the secondary market, sell for only a small fraction of what you paid. That is also the case now for the fancy shapes (pear, marquis, emerald cut, asscher, oval, heart, trilliant, baguette) and melee. They have little or no secondary market value. The top price you'll see for any commercial grade, fancy shaped, or melee diamonds will rarely be a penny more than 19.7 percent of the original dollar spent. While a good diamond (white, eye clean, Class 1 or 2, non-fluorescent, natural, fully bonded) will always bring you even money (100 percent of what you paid) as long as the vendor you bought it from stays in business. Even if they don't, you'll at least get 40 to 45 percent of what you paid as dump value (the average is 60 pecent) or 80 to 85 percent on the secondary market to an end consumer who is not looking to flip the rock. There is no question: if you are going buy a diamond, it makes no sense purchasing a crummy one with bogus "certificates" that don't guarantee you anything. It leaves you holding a piece gravel if you ever want to part with your rock.

Anyway, this is what the market (world) is dealing with. Good diamonds in entire categories are extinct except the onesies and twosies, and what is left could be gone as early as 2010. The following Buying Shy Price Lists are like an endangered species, they can become extinct over night.

Buying Shy Endangered Price List

.46 Carat
CLARITY

Color		IF	VVS1	VVS2	VS1	VS2	SI1	SI2	I1	I2	I3
D	1	3618	3223	2960	2631	2171	1710	1513	1118	789	592
	2	3519	3158	2894	2598	2138	1693	1497	1102	773	576
	3	3420	3093	2828	2565	2105	1677	1481	1085	757	560
	4	3320	3025	2762	2532	2074	1662	1464	1069	740	543
	5	3223	2960	2696	2499	2039	1644	1447	1052	723	526
E	1	3223	2960	2696	2499	2039	1644	1447	1052	723	526
	2	3172	2894	2631	2434	2006	1626	1429	1034	723	526
	3	3123	2828	2565	2368	1973	1610	1413	1018	723	526
	4	3074	2762	2499	2302	1940	1594	1397	1002	723	526
	5	3025	2696	2433	2236	1907	1578	1381	986	723	526
F	1	3025	2696	2433	2236	1907	1578	1381	986	723	526
	2	2960	2646	2383	2186	1875	1560	1363	968	705	508
	3	2894	2597	2334	2137	1842	1544	1347	952	689	492
	4	2828	2548	2285	2088	1809	1528	1331	936	673	476
	5	2762	2499	2236	2039	1776	1512	1315	920	657	460
G	1	2762	2499	2236	2039	1776	1512	1315	920	657	460
	2	2662	2401	2171	1974	1743	1480	1283	903	657	460
	3	2564	2302	2105	1908	1710	1447	1250	887	657	460
	4	2466	2203	2039	1842	1677	1414	1217	871	657	460
	5	2368	2104	1973	1776	1644	1381	1184	855	657	460
H	1	2368	2104	1973	1776	1644	1381	1184	855	657	460
	2	2285	2022	1890	1710	1594	1348	1166	837	640	460
	3	2203	1940	1808	1644	1545	1315	1150	821	624	460

Color		IF	VVS1	VVS2	VS1	VS2	SI1	SI2	I1	I2	I3
	4	2121	1858	1726	1578	1496	1282	1134	805	608	460
	5	2039	1776	1644	1512	1447	1249	1118	789	592	460
I	1	2039	1776	1644	1512	1447	1249	1118	789	592	460
	2	1923	1710	1594	1462	1382	1217	1085	771	592	442
	3	1808	1644	1545	1413	1316	1184	1052	755	592	426
	4	1693	1578	1496	1364	1250	1151	1019	739	592	410
	5	1578	1512	1447	1315	1184	1118	986	723	592	394
J	1	1578	1512	1447	1315	1184	1118	986	723	592	394
	2	1528	1462	1396	1265	1133	1067	954	705	574	394
	3	1479	1413	1347	1216	1084	1018	921	689	558	394
	4	1430	1364	1298	1167	1035	969	888	673	542	394
	5	1381	1315	1249	1118	986	920	855	657	526	394
K	1	1381	1315	1249	1118	986	920	855	657	526	394
	2	1331	1265	1199	1085	970	903	837	640	508	376
	3	1282	1216	1150	1052	954	887	821	624	492	360
	4	1233	1167	1101	1019	936	871	805	608	476	344
	5	1184	1118	1052	986	920	855	789	592	460	328
L	1	1184	1118	1052	986	920	855	789	592	460	328
	2	1151	1085	1019	954	903	837	771	574	442	311
	3	1118	1052	986	921	887	821	755	558	426	295
	4	1085	1019	953	888	871	805	739	542	400	279
	5	1052	986	920	855	855	789	723	526	394	263
M	1	1052	986	920	855	855	789	723	526	394	263
	2	1020	962	888	823	823	773	707	510	378	247
	3	988	958	856	791	770	757	691	494	362	231
	4	956	942	824	759	748	741	675	478	346	215
	5	924	926	792	727	716	707	659	462	330	199

E.G. 0.49 carat I-2 (clarity) G-1 (color) = $657

.65 Carat

Color		IF	VVS1	VVS2	VS1	VS2	SI1	SI2	I1	I2	I3
							CLARITY				
D	1	7064	5669	5112	4368	3996	3439	2788	1859	1394	929
	2	6691	5529	5019	4323	3972	3394	2743	1838	1373	908
	3	6317	5390	4926	4276	3949	3347	3696	1814	1349	884
	4	5943	5251	4833	4229	3926	3300	2649	1790	1325	860
	5	5569	5112	4740	4182	3903	3253	2602	1766	1301	836
E	1	5569	5112	4740	4182	3903	3253	2602	1766	1301	836
	2	5529	4923	4671	4113	3811	3184	2557	1745	1280	836
	3	5390	4880	4601	4043	3718	3114	2510	1724	1256	836
	4	5251	4833	4531	3973	3625	3044	2463	1699	1232	836
	5	5112	4740	4461	3903	3532	2974	2416	1673	1208	836
F	1	5112	4740	4461	3903	3532	2974	2416	1673	1208	836
	2	5019	4637	4344	3835	3439	2905	2347	1628	1184	831
	3	4926	4514	4228	3765	3346	2835	2277	1581	1161	790
	4	4833	4391	4112	3695	3253	2765	2207	1534	1138	767
	5	4740	4275	3996	3625	3160	2695	2137	1487	1115	743
G	1	4740	4275	3996	3625	3160	2695	2137	1487	1115	743
	2	4602	4135	3835	3484	3043	2626	2092	1463	1091	743
	3	4462	3956	3672	3345	2927	2556	2045	1440	1068	743
	4	4322	3857	3509	3206	2811	2486	1998	1417	1045	743
	5	4182	3718	3346	3067	2695	2416	1951	1394	1022	743
H	1	4182	3718	3346	3067	2695	2416	1951	1394	1022	743
	2	3997	3277	3208	2929	2593	2323	1928	1370	1022	743
	3	3811	3207	3068	2789	2503	2230	1905	1347	1022	743
	4	3625	3137	2928	2649	2413	2137	1882	1324	1022	743
	5	3439	3067	2788	2509	2323	2044	1859	1301	1022	743
I	1	3439	3067	2788	2509	2323	2044	1859	1301	1022	743

Color		IF	VVS1	VVS2	VS1	VS2	SI1	SI2	I1	I2	I3
	2	3253	2929	2695	2416	2254	2043	1835	1277	1022	743
	3	3067	2789	2602	2323	2184	1997	1812	1254	1022	743
	4	2881	2649	2509	2230	2114	1951	1789	1231	1022	743
	5	2695	2509	2416	2137	2044	1905	1766	1208	1022	743
J	1	2695	2509	2416	2137	2044	1905	1766	1208	1022	743
	2	2603	2440	2347	2069	1976	1824	1694	1184	998	719
	3	2510	2370	2277	1999	1906	1743	1625	1161	975	696
	4	2417	2300	2207	1979	1836	1662	1556	1138	952	673
	5	2323	2230	2137	1859	1766	1580	1487	1115	929	650
K	1	2323	2230	2137	1859	1766	1580	1487	1115	929	650
	2	2251	2158	2089	1835	1766	1580	1463	1067	905	626
	3	2182	2089	2043	1812	1766	1580	1440	1021	882	603
	4	2113	2020	1997	1789	1766	1580	1417	975	859	580
	5	2044	1951	1951	1766	1766	1580	1394	929	836	557
L	1	2044	1951	1951	1766	1766	1580	1394	929	836	557
	2	1973	1880	1880	1718	1718	1532	1370	905	812	533
	3	1904	1811	1811	1672	1672	1486	1347	882	789	510
	4	1835	1742	1742	1626	1626	1440	1324	859	766	487
	5	1766	1673	1673	1580	1580	1394	1301	836	743	464
M	1	1766	1673	1673	1580	1580	1394	1301	836	743	464
	2	1591	1598	1598	1530	1530	1368	1283	813	726	447
	3	1461	1523	1523	1480	1480	1342	1265	790	709	430
	4	1241	1448	1448	1430	1430	1316	1247	767	692	413
	5	1066	1373	1373	1380	1380	1290	1229	744	675	396

E.G. 0.69 carat SI-2 (clarity) G-1 (color) = $2,137

.80 Carat

CLARITY

Color		IF	VVS1	VVS2	VS1	VS2	SI1	SI2	I1	I2	I3
D	1	10296	8122	7436	6635	6177	5605	5033	3203	2059	1258
	2	9751	7979	7262	6519	6089	5547	4975	3172	2028	1258
	3	9208	7836	7091	6405	6004	5490	4918	3144	2000	1258
	4	8665	7693	6920	6291	5919	5433	4861	3116	1972	1258
	5	8122	7550	6749	6177	5834	5376	4804	3088	1944	1258
E	1	8122	7550	6749	6177	5834	5376	4804	3088	1944	1258
	2	7949	7407	6634	6089	5746	5288	4716	3058	1914	1228
	3	7778	7264	6520	6004	5661	5203	4631	3030	1886	1200
	4	7607	7121	6406	5919	5576	5118	4546	3002	1858	1172
	5	7436	6978	6292	5834	5491	5033	4461	2974	1830	1144
F	1	7436	6978	6292	5834	5491	5033	4461	2974	1830	1144
	2	7293	6805	6206	5746	5403	4945	4373	2944	1830	1113
	3	7150	6634	6120	5661	5318	4860	4288	2416	1830	1085
	4	7007	6463	6034	5576	5233	4775	4203	2888	1830	1051
	5	6864	6292	5948	5491	5148	4690	4118	2860	1830	1029
G	1	6864	6292	5948	5491	5148	4690	4118	2860	1830	1029
	2	6690	6118	5775	5348	5032	4602	4088	2802	1800	1029
	3	6519	5947	5604	5205	4918	4517	4060	2745	1772	1029
	4	6348	5776	5433	5062	4804	4432	4032	2688	1744	1029
	5	6177	5605	5262	4919	4690	4347	4004	2631	1716	1029
H	1	6177	5605	5262	4919	4690	4347	4004	2631	1716	1029
	2	5919	5404	5089	4776	4547	4231	3861	2600	1685	1029
	3	5662	5204	4918	4633	4404	4117	3718	2574	1657	1029
	4	5405	5004	4747	4490	4261	4003	3575	2544	1629	1029
	5	5148	4804	4576	4347	4118	3889	3432	2516	1601	1029

Color		IF	VVS1	VVS2	VS1	VS2	SI1	SI2	I1	I2	I3
I	1	5148	4804	4576	4347	4118	3889	3432	2516	1601	1029
	2	4862	4573	4375	4146	3945	3746	3346	2470	1591	999
	3	4576	4345	4175	3946	3774	3603	3260	2383	1543	971
	4	4290	4117	3975	3746	3603	3460	3174	2345	1515	943
	5	4004	3889	3775	3546	3432	3317	3088	2288	1487	915
J	1	4004	3889	3775	3546	3432	3317	3088	2288	1487	915
	2	3888	3774	3659	3430	3316	3174	2945	2172	1456	915
	3	3774	3660	3545	3316	3202	3031	2802	2058	1428	915
	4	3660	3546	3431	3202	3088	2888	2659	1944	1400	915
	5	3546	3432	3317	3088	2974	2745	2516	1830	1372	915
K	1	3546	3432	3317	3088	2974	2745	2516	1830	1372	915
	2	3373	3258	3144	2930	2858	2660	2428	1714	1315	884
	3	3202	3087	2973	2787	2744	2575	2340	1600	1258	856
	4	3031	2916	2802	2644	2630	2490	2258	1486	1201	828
	5	2860	2745	2631	2516	2516	2402	2173	1372	1144	800
L	1	2860	2745	2631	2516	2516	2402	2173	1372	1144	800
	2	2802	2687	2573	2459	2459	2344	2143	1342	1113	770
	3	2745	2630	2516	2405	2405	2287	2115	1314	1085	742
	4	2688	2573	2459	2345	2345	2230	2087	1286	1057	714
	5	2631	2516	2402	2288	2288	2173	2059	1258	1029	686
M	1	2631	2516	2402	2288	2288	2173	2059	1258	1029	686
	2	2592	2446	2334	2222	2222	2110	2024	1239	1012	675
	3	2553	2375	2266	2156	2156	2044	1989	1216	995	664
	4	2514	2304	2198	2090	2090	1982	1954	1195	978	653
	5	2475	2273	2130	2024	2024	1918	1919	1174	961	642

E.G. 0.80 carat SI-1 (clarity) I-1 (color) = $3,889

.90 Carat

CLARITY

Color	IF	VVS1	VVS2	VS1	VS2	SI1	SI2	I1	I2	I3
D 1	13513	10939	10296	9137	8365	7850	6821	4247	2960	1673
2	12869	10778	10102	8944	8268	7753	6756	4214	2927	1641
3	12225	10617	9908	8751	8171	7656	6691	4181	2894	1609
4	11581	10456	9714	8558	8074	7559	6626	4148	2861	1577
5	10939	10296	9523	8365	7979	7464	6563	4118	2831	1544
E 1	10939	10296	9523	8365	7979	7464	6563	4118	2831	1544
2	10810	10167	9394	8269	7914	7368	6498	4085	2799	1544
3	10681	10038	9265	8173	7849	7272	6433	4052	2767	1344
4	10552	9909	9136	8077	7784	7176	6368	4019	2735	1544
5	10424	9781	9009	7979	7722	7078	6306	3989	2702	1544
F 1	10424	9781	9009	7979	7722	7078	6306	3989	2702	1544
2	10231	9556	8848	7882	7626	6981	6209	3957	2655	1512
3	10038	9331	8687	7785	7529	6885	6112	3925	2608	1480
4	9845	9106	8526	7688	7432	6788	6016	3893	2561	1448
5	9652	8880	8365	7593	7335	6692	5920	3861	2514	1415
G 1	9652	8880	8365	7593	7335	6692	5920	3861	2514	1415
2	9395	8687	8204	7497	7239	6594	5856	3796	2497	1415
3	9137	8494	8043	7401	7143	6435	5791	3732	2480	1415
4	8880	8301	7882	7305	7046	6306	5726	3667	2463	1415
5	8622	8108	7722	7207	6949	6177	5662	3603	2445	1415
H 1	8622	8108	7722	7207	6949	6177	5662	3603	2445	1415
2	8283	7787	7400	6949	6691	6016	5501	3539	2413	1383
3	7944	7466	7078	6691	6433	5855	5340	3474	2381	1351
4	7605	7145	6756	6433	6175	5694	5178	3409	2349	1319
5	7267	6824	6435	6177	5920	5534	5019	3346	2316	1287

Color		IF	VVS1	VVS2	VS1	VS2	SI1	SI2	I1	I2	I3
I	1	7207	6824	6435	6177	5920	5534	5019	3346	2316	1287
	2	6994	6598	6242	5984	5727	5373	4890	3281	2284	1287
	3	6722	6372	6049	5791	5534	5212	4761	3216	2252	1287
	4	6450	6146	5856	5598	5341	5051	4632	3151	2220	1287
	5	6177	5920	5662	5406	5148	4890	4504	3088	2187	1287
J	1	6177	5920	5662	5406	5148	4890	4504	3088	2187	1287
	2	5887	5662	5437	5180	4923	4665	4279	2928	2123	1255
	3	5598	5404	5212	4955	4698	4440	4054	2768	2058	1222
	4	5308	5146	4987	4730	4473	4215	3829	2608	1993	1190
	5	5019	4890	4761	4504	4247	3989	3603	2445	1930	1158
K	1	5019	4890	4761	4504	4247	3989	3603	2445	1930	1158
	2	4826	4697	4568	4343	4086	3860	3507	2380	1866	1126
	3	4633	4504	4375	4182	3925	3731	3410	2315	1802	1094
	4	4440	4311	4182	4021	3764	3602	3313	2250	1738	1062
	5	4247	4118	3989	3861	3603	3474	3217	2187	1673	1029
L	1	4247	4118	3989	3861	3603	3474	3217	2187	1673	1029
	2	4150	4021	3892	3764	3538	3409	3152	2155	1641	1029
	3	4053	3924	3795	3667	3474	3345	3088	2123	1609	1029
	4	3956	3827	3698	3570	3410	3281	3024	2091	1577	1029
	5	3861	3732	3603	3474	3346	3217	2960	2059	1544	1029
M	1	3861	3732	3603	3474	3346	3217	2960	2059	1544	1029
	2	3817	3688	3558	3429	3301	3173	2915	2037	1523	1029
	3	3773	3644	3513	3384	3256	3129	2870	2055	1502	1029
	4	3729	3600	3468	3339	3211	3085	2825	1993	1481	1029
	5	3685	3556	3423	3294	3166	3041	2780	1917	1460	1029

E.G. 0.90 carat VS-2 (clarity) L-1 (color) = $3,603

To Thine Own Self Be True:

What Kind of Customer Are You?

In my years in the business, I've come across five basic kinds of folks who buy diamonds. Tell me what type you are, and I'll recommend what grade of diamond you should buy.

Customer #1 will tell me the three most important things about a diamond are size, size, and size. The bigger the better, never mind if the stone is yellow and has a few black spots or cracks!

My recommendation:

Weight 1 carat plus

Clarity I2

Color L–M

Diamond Myth

"Diamonds are a bad investment."

Diamonds are probably not a great investment for the average person, but they are not a bad investment for someone who buys wisely and well. Since the diamond crash of 1979, when one-carat flawless diamonds fell in value from $75,000 to $15,000, diamond prices have increased steadily. That's largely due to the tightly controlled world diamond market.

Customer #2 also wants a big diamond, but size isn't the only thing. A little quality wouldn't hurt. Maybe the diamond can be slightly yellow, but please, no obvious cracks or spots. Maybe some teeny spots that can hardly be seen.

My recommendation:
Weight .50 carat or bigger
Clarity SI2 to I1
Color K

Customer #3 is a balanced kind of person, yin and yang. Size and quality are equal values. The diamond doesn't have to be perfect, but it should be clean to the eye, white, and sparkly.

My recommendation:
Weight .50 carat or bigger
Clarity SI1
Color I(1) to J(3)

Customer #4 demands Quality, with a capital "Q." Everything else is secondary. The diamond must be not only eye-clean, but clean when viewed with a 10X loupe, and bright white without a hint of yellow.

My recommendation:
Weight .50 carat or bigger
Clarity VS1
Color G

Customer #5 isn't getting engaged, or buying an anniversary stone. The diamond is an investment, to be locked away and later resold for a profit.

My recommendation:
Shape Round (No other!)
Weight 1 carat or bigger
Clarity VVS1 to Flawless
Color D, E, or F

Take a look at this chart. Find your type, your budget, and the size diamond you'll be able to afford. This table will help you get the most bang for your buck, whatever type of customer you happen to be.

Buying Guide by Customer Type

	Type				
Budget	1	2	3	4	5
$250	.38 carat	.30 carat	.20 carat	.16 carat	n/a
$500	.50 carat	.46 carat	.29 carat	.24 carat	.22 carat
$750	.70 carat	.62 carat	.35 carat	.29 carat	.23 carat
$1,000	.89 carat	.65 carat	.41 carat	.30 carat	.29 carat
$1,250	.90 carat	.78 carat	.46 carat	.37 carat	.29 carat
$1,500	1.00 carat	.89 carat	.50 carat	.40 carat	.29 carat
$1,750	1.00 carat	.90 carat	.55 carat	.45 carat	.29 carat
$2,000	1.30 carat	.99 carat	.65 carat	.46 carat	.30 carat
$2,250	1.40 carat	1.00 carat	.65 carat	.46 carat	.30 carat
$2,500	1.40 carat	1.00 carat	.65 carat	.46 carat	.37 carat
$2,750	1.50 carat	1.10 carat	.65 carat	.50 carat	.38 carat
$3,000	1.65 carat	1.20 carat	.65 carat	.50 carat	.40 carat
$3,500	1.80 carat	1.40 carat	.65 carat	.60 carat	.46 carat
$4,000	2.00 carat	1.40 carat	.80 carat	.65 carat	.46 carat
$4,500	2.00 carat	1.50 carat	.80 carat	.70 carat	.46 carat
$5,000	2.00 carat	1.70 carat	7.00 carat	.75 carat	.46 carat

Type					
Budget	1	2	3	4	5
$5,500	2.00 carat	1.80 carat	.90 carat	.80 carat	.50 carat
$6,000	2.00 carat	1.80 carat	.90 carat	.80 carat	.50 carat
$7,000	3.00 carat	2.00 carat	1.00 carat	.80 carat	.65 carat
$8,000	3.00 carat	2.00 carat	1.00 carat	.90 carat	.65 carat
$9,000	3.00 carat	2.00 carat	1.00 carat	.90 carat	.65 carat
$10,000	3.00 carat	2.00 carat	1.00 carat	.90 carat	.75 carat
$11,000	n/a	2.00 carat	1.00 carat	.90 carat	.80 carat
$12,000	n/a	3.00 carat	1.00 carat	1.00 carat	.80 carat
$13,000	n/a	3.00 carat	1.00 carat	1.00 carat	.80 carat
$14,500	n/a	3.00 carat	1.50 carat	1.00 carat	.90 carat
$15,000	n/a	3.00 carat	1.50 carat	1.00 carat	.90 carat
$15,500	n/a	n/a	1.50 carat	1.00 carat	.90 carat
$16,000	n/a	n/a	1.50 carat	1.00 carat	.90 carat
$16,500	n/a	n/a	1.50 carat	1.00 carat	.90 carat
$17,000	n/a	n/a	1.50 carat	1.00 carat	.90 carat
$17,500	n/a	n/a	1.50 carat	1.00 carat	.90 carat
$18,000	n/a	n/a	1.50 carat	1.00 carat	.90 carat
$18,500	n/a	n/a	1.50 carat	1.00 carat	.90 carat
$19,000	n/a	n/a	1.50 carat	1.00 carat	.90 carat
$19,500	n/a	n/a	1.50 carat	1.00 carat	.90 carat
$20,000	n/a	n/a	1.50 carat	1.00 carat	.90 carat
$25,000	n/a	n/a	2.00 carat	1.50 carat	1.00 carat
$30,000	n/a	n/a	2.00 carat	1.50 carat	1.00 carat
$35,000	n/a	n/a	2.00 carat	1.50 carat	1.00 carat
$40,000	n/a	n/a	2.00 carat	1.50 carat	1.00 carat
$45,000	n/a	n/a	3.00 carat	2.00 carat	1.50 carat
$50,000	n/a	n/a	3.00 carat	2.00 carat	1.50 carat

			Type		
Budget	1	2	3	4	5
$55,000	n/a	n/a	3.00 carat	2.00 carat	1.50 carat
$60,000	n/a	n/a	3.00 carat	2.00 carat	1.50 carat
$70,000	n/a	n/a	3.00 carat	2.00 carat	1.50 carat
$80,000	n/a	n/a	3.00 carat	2.00 carat	1.50 carat
$90,000	n/a	n/a	3.00 carat	3.00 carat	1.50 carat
$100,000	n/a	n/a	3.00 carat	3.00 carat	2.00 carat

Too Good to Be True

Is it actually possible for a diamond to be priced too low? You'd think not, but be careful. The prices in this book are wholesale, not retail. If the price of a diamond is dramatically lower than the prices in this book—beware! Nobody gives away a good diamond; they discount the stinkers. Notice how much the price of a diamond drops when it's a Class III or a Class IV, versus a Class I or Class II.

At least one of the following is most likely going on:
1. The clarity, color, or weight has been overgraded.
2. It's an off-make (poorly proportioned) Class III or Class IV.
It is poorly warranted (bad return, trade-in, or breakage policy).

How Much Is a 1 Carat VS1, G?

This may seem like a reasonably easy question for someone in the jewelry industry to answer, but it's actually quite difficult if the quote is to be accurate. In fact, an accurate answer cannot be derived due to lack of information. Probability comes into play when we don't have the information needed to make an informed decision. When we don't have enough data, all we are left with are "reasonable guesses." Here are just some of the things we don't know: For starters, what type of 1ct are we talking about: a shy, full, heavy, or true? What type of VS1 are we talking about: a hard, lab, bonded, paperless, partial, or split? What type of G: G1, G2, G3, G4, or G5? How well proportioned is it: Class I, Class II, Class III, Class IV, Ideal, Signature, Hearts and Arrows, Eight Star, High Definition, or Kaplan? If they use one of these titles to advertise the diamond is well-proportioned, what are the specifics in angles, percentages, and ratios of that brand? Once you know the specifics (proportions), do they give you enough measurements to determine if the crown angles and pavilion angles are universal or if the diamond is warped? Please don't forget about fluorescence. Is the diamond fluorescent? If it is, is it strong, medium, or faint fluorescence? Was the diamond annealed, fracture filled, bleached, assembled, or laser drilled? What equipment was used to measure the diamond? Was the equipment calibrated before it was used? Does the paperwork that comes with the diamond really match the stone? Where did the diamond come from? Is it a blood diamond? Is it a secondary market diamond? Finally, once you ask every last detail, how can you know what you've been told is factual?

Time for a joke. There are three men on a train—an economist, a logician, and a mathematician. They have just crossed the border into Scotland and they see a brown cow standing in a field. The cow is standing parallel to the train.

The economist says, "Look. The cows in Scotland are brown."

The logician says, "No. There are cows in Scotland, of which at least one is brown."

The mathematician says, "No. There is at least one cow in Scotland, of which one side appears to be brown."

How much is a 1ct, VS1, G? If you were to ask the economist, he might give you more than one answer. If you were to ask the logician, he would be smart enough to ask what type of 1ct, VS1, G you were talking about. And finally, if you were to ask the mathematician, he would say, "Did you forget about one thing? How much profit does the seller want to make?"

Inflation Beaters

According to Bottom Line Personal *magazine, in the last twenty years,*

only two categories of collectibles have stayed ahead of inflation. Stamps, at an

average return of 9.1 percent, and diamonds, at 7.9 percent per year!

Chapter 3

Ring Settings

O nce you have decided on a diamond, you'll need to select a setting. I mean, diamonds are beautiful, but what good are they unless you can wear them?

There are three basic types of ring settings: the Tiffany Setting, Bridal Sets, and Diamond Wedding Rings.

Tiffany
The Tiffany Setting, named after the famed jeweler Louis C. Tiffany, is a simple, elegant setting that lets the diamond be the star of the show and be in the spotlight. In a Tiffany Setting, the stone is held by four to six prongs, depending on the shape of the diamond.

Three basic styles of settings: Bridal Set (far left), the Tiffany (middle), and Diamond Wedding Ring (right).

Note: When buying a ring that uses prongs to hold the diamond, make sure the prongs are white gold or platinum. Yellow gold prongs will give the stone a yellow cast.

Bridal Sets

The bridal set is a perennial favorite. It consists of an engagement ring and a wedding band made to fit together to look like one ring.

Diamond Wedding Rings

The diamond wedding ring is large enough to be worn by itself, and can serve as the engagement ring and the wedding ring all in one. In many of these settings there is a main diamond surrounded by several smaller stones.

Accents: Baguettes, Melees, Trilliants

These are small diamonds that are set around the main stone.

Baguettes are small, elongated diamonds, usually under .15 carat in weight, either tapered or nontapered. Melees are round diamonds, under .20 carat. Trilliants are triangular in shape, usually under .33 carat.

Baguettes under .15 carat cost approximately $2,000 per carat. Trilliants under .33 carat cost approximately $3,000 per carat. Melees under .20 carat cost around $1,500 to $1,750 per carat. (Wholesale prices, based on SI1, H through I(3) color grade.)

Adding Color

Of course, diamonds are a girl's best friend, but rubies, sapphires, emeralds, and other colored stones are pretty good pals, too! Many women like to surround their diamonds with colored gems, or

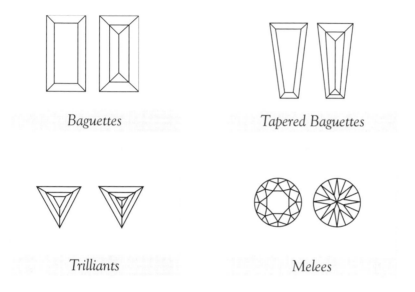

Baguettes

Tapered Baguettes

Trilliants

Melees

vice-versa, and your True Love might like her diamond accented with her birthstone. There are some stunning combinations of diamonds and other precious stones. Ask your jeweler to show you some.

A Word About Gold...

Most engagement rings and wedding bands are made of gold. Pure gold is stamped 24K (24 Karat), which means it has not been mixed with any other metals. We don't use 24K gold for jewelry because it's too soft, and will bend too easily.

18K gold is 75 percent pure gold. Other metals such as copper, zinc, or nickel have been added for strength.

14K gold is 58.5 percent pure gold, and 41.5 percent other metals for strength.

10K gold is mostly other metals and should not be considered for jewelry.

You might see gold jewelry stamped with a number—750 or 585. This is the European system of grading gold. Pure gold is 1000, or 24K; 750 is 75 percent pure gold, or 18K; 585 is 58.5 percent pure gold, or 14K.

...And Platinum

Platinum is a rarer metal than gold, and somewhat harder for a jeweler to work with. As you might guess, this makes it more expensive than gold. It is stronger than gold and therefore holds the diamond more securely—and some women prefer platinum because they feel it shows off the diamond better than gold.

Platinum Doping

The platinum world is being turned upside down and I thought someone should let you know. But, before we get into that, I need to make you a platinum aficionado. So, I went to Google and typed in "what is the definition of platinum?"

This is some of what I got:

• "One of the rarest precious metals, platinum is also one of the strongest and heaviest, making it a popular choice for setting gemstone jewelry and watches. It has a rich, white luster and an understated look. Platinum is hypoallergenic and tarnish resistant. Platinum used in jewelry and watches is at least 85 to 95 percent pure. Many platinum watches are produced in limited editions due to the expense and rarity of the metal."

• "Rare, silvery white metallic element of great strength, weight, and resistance to corrosion. Difficult to alloy, cast, and work owing to its very high melting point. The standard of platinum in the US and most western countries is 95 percent pure and is marked PLAT. From platina, little silver, the word the Spanish gave it when first seen in South America in the eighteenth century."

• "Platinum is a white metal, but unlike gold it is used in jewelry in almost its pure form from 85, 90, or 95 percent pure. Platinum is very hard and is extremely long wearing and is very white, so it does not need to be rhodium-plated like white gold. Platinum is very dense making it much heavier than 18k gold. Because platinum is hard it is best suited for setting the large, valuable stones. The platinum prongs for setting stones would be stronger than the setting made with softer gold."

• "A dense (heavy) silvery grey metal, atomic number 78, atomic weight 195.078 , used by pre-Columbian South American Indians, and rediscovered in the eighteenth century. Its first use for coins was by Russia in 1828, following the discovery of large platinum deposits in the Ural Mountains in 1822."

Platinum was never less that 85 percent pure under any definition. Well, now platinum is being DOPED! Large metal manufacturers are taking pure platinum and cutting it with copper and cobalt! The product is being sold as 585 platinum. The 585 stands for 58.5 percent pure platinum and 41.5 percent copper and cobalt. The C&C (copper and cobalt) is used as a filler. By diluting the platinum with cheaper alloys the manufacturer can practically double his profits. This comes at the expense of you, the consumer, if you think you are getting the real McCoy. The large manufacturers that are producing this product tell me that they are not breaking any Federal Trade Commission guidelines as long as they inform the consumer (you) that you are buying watered down platinum with the 585 stamp inside the ring. The problem comes in when the doped platinum gets sold over and over down the supply chain and less scrupulous vendors decide to remove the 585 and leave just the plat stamp. (This can be done in less than sixty seconds on a polishing wheel). Then you decide to go online and buy what appears to be a great deal on a platinum band only to possibly find out later (when it cracks, craters, discolors, or your finger breaks out in a rash) that you have been duped by doping!

How can you protect yourself

• Only buy a platinum ring from a well know manufacturer (Novell, Benchmark, etc.) or from a vendor that will put in writing and guarantee the platinum content of your ring (90 to 95 percent pure is a good measuring stick with 5 to 10 percent iridium).

• A standard 6mm (¼ inch) comfort fit platinum band weighs 12–13grams. A doped platinum ring will come in weighing over 33 percent less at 8.6 grams (approximately).

• The color can also be a dead give away; all the pieces I examined couldn't be polished up to hold a true white luster but more of a grey luster. What makes visual identification so difficult is 585 can be dipped in rhodium (a platinum group metal) to mimic the look of real platinum.

• Melting point. Since the melting point of true platinum is so much higher than that of doped platinum, the minute a torch touches the imposter its shell will oxidize (crust with black film). Of course this test requires a jeweler and a torch; not necessarily things you have laying around your garage.

Let's look at this another way: when does milk stop becoming milk? We all know what it is—a whitish liquid containing proteins, fats, lactose, and various vitamins and minerals. Should there be a point when, if we tamper with its composition, we should no longer be allowed to call it milk? The answer would seem to be no if you go to your local grocer. There is soy milk, 2 percent, low-fat, skim, lactose-free, and whole milk just to name a few. There appears to be no end to the amount of diluting or modifying of milk that will cause the consumer to yell foul. But what if they start marketing a type of milk called "Royal Milk," "Tru Milk," or "Simply Milk" and told you it was "dip your chocolate chip cookie in it" good! Tasty and more affordable than regular milk. Would you go buy it? What if you discovered that these new milk products were simply one gallon of fresh, cold, delicious milk and one gallon of tap water; does that sound like "Royal Milk," "Tru-Milk," or "Simply Milk"? How much tap water would you allow to be mixed with your precious milk before you simply wouldn't drink or buy it anymore? One gallon? Two gallons? Or would you allow three gallons of tap water with your milk?

A few months ago I raised my hand (politely) and helped tell anyone who would listen that companies were watering down platinum and I didn't think it was right. I explained all the pitfalls to diluting platinum and how you the consumer could protect yourself. Unfortunately, manufacturers are trying to stay one step ahead of all of us. Instead of picking a new name for their product that would easily identify it for what it is, they are riding platinum's coattails and clever marketing to get you to purchase their product. It reminds me of the folks who like to put "low fat" in front of everything they sell to make you feel better about eating an Oreo cookie. "Low fat" and "No fat" are hardly the same thing. Platinum and low platinum aren't either. By introducing products into the market under the brand name "Royal Platinum," "Tru-Platinum," or "Simply Platinum" when they aren't royal, 100 percent true, or just simply platinum is crossing the line. In my last article I reported how copper and cobalt were being used to dope platinum. Now these pseudo-platinum products are being created by mixing $889-an-ounce platinum with $200-an-ounce palladium, then marketing them with a lot of interesting claims: "As good as," "100 percent hypoallergenic," and "Pure precious metal."

If just one person gets a piece of cheap imitation platinum jewelry and believes it to be the real thing it is one person too many in my book. Obviously, we all understand what the marketers are trying to do. They are trying to bring platinum to the masses. If the masses can't afford it we'll just dope it down and dilute it 'till they can. They believe that the average Joe is just too stupid to understand he's being screwed! Guess what? I'm an average Joe and I'm not stupid. I'll write a new article every time someone pulls a fast one. I'll keep you informed. In the mean time, if someone wants to put the word "Royal," "Tru," or "Simply" in front of your platinum please know it isn't really platinum. Now I've got one more question for you:

"Got milk?"

How Do I Get My True Love's Ring Size?

The simplest way, of course, is to ask her. The only problem with this method is that it might tip her off that you're going to propose. For many suitors, that would be a disaster—statistics show that seven out of ten men shop alone and plan to surprise their intended. The other three take the low-risk route—they propose first, then shop for a diamond with the lady. If you're in the latter group, you can check her ring size at the jeweler's.

Another way is to get your hands on a ring she has worn on her third finger, left hand. Take it to a jeweler, who can quickly tell you the ring size. Don't forget to return the ring promptly!

A third way is to ask her mother. This might be even scarier than proposing, but going to her mom first can be a great idea. It can often tell you three key things: One, your beloved's ring size. Two, how the parents feel about you as a potential son-in-law. And, three, the mom can give you a pretty good reading on how your proposal will be received. This way you'll be a lot more sure of the outcome before making this expensive purchase.

Gold "Allergy"

Some women, after wearing gold jewelry for awhile, will find that it leaves a black mark or smudge on their skin. This is caused by perspiration reacting with the metals mixed with the gold, and not from a "gold allergy." Usually a switch from 14K to 18K gold will solve the problem. But if you are the one-in-a-million who still reacts to 18K, switch to platinum. Your body has expensive tastes!

Chapter 4

Picking the Jeweler

N ow that you know what you're looking for, and how to look, the next step is to determine where to shop for your diamond. Before you visit every jeweler in the area, "let your fingers do the walking." You'll find lots of jewelers in the Yellow Pages, under "Jewelers, Retail," and also under "Diamonds, Wholesale." Many merchants advertise in both places. You'll see a variety of information in the advertisements. Some will only mention their "lowest prices." Others will note that the jeweler is a "Graduate Gemologist," or that they sell "GIA Lab Graded" diamonds. To narrow down your search, limit it to jewelers who advertise their GIA and Gemologist credentials.

Using the following questionnaire sheet, spend an hour on the phone calling jewelers and screening them to make sure they have the qualifications you're after. Add up the scores, and visit the top three on your scoreboard.

Jeweler Questionnaire Sheet (J.Q.S.): A Worksheet

Enter the points earned for each answer.

Score

_____1. *How do their prices compare to the wholesale prices listed in this book?*

At wholesale (75 pts)

10% over wholesale (25 pts)

50% over wholesale (10 pts)

Double wholesale (-10 pts)

_____2. *Can they supply a lab grading report with the diamond?*

Yes (15 pts)

No (0 pts)

_____3. *Can they provide an appraisal by a GIA graduate?*

Yes (15 pts)

No (0 pts)

_____4. *Do they have a gem laboratory where the stone can be viewed?*

Yes (15 pts)

No (0 pts)

_____5. *Do they have a master set of diamonds for color grading?*

Yes (15 pts)

No (0 pts)

_____6. *Do they have a gem diamond light for color grading?*

Yes (15 pts)

No (0 pts)

_____7. *Do they have an ultraviolet light to check for flourescence?*
Yes   (15 pts)
No   (0 pts)

_____8. *Do they have a 10X 20.5mm triplet loupe?*
10X 20.5 triplet   (15 pts)
Any 10X loupe   (10 pts)

_____9. *Do they have a gem scope or microscope to view diamonds?*
Yes   (15 pts)
No   (0 pts)

_____10. *Do they use the GIA grading scale for color and clarity?*
If they use the GIA scale   (15 pts)
An automatic disqualification if they do not.

_____11. *Are the diamonds loose (not mounted)?*
If the answer is yes   (15 pts)
If the answer is no, this is an automatic disqualification!

_____12. *Do they have an electronic scale to weigh the diamonds?*
If the answer is yes   (15 pts)
If the answer is no, this is an automatic disqualification!

_____13. *Do they custom-cut diamonds to order?*
Yes   (15 pts)
No   (0 pts)

_____14. *Do they make their own jewelry on the premises?*
Yes   (15 pts)
No   (0 pts)

_____15. *How large is their loose-diamond inventory?*
$250,000 and over (50 pts)
Under $250,000 (0 pts)

_____16. *Do they own the inventory, or are they dealing in memorandum diamonds?*
If they have their own inventory (25 pts)

_____17. *What is their trade-in policy?*
Equal to what you pay for the diamond (20 pts)
Less than what you pay for the diamond (0 pts)
No trade-in policy (-25 pts)

_____18. *Do they have a return policy?*
If they have a 30, 60, or 90-day unconditional (20 pts)
return policy
For a return policy based on possible (15 pts)
misrepresentation, that is, if you find that the stone isn't
exactly what the jeweler said it was
Automatic disqualification for no return policy.

_____19. *Do they have an unconditional buy-back policy?*
Yes (100 pts)
No (0 pts)

_____20. *Does the store specialize in diamonds (or do they also sell watches,*
gold chains, etc.)?
Yes (10 pts)
No (0 pts)

_____21. *Where is the store located?*

If the store is in an office building, such as (15 pts)
Boston's Jewelers' Building

If the store has an ordinary street address (0 pts)

If the store is in a mall (-10 pts)

_____22. *How long has the store been around?*

More than two years (10 pts)

Less than two years (0 pts)

_____23. *Is the jeweler American Gem Society (AGS) rated?*

Yes (10 pts)

No (0 pts)

_____24. *Do they have a GIA graduate on staff?*

Yes (15 pts)

Automatic disqualification if they do not.

_____25. *Do they see customers by appointment only?*

Yes (15 pts)

No (0 pts)

_____26. *Do they have a breakage guarantee on the diamond?*

Yes (40 pts)

No (0 pts)

_____ Total Score

Rating
500–600 points = Superior
460–499 points = Excellent
375–459 points = Good
325–374 points = Acceptable
275–324 points = Marginal
Below 275: Keep looking!

Bonded Jewelers

In every organization there are always the elite few who stand out in the crowd. In the Army, you've got the Rangers. In the Navy, you've got the Seals. In the Air Force, you've got the P.J.s, and in a world filled with ordinary jewelry stores, you have super jewelry stores called bonded jewelers! Why, Fred, are bonded jewelers better than the rest? What are they bonded for? Well, hold on to your hats and I'll tell you.

For starters, only approximately 5 percent of the jewelers in the world are bonded. Only one out of every twenty! "Bonded" refers to the fact that they sell bonded diamonds, and bonded diamonds, my friend, are the way to go if you can afford them. They typically cost 10 percent to 15 percent more than nonbonded diamonds.

A bonded diamond is just a fancy way of describing a fully guaranteed diamond.

This is what you get with a bonded diamond

1. All bonded diamonds come with a lifetime breakage policy. You bust the stone, the jeweler gives you a new one. (One bust per customer.) This is a wonderful policy since treated stones tend to be brittle, and no jeweler would give you this guarantee on an easily broken (and therefore less than 100 percent natural) stone.

2. You're going to love this: all bonded stones come with a lifetime buy-back policy. Translation: for the life of the diamond, you can take it back to the jeweler and get 100 percent of your money back!! (Mountings and sales tax are not included.) How wonderful this is! If you're not 100 percent satisfied for the life of your purchase, you get your money back. Now you might ask, "How can a jeweler afford to do this?" How can he not? Great diamonds are in demand, very liquid, and easy to resell. Any jeweler worth his salt will be glad to buy back a good diamond. If a jeweler doesn't want to buy your diamond back, then there was probably something wrong with it in the first place.

3. All bonded diamonds come with an unconditional lifetime exchange policy. This is great! If your fiancée ever gets bored with her shape, the jeweler will allow even exchanges. (You have to pay for resetting fees.)

4. Bonded diamonds come with a lifetime trade-in policy with a fixed appreciation rate to keep up with inflation.

5. Bonded diamonds come with a market crash protection policy. If the diamond market ever crashes and your diamond depreciates,

the jeweler will refund the difference between what you paid from the new market value.

6. All bonded stones are guaranteed to be natural and untreated.

7. All bonded stones are guaranteed to be 100 percent conflict free.

If you can find a bonded jeweler, they are the way to go. Dishonest jewelers thrive knowing that it's possible to take a bad diamond and make it look good. But looking good and staying looking good are two different things. That diamond needs to pop as much your twenty-fifth anniversary as it did the day you bought it. With a bonded diamond, if the diamond doesn't always meet your expectations or surpass them, you get your money back.

Who Will Help Me Now?

You've probably already realized there are two components that must be evaluated before you sign on the dotted line: the diamond and the setting that holds it. The funny thing is that more and more people are buying the setting from one place and the diamond at another, which leaves us with some serious questions:

1. Who should set it?

2. Who should be responsible for the diamond during the setting?

3. Who will service the ring after it is set? (Who will size it if it needs sizing, who will repair it if it gets damaged? Who will do the annual checkup? If you were lucky enough to buy a bonded diamond, is the bonding still in effect if the seller doesn't do the setting?)

The seller of the setting may or may not agree to set the diamond. Many jewelers won't set someone else's diamond because they don't want to be responsible for any chipping or nicks that may result in the setting process. In fact, many jewelers will only set the diamond if you sign a "hold harmless" agreement. The rest of the jewelers, in order to pressure you to also buy the diamond from them, won't agree to set someone else's diamond under any circumstances.

Jewelers carry exclusive lines of designer jewelry no one else in their region can carry to lure you into the store. Their hope is to hook you with the setting and reel you into a diamond.

The reasons the settings are so expensive are because even though the jeweler hopes to sell you their diamond, they are well aware of the commoditization of commercial diamonds and the difficulty of competing against consolidators that are now selling direct. With the loss of the "rock" profit, they must compensate with an overpriced semi-mount.

I don't blame the jeweler. I wouldn't want to set someone else's diamond unless I had insurance to protect me. Plus, even if I am covered, where is the incentive for me to service some guy who blatantly didn't consider me for the major purchase—the diamond?

As the customer, I wouldn't even ask the jeweler who sold me the setting to set the diamond for one very good reason: he's probably upset with me for not buying my diamond from him, and his setter may take it out on my beautiful new diamond with "torquing." (Torquing is the over-application of pressure to a prong in order to cause permanent damage to the girdle of the diamond.)

So the answer to who should set the diamond is easy: it's the seller of the diamond. And not just for the setting, but all servicing as well. Furthermore, if the diamond is bonded, the diamond seller's insurance company requires him to set it or it voids the warranty. If the diamond seller refuses responsibility, then buy your diamond somewhere else.

The Gift of Jewelry

The engagement ring may be the first piece of fine jewelry you buy, but chances are, it won't be the last. A gift of fine jewelry is appropriate at any season of the year and in any season of life. Birthdays, anniversaries, Christmas, Chanukah, the first day of spring, Mother's Day, Valentine's Day—jewelry is always an excellent gift.

You should take as much care buying a birthday gift as you do when you shop for an engagement ring, to make sure you get the most value for your loved one and your budget. Whether it's a diamond or some other precious stone, many of the same rules apply. And always keep the recipient uppermost in your mind. Use the Gift Questionnaire Sheet below. It'll help you match the gift to the person, and ensure that the gift will be happily received and worn with pride.

Gift Questionnaire Sheet:
A Worksheet

Here are some things to think about before making an expensive jewelry purchase, whether it's an engagement ring, a birthday gift, or a gift for some other special occasion. You may already know all or most of this information, but you probably haven't thought about it in terms of buying a ring. Take the time to fill out this questionnaire, and you're almost guaranteed to be on target with your purchase.

1. *Birth date:* _____

The birth date tells you the birthstone. Sometimes women like their engagement ring or wedding band to have their birthstone mixed with diamonds. Or, a birthstone ring is a nice gift by itself.

2. *Height & Weight:* _____

You can guess at these if you have to. Sometimes these vital stats will help you make an educated guess of someone's ring size, if you don't know it. It also helps you get a ring that's in proportion with body type. For example, a half-carat diamond may look fine on a person of average build, but might look small on a larger person.

3. *Favorite color:* _____

This is important information! If your True Love's favorite color is blue, a diamond set with sapphire accent stones might be perfect. In some cases, the color might be so important she'll want the colored stone as the main stone.

4. *Personality type:*
( ) Conservative ( ) Traditional ( ) Flamboyant
( ) Contemporary ( ) Trendsetter

The choice of settings is virtually unlimited. The personality type will narrow down the search. For example, if the person is conservative and very traditional, a diamond solitaire in a Tiffany setting might be perfect.

5. *Ring size:* _____

Very important. The last thing we want to do is take the ring back to have it sized.

6. *Profession:* _____

Some professionals can't wear jewelry to work, or must wear modest jewelry. A ring might actually interfere with some jobs, so the person should be able to remove it easily. In some professions (real estate broker, stockbroker, model) a "knockout" ring is an indicator of success.

7. *Diamond shape:* _____

Ask if you must, but find out what her favorite diamond shape is. Personality type can be an indicator—the traditionalist would probably favor a round stone (65 percent of all engagement rings have round stones) while a trendsetter may like a fancy shape. After round, the most popular shapes are box radiant, standard radiant, princess, emerald cut, oval, pear, marquise, and heart. Don't buy her a heart-shaped diamond unless she specifically asks for it—it's probably the least attractive.

8. *Carat size:* _____

Ask a woman what size diamond she wants, and she's likely to ask, "How big can I get?" The best way to go about this is to determine your budget and check the price guides in this book.

Size Scale:
Average: .38 points
Yuppie: Around one carat
Ultimate Dream: One and a half to three carats
Filthy Rich: Three to five carats

Is the recipient *size*-conscious or *quality*-conscious? You'll need to have some idea, to know whether you can trade off a little quality for a bigger carat size or vice-versa.

9. **Setting color:**
( ) Yellow gold ( ) White gold ( ) Platinum

Nine out of ten women like yellow gold, but it's important to be sure. Look at her other jewelry. (Don't forget, on a yellow gold ring make sure the prongs are white gold or platinum so they don't make the diamond appear yellow.)

10. **Purity:**
( ) 10K ( ) 14K ( ) 18K ( ) 22K

Most jewelry worn by most women is 14K. 18K is a little softer and a little yellower. Platinum is white. Unless she specifies 18K or platinum, 14K is a safe choice.

11. *Other favorite jewelry:* _____

You might want to match the color or style of other favorite pieces of jewelry.

12. *Is there a particular ring she has admired?*

Pay attention to your True Love and you'll learn a lot about likes and dislikes, and you may hear her admire someone else's ring, or a picture of a ring in a magazine. If you're lucky she may even say, "That's exactly the kind of ring I'd love to have."

The New York Diamond District
"Bargains Galore" or "Buyer Beware"?

The fabled New York Diamond District, centered on 47th Street in Manhattan, probably has more diamond dealers per square foot than any place on earth. For a couple of bustling blocks, the streets are teeming with diamond sellers, practically hawking their wares as if they were selling hot pretzels. The diamond trade here is dominated by hastening figures who lend the place an unmatched mystique as they shuttle between cutting houses and shops, carrying hundreds of thousands of dollars worth of diamonds in their pockets and satchels. But is this a good place to buy a diamond?

In my experience, it is probably the most difficult place in America to get a good deal on a good diamond. You have a better chance of winning the lottery or getting hit by lightning than getting a good diamond deal on 47th Street!

The whole place is attitude and hustle. They employ a kind of reverse psychology—here, the dealer doesn't trust the customer! The dealers give you the impression they haven't really got the time or the inclination to deal with you. "You really want a diamond? Okay, hurry up and pick something out, pay me, and please leave. I have more important things to do than sell you one measly diamond.

Lab grading reports? Guarantees? Whaddya want, papers or diamonds? You want to buy—here, take it. You don't want to buy—try the guy down the street, maybe he has time to deal with papers, I deal with diamonds!"

I bought a diamond on 47th Street one day. Dressed in a business suit, I went shopping, settled on a dealer, and asked for a one-carat, VS1-G. I was given a stone that was said to fit my specs. When I asked for paperwork, the dealer gave me something that fudged on the grades, that said the stone was "VS," but not VS1, and "G-H," not G. Two days later, dressed in jeans, I returned to the same dealer. He didn't recognize me. When I showed him the stone and told him what I'd paid for it, he immediately started berating me: "You got taken! You paid too much for this diamond! You should have come to me in the first place!" When I pulled out my receipt and reminded him I'd bought the stone from him two days ago, he practically pushed me out of the store.

Everyone in New York "knows a guy on 47th Street" who will allegedly give you the diamond deal of a lifetime if you mention the right name. Friends, it ain't that easy.

I've found that if you get above street level on 47th Street, up to the dealers on the higher floors, you can get a decent deal on a diamond if you're a shrewd buyer. Even up there, above the hustle and bustle, dealers pressure you to move quickly on a purchase. Take your time. Examine the stone closely, go through all the steps outlined in this book, *pay by credit card—never cash!*—and get an independent appraisal immediately.

Every major city has its diamond center, and some of them are excellent places to purchase diamonds if you shop for the right dealer and ask the right questions. But the New York Diamond District? Toughest place I know to buy a diamond.

Inside the Diamond Business

A few years ago, an industry group conducted a national survey to see how honestly diamond dealers were doing business with the public. The bottom line: not very.

The group sent diamond experts posing as ordinary customers into jewelry stores across the country. The experts found that the average dealer gave his diamonds a "two-grade bump." That is, they sold their diamonds two grades higher than they actually were. For example, if a GIA gemologist rated a stone's clarity and color as SI1-J, the jeweler would tell you it was a VS1-H—two grades higher, and a lot more expensive. The investigators quietly told jewelers to clean up their act.

But is this stuff still going on? You bet it is! The "bumps" are almost always in clarity and color, because those are the hardest things for the average customer to judge. Beware, and be doubtful of the jeweler's grading. Compare color against a master set, and look carefully at the stone with a 10X loupe for inclusions and blemishes that can affect clarity.

Disposable Jewelry

Ask yourself a question, "Why do people buy jewelry?" Personal adornment? Possibly beauty? Certainly investment? These may be reasons for some, but the number one reason for the purchase of jewelry is status. Pure and simple. If I can have something you can't have I'm better than you. I don't agree with it but it's a fact. People buy jewelry to impress. If not others, themselves. I've heard more than one woman in my day, at a big tenth or twenty-fifth anniversary, say, I deserve this diamond; I've earned it. *When I wear it I feel complete, when I don't I feel naked. Diamonds make me feel special.* Why doesn't paste or glass or cubic zirconia make a woman feel special? They certainly look pretty. They certainly cover the personal adornment category. So why diamonds? Why gold? Why platinum? Because they are supposed to be valuable. They are supposed to be heirlooms. They are supposed to look beautiful, be durable, and maybe if we are lucky, we will have something to pass down to our loved ones along with a story of the special day that piece of jewelry came to be. Jewelry is bought and sold every day because it is supposed to be valuable; it is supposed to be worth something. Then it's our job to weave it into the personal folklore that we can pass down through the generations. But what if it's not?

What if all the big retailers put together a lot of pretty, shiny jewelry, ran expensive ads at Christmas and Valentine's Day and Mother's Day, and told everyone to buy this seven-carat tennis bracelet for $1,000.00, buy this diamond drop necklace for $199.00, buy these 1 carat diamond stud earrings for $499.00 to make your loved one feel special? And what if that jewelry was junk? Hollowed out metal, under-carated gold, treated diamonds with no value. Would your loved one feel special then? When the ads on TV say we only choose the best diamonds for your loved ones and it isn't the truth, is it fraud? Is it?

It is! Plain and simple. When someone buys something and thinks it has an inherent value and it doesn't, the vendor is stealing from you. They might as well have stuck a gun to your side at an ATM. But this is worse. These are our mothers, daughters, wives, sisters, our family that is being taken every time a national chain pushes a piece of junk at a low price and has the gall to call it fine jewelry. I don't have to mention these chain's names, you know who they are, and it's horrendous.

Fine jewelry shouldn't have an expiration date. Paper cups, razors, newspapers, these are things you use and throw away, not jewelry. For the first time in the history of man you can buy diamonds with blue book values so you won't get ripped off. Jewelry should have that same guarantee. I started this section with a question, now I'll end it with one. Would you buy a piece of jewelry if five years from now it was worth less than 17 percent of what you paid for it? Ninety-nine percent of the jewelry bought today falls into that category. The only question left is are you going to buy disposable jewelry or demand something better?

Buying Diamonds on the Internet

Seems like yesterday (it was) when companies selling diamonds over the Internet were a novelty, but today there are literally thousands of such sites. This is how it works: you locate a diamond merchant on the web and look over a selection of stones. Full-color, high-resolution images of the diamonds are displayed on your screen. The diamonds are graded by carat weight, cut, clarity, and color. You select the stone you like, enter your credit card number, and your diamond will be shipped.

My major concern is the quality of the stone's proportions. In my cyber travels, I find lots of "off-makes" (poorly proportioned stones). I could tell they were taking rough stones, which, if properly cut, would have yielded shy-carated diamonds, and creating full-carat stones and in the process sacrificing sparkle for size.

In the process, they offer lots of full-carated diamonds and very few opportunities to "buy shy." If you want a .90ct SI1, I(1), then don't be pushed into a 1ct SI1, G(1), unless you get it for the .90ct price and all the parameters of cut are at least Class II.

In short, you're forced to hunt for the needle in the haystack. Carefully consider the following pros and cons before you decide if it's worth the search.

Cons

1.) *The Scams:*

    A. *Treated Diamonds:* Every form of treated diamond is detectable by a lab, with the exception of a baked or heat-treated diamond. These are diamonds that two weeks ago might have been yellow but are now miraculously white! Baked diamonds are brittle and can break and, therefore, must be avoided. The only way to avoid being stuck with one is to make the sale contingent on a breakage guarantee and/or a money back guarantee.

    B. *Fake or Duplicate Lab Grading Reports:* Diamonds are popping up all over the country that don't match their lab grading reports. A lot of people believe that if a diamond has been graded by a third party, there is no need to have it independently checked when you get it. What good is a lab grading report that says a diamond is great if it doesn't match the diamond? With the technology of today's personal computers, knocking off lab grading reports has become a piece of cake. Or, a crook can take a good diamond and obtain a lab grading report two or three times, then take the extra lab grading report and put it with a similar-looking, but lower quality diamond.

C. *"Hot" Diamonds:* Another quick hustle online vendors use is selling diamonds they haven't paid for and never plan to pay for. In the jewelry industry, diamonds are routinely handled on consignment. This means the owner loans diamonds to a retailer, with the agreement that he will be paid when the retailer sells the stone. But the dishonest vendor sells the diamond online below his cost to attract a quick sale, but never pays his supplier. In a few months, he declares bankruptcy and the spoils are his. In this case, you might get a nice diamond at an unbelievably low price, but not for long. The FBI is now looking at these cases as interstate theft. How would you feel if in a year and a half someone knocked on your door, demanding your stolen diamond? You're out the money and the rock!

D. *The Shell Game:* You order a diamond online, get it appraised, and the appraiser says it's a fake! "Cubic Zirconia!" You scream foul play, go to the police, and the retailer claims he's innocent. But the police have no way of knowing who the real crook is. Did the seller mail a fake like the appraiser says? Or did the appraiser switch the real diamond for a fake, or better yet, did the customer switch the diamond for a fake before going to the appraiser? What a mess indeed.

E. *Handling Fees Scam:* Some online jewelers build their profit into handling fees, not the diamond. That way whether you keep it or not, they just made a sale. Avoid jewelers who charge handling fees that are not refundable.

F. *The Return Authorization Number:* R.A.N. for short. Here's what some "smooth operators" do—they say your satisfaction is the only thing important to them and if you're not happy you can return your diamond for a full refund. Then they stick it to you by using a R.A.N., which is a way for an outfit to deter or even eliminate returns. These companies make you call back to get an authorization number for return approval or you can't return the item. This benefits the vendor in two ways:

1. In most cases anyone who uses R.A.N.s has limited return policies, usually around thirty days. They know that the more difficult they make it for you to use it, or the more procedures you have to undertake, the clock will always be ticking—usually from the very second it was postmarked. If they can stall long enough to make the return policy lapse, they win.

2. Also, if you want to return something, they shuffle you off to another department. Forget about talking to that nice salesman who sold it to you, you're about to get the gorilla of a salesman on the line who will do everything in his power to talk you out of it. Look, if I want to return something, I don't want to spend an hour justifying my return.

Oh, one more thing—believe it or not, a lot of vendors use one more little hurdle on returns. They tell you all returns must be mailed back in the original packaging. Then, they pack it in such a way as to make it impossible to not destroy the packaging and hope you will accidentally throw it away so they can avoid a refund altogether.

2.) *Lack of Multiple Stone Viewing:* I've yet to find an Internet diamond company that has said, "Let me mail you a dozen diamonds, keep the one you like, and mail the rest back." Comparative shopping is the American way. How can we appreciate anything without something to compare it to? Unless you're willing to do your comparative shopping locally before buying online, the only other option is to have one stone mailed to you at a time—and that is an enormous waste of time.

3.) *Poor Warranties:* The best these companies seem to be able to come up with are thirty- to ninety-day return policies. That's it— period! What if your fiancée breaks up with you after four months and you don't need the diamond anymore? Tough! What if a couple years from now you want to exchange or upgrade? Tough! What if your diamond is chipped or breaks? Tough! What if the diamond turns out to be treated? Tough! Tough! Tough! After the limited return policy is over, if anything goes wrong you're stuck with a diamond you don't want. Compare that to bonded jewelers that offer lifetime breakage guarantees, lifetime buy-backs, lifetime trade-ins, and exchanges, and online jewelers are outmatched. Who cares how good a deal something is if you don't need or want it? Ask yourself this question—would you buy a car with only a thirty-day guarantee?

4.) *Service:* I need my prongs tightened, I need my ring sized, my ring broke. What's the Internet company going to do for you now? All they can say is mail it back. What about the annual inspection a ring needs? I haven't found one online jeweler that brings this up, much less says they will take care of it free of charge. When it comes to service after the sale, there is no beating a local jeweler. I know some people live in remote areas, and finding a good jeweler is hard, but that should always be the first place you begin your search. Remember, only buy out of town when local jewelers let you down.

5.) *Will they be here tomorrow?* According to the *Bloomberg Network*, only 2 percent of online retailers will survive. What are the odds you'll pick the right one? Is it important to you that one of the biggest purchases you'll ever make is from somebody that will stay in business? Look at Levi Strauss—they threw in the towel. They couldn't sell blue jeans online! In the end, they realized there is no way to know a perfect fit unless you try it on. Can't do that on the Internet! So if an American icon like Levi Strauss can't make it on the Internet selling $45 blue jeans, what makes these non-brick-and-mortar cyber peddlers think they will? If I were dealing with an online retailer, I'd be pretty damn sure they had an actual location I could visit and had been around for awhile. Because for my money, I want to do business with someone who's going to stay in business.

Pros

1.) *Price:* Certainly the prices on these Internet sites are very appealing. They lure you in like bees to honey. The one thing all these diamond companies must believe is the man with the lowest price wins. They should, however, check their stats. In a recent customer survey conducted by *Jewelers Circular Keystone*, only 35 percent of jewelry buyers said finding the lowest price was their primary concern. Regardless, the frosting on the cake looks very appealing and I've seen little or no price gouging online.

2.) *Selection:* The companies seem to have endless inventories. Walk into your typical jeweler and ask to look at a specific loose diamond and you're lucky to see two or three stones. In some cases, they don't have any and say they have to bring some in. The one thing I find interesting, though, is on several occasions I decided to add up these virtual inventories that many companies claim are theirs and in one case the total value of one inventory exceeded $2.1 billion and in another case their inventory exceeded $5 billion. How does a typical start-up Internet diamond seller get billions of dollars worth of inventory with start-up capital of $15-$20 million? That's a nifty trick!

3.) *Lab Grading Reports and Appraisals:* Every diamond bought online has some kind of piece of paper talking about how good it is. Considering there are a lot of jewelers that only hand over a sales receipt with purchase, a third independent evaluation is a plus.

4.) *Sales Tax:* It's hard to overlook, at least for the time being, that buying a piece of jewelry online from an out-of-state vendor can save a lot of money. In Texas, where the sales tax is 8.25 percent in some places, purchasing a $10,000 diamond online would save you $825! It's important, however, to not let shipping charges, credit card charges, and handling fees eat up this legitimate cost-saving feature.

Conclusion

These are still shark-infested waters—unless you have to surf the net, stay on dry land.

Final Thoughts

Well, Fred, are you telling me there is no way you would recommend buying online? No, I'm not saying that, but before I did, these would be my requirements.

1.) The retailer would have to be in business, with a brick-and-mortar location for at least ten years. (That way I would know they weren't going anywhere.)
2.) A clean Better Business Bureau record.
3.) A lab appraisal or lab grading report with the purchase. Also, never accept a lab grading report older than six months! You never know where that diamond has been or what's been done to it since it was graded. If they are convinced their old diamond is so wonderful, have them regrade it.
4.) A bonding document guaranteeing the diamond is 100 percent natural and not treated.
5.) Lifetime breakage guarantee to guard against baked diamonds.
6.) Lifetime cash buy-back to guarantee against any future customer dissatisfaction.
7.) A lifetime exchange policy.
8.) A lifetime trade-in policy.
9.) A fair, provable price.
10.) Free annual service.
11.) Knowledgeable salespeople.
12.) Good store reputation.
13.) Takes all major credit cards.

Diamond Guy ® Seal of Approval

Many unscrupulous websites are attempting to make money off my name—Fred Cuellar. When in doubt, if you don't see The Diamond Guy®, I have not endorsed it.

Fully Bonded Diamonds™

They are the first fully bonded diamond dealer on the Internet. Fully Bonded Diamonds™ is a subsidiary of Canary Investments Inc., the parent company of Diamond Cutters International.

Honorable Mention: Costco

While generally Costco does not sell the quality diamonds that other fully bonded jewelers do, on occasion I have found a few diamonds that meet my criteria. They are still the first and only major brick-and-mortar retailer to offer an unconditional buy back policy on their diamonds. Way to go, Costco!

Certifiable? Lab Grading Reports:
Are They Just a Piece of Paper?

Every day thousands of people go to work in the major gem labs in the United States. They are there for only one purpose, to serve the gem and jewelry industry and above all the consumer. However, there are limits to what they can do. Can you separate fact from fiction in terms of their capabilities? Here's your chance. Armed with information provided by the experts at Gemological Institute of America (GIA); European Gem Laboratory (EGL); International Gemological Institute (IGI); and American Gem Society (AGS) I developed the following quiz.

Each statement is either fact or fiction. Mark which statement you believe to be true and compare your answers to what the experts have to say at the end of the quiz. Good luck!

136

1.) A lab grading report isn't a guarantee.

_____ Fact _____ Fiction

2.) GIA's mission statement is to ensure the public trust by educating and serving the gem and jewelry industry worldwide. As a nonprofit institution, GIA provides knowledge and professionalism that will maintain the long-term stability and integrity of the industry while strengthening and securing consumer confidence.

_____ Fact _____ Fiction

3.) Grading a diamond can be so subjective some of the labs use four or more graders to get a consensus.

_____ Fact _____ Fiction

4.) Lab grading reports only represent a snapshot of the opinion of the graders at the time the report was taken.

_____ Fact _____ Fiction

5.) A lab grading report and a certificate are the same thing.

_____ Fact _____ Fiction

6.) No major labs will do a lab grading report on synthetic diamonds.

_____ Fact _____ Fiction

7.) GIA does not certify any person, place, or thing.

_____ Fact _____ Fiction

8.) At an additional cost all the labs allow diamonds to be resubmitted for re-grading if the submitter is unhappy with the original results.

_____ Fact _____ Fiction

9.) All labs use the same criteria to evaluate a diamond.

_____ Fact _____ Fiction

10.) GIA uses proprietary Sarin machines to assist in determining the diamond's measurements.

_____ Fact _____ Fiction

11.) All major labs calibrate their equipment before each diamond is graded.

_____ Fact   _____ Fiction

12.) Lab grading reports could be null and void if a diamond is worn.

_____ Fact   _____ Fiction

13.) Lab grading reports are 100 percent accurate within one grade in either direction in clarity and color listed on the report.

_____ Fact   _____ Fiction

14.) Lab grading reports lose their purpose (even if the diamond isn't worn) as they get older.

_____ Fact   _____ Fiction

15.) Physical measurements like weight, dimensions, and proportions are absolutely objective.

_____ Fact   _____ Fiction

16.) If a lab grading report "reads" well, the diamond must be beautiful.

_____ Fact   _____ Fiction

17.) If the lab grading report "reads" poorly, the diamond must be ugly.

_____ Fact   _____ Fiction

18.) A lab grading report tells you everything you need to know to determine the value of a diamond.

_____ Fact   _____ Fiction

19.) A lab grading report makes the diamond more valuable.

_____ Fact   _____ Fiction

20.) The labs can detect all forms of treatment 100 percent of the time, including baking.

_____ Fact   _____ Fiction

21.) The labs can with almost 100 percent accuracy determine if a fancy color diamond is natural.

_____ Fact   _____ Fiction

22.) A lab grading report is an appraisal.

_____ Fact   _____ Fiction

23.) A fully bonded appraisal based on the GIA grading system is more valuable than any lab grading report.

_____ Fact   _____ Fiction

24.) To ensure the diamond is worth what you paid and holds its value in the future it must come with a lab grading report.

_____ Fact   _____ Fiction

25.) A lab grading report will ensure that the diamond is not a blood diamond.

_____ Fact   _____ Fiction

26.) All the major labs use colorimeters to be as precise as possible.

_____ Fact   _____ Fiction

Answers

1.) *A lab grading report isn't a guarantee.*

Fact

The opening line on a GIA lab grading report states, "This report is not a guarantee, valuation, or appraisal." No lab wants to guarantee anything or leave you with the impression that they do, because if something goes wrong in the transaction they don't want to be held responsible.

2.) *GIA's mission statement is:* To ensure the public trust by educating and serving the gem and jewelry industry worldwide. As a nonprofit institution, GIA provides knowledge and professionalism that will maintain the long-term stability and integrity of the industry while strengthening and securing consumer confidence.

Fact

3.) *Grading a diamond can be so subjective some of the labs use four or more graders to get a consensus.*

Fact

In some cases not even the four graders can agree so they bring in more people to break the tie!

4.) *Lab grading reports only represent a snapshot of the opinion of the graders at the time the report was taken.*

Fact

Where that diamond came from and what it's been through (mounted, dropped, nicked, etc.) cannot be determined from the date it was graded to the date you receive it.

5.) *A lab grading report and a certificate are the same thing.*

Fiction

A lab grading report is not a certificate. A certificate would authoritatively confirm the facts and a lab grading report states a few facts but mostly subjective opinions. It was the jewelry industry (not the labs) who started the slang use of the word "certificate" in reference to lab grading reports. GIA categorically states that they do not certify any person, place, or thing. In the past, I have often used the word "certificate" incorrectly. To be perfectly accurate, we should all be saying lab grading report or document if what we are saying is opinion based. EGL USA does use the word "certificate" on their grading reports, but they disclaim any responsibility for any errors or omissions in the report.

6.) *No major labs will do a lab grading report on synthetic diamonds.*

Fiction

According to Lynn Ramsey, publicist for EGL, "EGL USA is the only lab in North America to certify synthetic diamonds. However, we do not certify diamonds that have been fractured filled or any treated stones in which the treatment is known to be unstable under certain circumstances."

7.) *GIA does not certify any person, place, or thing.*
Fact
As stated in the response to question #5.

8.) *At an additional cost, all the labs allow diamonds to be resubmitted for re-grading if the submitter is unhappy with the original results.*
Fact
(*GIA's Response*) "There are times when the grade of a diamond is at, or close to, a boundary point between grade ranges. For this reason, we offer services whereby a client may resubmit a diamond to be subsequently examined by additional independent experts, who may or may not render an opinion that differs from the original grading."

(*EGL's Response*) "Diamonds may be resubmitted at least two times if the owner disagrees with our grading. After two submissions, the owner can have a consultation with the senior graders."

(*AGS's Response, Peter Yantzer*) "It's very simple. If the customer is not happy with our results and believes we are wrong they can resubmit it for evaluation again."

9.) *All the labs use the same criteria to evaluate a diamond.*
Fiction
A.G.S. uses their own in-house system (such as A.G.S. 000) while EGL

recognizes an SI-3 grade. In addition, none of the labs agree with each other on one standardized system for measuring proportions.

10.) *GIA uses proprietary Sarin machines to assist in determining measurements.*
Fact
Sarin and Megascope machines can be ordered from the factory calibrated to specific tolerances as requested by the customer.

11.) *All major labs calibrate their equipment before each diamond is graded.*
Fiction
"Once a day would be ideal for us, but at least once a week," says Peter Yantzer of American Gem Society. "We fully service them once a year. With hundreds of diamonds being graded a day it is not cost-effective for any lab to calibrate before each evaluation."

12.) *Lab grading reports could become null and void if a diamond is worn.*
Fact
Since a diamond can be damaged during setting and while being worn, in my opinion any grading report becomes invalid at that point.

13.) *Lab grading reports are 100 percent accurate within one grade in either direction in clarity and color listed on the report.*
Fact
Pin-pointing a diamond to an exact grade is subjective but pin-pointing it to a range is not. Example: To say a diamond is SI-1 is subjective, but to say it is not any worse than an SI-2 or better than a VS-2 is objective. The FTC regulations state that a diamond must be within one clarity and one color grade.

14.) *Lab grading reports lose their purpose (even if the diamond isn't worn) as they get older.*

Fact

As was stated earlier, the time frame between the diamond's evaluation and its purchase date is unaccounted for. Lab grading reports older than six months tell the consumer one of two things: A. The diamond isn't beautiful enough to be snatched up right away and/or B. The lab grading report is no longer a legitimate reflection of the quality of the diamond. Old grading reports are a red flag.

15.) *Physical measurements like weight, dimensions, and proportions are absolutely objective.*

Fact and Fiction

Leverage gauges, Megascopes, Sarin machines, and scales are temperamental. According to the manufacturers, if (and this is a big if) the equipment is clean and calibrated before each testing the results are 99.9 percent accurate. If hundreds of stones are tested between calibrations then measurements may be off plus or minus 3 percent. Since we already know that it is financially infeasible for a lab to calibrate their equipment for every stone, a separate Megascope or Sarin report must accompany or replace the lab grading report to confirm its physical measurements.

16.) *If the lab grading report "reads" well, the diamond must be beautiful.*

Fiction

No one lab grading report provides all the vital information. Therefore, it is possible for a diamond to appear to look good (read well) on its lab grading report when in actuality it is unattractive to the eye.

17.) *If a lab grading report "reads" poorly, the diamond must be ugly.*

Fiction

The lab grading report may have judgments which are misleading. Also, beauty is still in the eye of the beholder. There are a lot of diamonds that technically return a poor amount of light, are off color and heavily included, but are loved anyway by their owner. Never forget it's what a diamond represents that is its real beauty.

18.) *A lab grading report tells you everything you need to know to determine the value of the diamond.*
Fiction
A lab grading report is not a guarantee, valuation, or appraisal.

19.) *A lab grading report makes the diamond more valuable.*
Fiction
Don't confuse a bonding document (fully-bonded), which does guarantee value, and a lab grading report. A lab grading report is an opinion on the overall quality of the diamond and does not increase the diamond's worth.

20.) *The labs can detect all forms of treatment 100 percent of the time, including baking.*
Fiction
Nothing is 100 percent, but the labs are probably 99.9 percent accurate on all forms of treatment with the exception of baking, where they are batting .750.

21.) *The labs can with almost 100 percent accuracy determine if a fancy colored diamond is natural.*
Fact and Fiction
Fact on all colors except green.

22.) *A lab grading report is an appraisal.*
Fiction

23.) *A fully-bonded appraisal based on the GIA grading system is more valuable than any lab grading report.*
Fact
The fully-bonded appraisal is the most comprehensive document you can get on the quality of the diamond. It includes every measurement (taken from a calibrated Sarin or Megascope machine), and a colorimeter reading where grade and type are listed and a consensus of four graders who all must agree on what the worst case scenario is on the clarity grade. Then, it is accompanied with an unconditioned lifetime bonding document to guarantee current market value and secondary market value.

24.) *To ensure the diamond is worth what you paid for it and holds its value in the future it must come with a lab grading report.*
Fiction
Don't confuse a fully-bonded diamond and a lab grading report. They are two different things. Any quality diamond can come with a lab grading report, but only about 2 percent of all gem-quality diamonds come with a bonding document.

25.) *A lab grading report will ensure the diamond is not a blood diamond.*
Fiction
The only document in the world that can do that is a country of origin certificate.

26.) *All the major labs use colorimeters to be as precise as possible.*

Fiction

Officially, the labs do not use colorimeters at this time. Colorimeters do require constant maintenance and calibration.

Conclusion

Lab grading reports came into the marketplace to stop widespread misgrading. Did it work? Yes, I think so. However, lately it has become more important what letter or number or percentage shows up on a piece of paper than whether or not that little shiny rock has personality or takes our breath away. It didn't happen all at once; it happened slowly. I see people make decisions on how much they will love their diamond based on what someone else's opinion is. When did we give up our opinion of what's beautiful; when did we relinquish our judgment? Any paper that comes with a diamond can only give you an idea of what you have. Want guarantees? Fine, make sure it's fully bonded. Want beautiful? Make sure it takes your breath away! Make sure every time you look at the rock it reminds you of why you bought it in the first place; you found love, it found you. You're damn lucky! That rock, regardless of size or quality is a symbol of that love. It shouldn't be a contest about how big your bank account is or how smart you think you are. Are lab grading reports or appraisals or documents just a piece of paper? No. They are tools, guides, sign posts. No piece of paper in the world should ever try to tell you how you feel about your diamond. If it talks to you, listen up. It's letting you know that you are loved.

Fine Print

Are You Really Getting What You're Getting?

They say that the devil is in the details. If they are referring to the fine print found in contracts, grading reports, catalogs, and bills of sale, they are right. Recently, *ABC News* did a week-long special on how consumers are literally signing away their rights when they acquire a new product. Look at the fine print in the stack of papers you sign when you buy a new car or a catalog you receive in the mail. Fine print is everywhere! TV commercials that last sixty seconds give us one second to read the tiny print at the bottom of the screen. Lifetime warranties may have an expiration date (it's in the fine print). Many of us don't read the fine print and if we do read the teeny-weenie sentences, they don't necessarily make any sense to a layman. They are written with such legalese that even a lawyer could not pin down the meaning.

In sum, people buying products are not getting what they think they're getting. When they eventually figure out they've been bamboozled, there isn't anything they can do about it. You didn't send in the registration card so there is no warranty, or if you did they have no record of it, or there is a catch-all phrase that leaves them hold harmless and you holding the bag.

The following thirteen fine print sentences are the most prevalent and destructive to your rights as a consumer in the world of jewelry, lab reports, and jewelry insurance. If any item you contemplate buying is saddled with one or more of these fine print "viruses," then the potential purchase and subsequent enjoyment of that purchase will likely be compromised.

1. "Original prices may not have resulted in actual sales."

This one kills me! You almost have to read it a few times to under-stand what they are actually saying. This fine print statement shows up in many consolidators' websites and in brick-and-mortar store catalogs. It means the price listed as the original price is bogus! Nobody on this planet or any other one ever paid sticker! The price exists to give you a sense of savings when you compare the "sale" price to the "original" price. This is how stores run those fake 50 to 75 percent off sales and still make a nice profit. Anytime some-one says you are getting a sale price, ask them to put in writing the fact that someone in this universe actually paid the original price. If they won't, the asking price is the real price; there isn't a real sale going on and you need to take your business elsewhere.

2. "Diamond carat weights (ct) represent the approximate total weight of all the diamonds in the setting and may vary no more than .07 below the stated weights." Or

3. "All total carat weights are approximate."

While the law (Federal Trade Commission) says that any diamond piece of jewelry sold has to weigh within .005 ct of its actual weight, there is an exception. The exception is when stated other-wise. Translation: Any jeweler can tell you a diamond weighs any amount regardless of whether it weighs that amount if and only if this fine print virus is posted on their website, in their catalog, or in any paperwork they give you! If you see it or ask if the weights they sell are approximate and they reply affirmatively—RUN!

4. "The genuine gemstones in this catalog may have been treated or enhanced by heating."

This one is sneaky! Usually this paragraph is followed by, "Generally, diffusion (sapphires), oiling or waxing (emeralds and opals), irradiation (blue topaz), or surface enhanced (mystic or twilight topaz)." The key here is generally. By using "generally" it means they can treat their diamonds with no further acknowledgement than this statement. Translation: You could spend thousands of dollars on a diamond that has actually been baked and is brittle! If you're after quality, stay away from any jeweler that alters their gemstones and hides the fact in the fine print.

5. "This report is not a guarantee, valuation, or appraisal and _____ has made no representation or warranty regarding this report, the article(s) described herein or any inscription described in this report." Or

6. "_____ Lab and its employees and agents shall not be liable for any loss, damage, or expense for any error in or omission from this document or for its issuance or use even if caused by or resulting from the negligence or other fault of _____ Lab and its employees." Or

7. "The client declared and accepts that a certificate, drawn up in accordance with the scientific methods applied by _____, cannot as such be disputed before _____, and _____, its appointees or _____ are on no account responsible for possible dissimilarities and/or differences that could appear from repeated examinations or as a result of other methods applied." Or

8. "All clarity characteristics may not be shown."

These fine print viruses were all taken directly from lab grading reports. Lab names have been deleted to protect the guilty. The purpose of a lab grading report is to offer declarative objective information that the purchaser can rely on in order to make an informed decision. As consumers, we're looking for guarantees. If we are told it's X, it should be X. We shouldn't be told it's X and then in the fine print find out it might be X and if it's not, the vendor cannot be held liable. Any lab report that has these slimy small print viruses should be disregarded as nothing more than propaganda. Any lab report whose opening sentence is "This report is not a guarantee, valuation, or appraisal," is as useful as a college degree purchased on the Internet. A lab unwilling to stake their reputation on what they say in their document serves no purpose. This is why the guild stores like Tiffany, Cartier, and Harry Winston are all using internal labs where the grading can be quadruple checked in order to guarantee your purchase. If the labs don't clean up their act and lay down some hard and fast guarantees with their reports, the steroid baseball scandal will seem minor in comparison when tens of thousands of clients realize their diamond doesn't really match the report and their rock is worth less than 20 percent of what they paid.

9. "Diamond grades may vary."

I saw this little ditty in many department store (jewelry department) catalogs and mall jeweler catalogs. "Diamond grades" can refer to the clarity, color, and class of cut, so this little number can create a pandemic of problems. This statement literally allows the vendor to call the diamond any type of quality they want! "Vary" is so subjective that the deceptive jeweler could argue that "vary" means any number of grades off in any direction. Very simple solution here—tell the jeweler to put in writing that they guarantee every single characteristic they are telling you about or giving you in a lab grading report and if it is disputed by any accredited appraiser that you can get your money back or a replacement—no questions asked. If they blush or hem and haw, get walkin'!

10. "Some styles may contain single cut diamonds."

Single cut diamonds only have 16–17 facets (these are usually small diamonds) instead of the standard 58. Little diamonds that don't have enough facets flatten out and fog out very quickly when they get a little bit dirty. No brand new ring should come with single cut diamonds. If sparkle is important to you in your rocks, avoid these.

11. "Gemstone products are often treated to enhance their beauty. Some treatments may not be permanent and require special care."

This one is horrendous! They are saying that anything under the sun might have been done to your rock (baking, laser drilling, bleaching, etc.) and any side effects are not their responsibility. Not only that, they are stating their "enhancements" might not be permanent (the rock could fall apart) if you aren't careful. Any diamond, I repeat, any diamond that may have been treated needs to be avoided! Period.

12. "Photos may be enlarged and/or enhanced."

OK, I get the enlarged part, so I can see what I'm buying better. But the enhanced part crosses the line! The whole point of enlarging is to see the fine detail. If the true detail has been altered to look better, then how do I know what I'm getting? Look, if I'm in a chat room and someone emails me a picture of Christy Brinkley and tells me it's them, aren't I going to be a little disappointed when I meet them in person?

13. "If the merchandise is lost, stolen, or damaged, it will be replaced with like merchandise or what it costs us to replace it."

This is known in the industry as the "like clause." Mid-cap insurance companies place it in the fine print so they don't have to match exactly what you originally had. With some insurance companies "like" means within one clarity grade, one color grade, ten points of carat weight, and no provisions for class of cut, treatment, or fluorescence. Your half-million dollar home burned down and they want to give you a tent to live in, arguing that it is "like" merchandise because it also provides shelter! Any insurance policy with the-like clause" is practically worthless. Premium policies from Lloyds of London or Chubb do not have "like" clauses.

Knowledge is power. Now that you are aware of these fine print viruses they'll be easier to find and recognize.

Real versus "Fake" Diamonds

The Bellataire Diamond

"Should Jewelers start warning customers that the diamond they're buy-ing could be treated for color, but there is no way of knowing for sure?"

That's a direct quote from *Jewelers Circular Magazine*, September, 1999, page 92. What they are talking about, along with everyone else, is what could be "the greatest gemological crisis to hit the diamond industry!" That's at least what Gemological Institute of America President William Boyajian said at a symposium.

The Bellataire Diamond (formerly known as Monarch Diamond, previously Pegasus) is a non-detectable, color-enhanced, treated diamond that is now on the market and wreaking havoc.
The diamond is the brainchild of General Electric and Lazare Kaplan and is sold through a company called Pegasus Overseas Limited.

In a nutshell, here's what they do. They take an inexpensive brown or yellow diamond, heat it at high temperatures and pressure, and bake out the nitrogen or boron present to make it white. Like a twice-baked potato, with one exception—this one will leave a bad taste in your mouth!

Baked diamonds, or annealed diamonds as some people refer to them, though they are undetectable to labs or independent appraisers, have one major flaw: they are brittle! Moreover, treated diamonds have little or no secondary market value.

Insist your diamond comes with a bonding document to guarantee that it is natural, or you could just wind up buying one of the most expensive pieces of costume jewelry ever.

"Fake" Diamonds

Many customers want to be reassured that their diamond is really a diamond. This should not be a major worry, unless you bought your diamond from a guy on the street. No legitimate jeweler, even one who might try to cheat on color and clarity grades, is going to slip you a piece of glass, a cubic zirconia, or even a synthetic diamond and try to pass it off as a real diamond.

Diamond Substitutes

Cubic Zirconia (CZ)

A CZ is not a "man-made diamond." It's a diamond simulant that looks similar to a diamond. It does not have any of the properties of a diamond—it simply looks like a diamond. And while a well-made CZ looks pretty darned good, it doesn't have anywhere near the hardness of a diamond and will quickly become worn and dull. Any good jeweler can spot the difference between a diamond and a CZ in a moment. I think the CZ has a plastic look, and has a light blue cast through the entire stone. The sure way to tell is to weigh the stone— a CZ will weigh 55 percent more than a diamond of the same size!

The Yehuda Diamond

The Yehuda diamond, relatively new to the diamond marketplace, is named for Zui Yehuda of Israel. He's the man who developed the process of "filling" a flawed diamond to make it more attractive.

The Fall of the Tablet of Truth

Once upon a time, a long time ago, in a land far away, lived the house of

GIA. In this house were the most respected and honorable knights. Every day

they went into battle to uphold honor, credibility, and the search for the tablet

of truth. Many would come from faraway lands to the house that GIA built

and ask but one question, "Does my rock of honor speak the truth? For if

my rock is a mere pebble then I shall send it back from where it hath come

and choose another." All were happy in the land of Debeerios until another

family built another house that said their knights could find the truth as well.

Soon there were many houses. The houses of IGI, EGL, AGS, HRD, and

others all proclaimed that their knights could foretell the truth of the stones

of destiny better than the other. The land of Debeerios was in a state of con-

fusion. Does truth have many faces? And if so, which face tells no lies? All

the country's men and women were lost.

Then one day a great man rode into Debeerios on a white stallion. His name was King Bonding. Everywhere he went the villagers would follow. He went to every house and spoke with every knight and when he was done he made a proclamation: "There are some knights in all houses that do not speak the truth, or hold their tongues and speak only partial truths. To bring honor back to the stones of destiny, I will bless only the mightiest of stones. These stones of destiny that have been blessed by King Bonding will forever be known as The Fully Bonded Stones of Destiny! These stones can tell no lies for their value can never be disputed!" The land of Debeerios rang with happiness and joy for truth had been restored. No longer could the knights of the houses distort the truth for their own selfish reasons, because if they did, they would never win the final battle with King Bonding.

Here's how it works. Yehuda takes a diamond that has cracks on the outside and fills the cracks with clear molten glass. The cracks disappear. Using this process, Yehuda can take a stone with an I1 clarity grade and make it look like an SI2. The advantage of the Yehuda diamond is that you can get a slightly better-looking diamond without paying a higher price.

The disadvantages of the Yehuda diamond:
- You don't know how long the treatment will last. You might be wearing the diamond one day and it will look great, and the next day the filler will fall out, leaving you with a flawed stone.
- Any repair work on the setting could damage the filler.
- Most people don't like the idea of having a diamond that's not all diamond. If you buy a Yehuda diamond, you might have a very hard time reselling it.

The Federal Trade Commission requires a jeweler to disclose whether a diamond has been treated. But many jewelers don't have the expertise to know if a stone has been treated, and may buy or sell a Yehuda diamond unknowingly.

Synthetic Diamonds

In 1954, General Electric produced the first synthetic diamonds. A synthetic diamond is a rock that has all the properties (durability, hardness, refractive index, etc) of a natural diamond but was made by man. Not to be confused with simulants (those that look similar to a diamond but don't have the same properties) like glass, cubic zirconia, or moissanite. Think about it: Man was able to create in a laboratory what it took Mother Nature one hundred million years (minimum time required for a natural diamond to incubate) to do. I'll tell you something more incredible! What didn't happen in 1955? Can you guess? That's right, no synthetic diamonds in the market place! Not in '56, '57, '58, or in the '60s, '70s, '80s or early '90s! Man figures out how to make diamonds then man doesn't do anything with the discovery? Why?

Let's look at the facts. Right after General Electric learns how to synthesize a diamond (which, by the way, wins a Nobel Prize for P. W. Bridgeman of their company), GE is interviewed about the details. They say, "We've only learned how to grow industrial quality diamonds (not sufficient quality to be cut into a gem for a piece of jewelry but rather to be used for drill bits, semi-conductors, and such)." It would be sixteen long painstaking years before man would not only walk on the moon, but also create a gem quality diamond the likes of Mother Nature. GE is interviewed again and I quote, "We've conquered the next hurdle; we can now produce transparent gem-quality diamonds in an attractive size. There's only one problem. They cost more to grow than to find, cut, and polish." End of story? Hardly! Another quarter century would go by when a little company called Gemesis Corporation would raise their hand and say, "I think I can do it. I think I can figure out how to grow a diamond cheaper than it costs to find one." The problem was very few people were listening and those that did just scoffed. "If General Electric in partnership with DeBeers can't figure out the secret to growing diamonds at a profit, there's no way some little start up company is going to figure it out!" Know what? They were wrong! Flash forward to present day. Not only has Gemesis figured out how to grow white diamonds, but they've also figured out how to grow the tremendously expensive fancy colors—the blues, canary yellows, oranges, and even the million-dollar-per-carat reds! I know what you're probably saying, "Fred, if this is true, why isn't it in all the newspapers, on TV, and radio?" Well, the reason is only now have companies like Gemesis grown enough raw diamonds to be able to meet the inevitable demand onslaught! It makes no sense to go public when you don't have enough supply to meet the demand.

The Interview

I once had the honor and privilege to talk to Carlos Valeiras (the President and CEO of Gemesis). Here is a portion of my interview.

Question: Mr. Valeiras, I know you've unlocked the secrets to growing diamonds that encompass all the colors of the rainbow, so what will you serve up as a first course to the diamond-buying public?

Answer: While certainly there is a strong demand for the whites, the canary diamonds (yellow) are easier to grow and will offer the best price point to the public. Using your words, that will be our first course along with the oranges.

Question: What kind of price breaks will you be able to offer from the naturals?

Answer: The canaries and oranges will be offered at about 1/3 the going price of the naturals.

Question: You said that you can grow the whites. What's keeping you from offering the whites right now?

Answer: We can currently produce about six hundred carats of rough a month and we're moving every piece! Since the canaries are more profitable for us and offer the best savings to the end consumer, we're not going to add the whites till we can fulfill the demand for the yellows.

Question: How would anybody know they are looking at a synthetic versus a natural?

Answer: All of our synthetics will most likely be laser inscribed identifying them as lab created. The diamonds will be marketed under the brand name Gemesis Cultured Diamond.

Final Thoughts on Synthetics

Synthetics do not appreciate in value and have no trade-in value. In April 1995, synthetic diamonds became available to the public, selling for about two-thirds the cost of natural diamonds. There is no secondary market for these stones, so if you buy one you're stuck with it forever. If you tried to resell it you'd get back only 10 percent of your initial investment, versus an 80 percent resale average for a good quality natural diamond that was correctly purchased. For the latest on synthetic diamonds, go to my website, www.thediamondguy.com.

Making the Purchase
A Final Review

1. Fill out the Gift Questionnaire Sheet.

2. Call all potential jeweler candidates on the phone and have them answer questions on the Jeweler Questionnaire Sheet.

3. After you've called all the jewelry stores that you're planning to compare and have filled out a Jeweler Questionnaire Sheet on each one, pick the top three rated stores.

4. If for any reason you cannot find a jeweler in your area that

satisfies all the requirements, call my HelpLine for assistance (800-275-4047).

5. Before you visit your jeweler choices, call each one and make an appointment. By making an appointment you can be assured that you will get individual attention.

6. Once in the jewelry store, look at the diamonds they have to offer. Write down the clarity and color grade of each stone you like and fill out the Proportion Questionnaire Sheet on each stone. Only consider purchasing diamonds that match the carat weight, clarity, and color you like and pass the Proportion Questionnaire Sheet. Their prices should also be close to the reccomended prices listed in this book.

Chapter 5

Tricks of the Trade

Blue Diamond Blues

Some jewelers may try to market a "blue-white" diamond as though it were a white diamond with a hint of blue, and more valuable than a plain white diamond. It's not! It's a diamond that fluoresces blue and is therefore less valuable. Avoid it!

The "50% Off" Sale

Browsing through your Sunday paper you spot an exciting ad: a local jeweler is having a "50% Off" sale on diamonds! Wow! You jump into your car, drive to the store, and you make what you are sure is an incredible buy on a one-carat diamond.

You're still patting yourself on the back a week later when you happen to walk past another jewelry store where you see the same size, same quality diamond selling for less than what you paid—*and it's their regular price!* What happened?

You were taken in by a fake sale. Many jewelers run these sales. They'll take a diamond that is worth, say, $1,000 wholesale and instead of marking it up 100 percent, which is standard practice, they'll mark it up 400 percent and tell you that $4,000 is the regular price—when in fact the regular price for such a stone would be $2,000. Then the jeweler takes 50 percent off the inflated price and sells it to you for full retail, $2,000.

The way to know if you're really getting a sale price is to compare the jeweler's price with the wholesale price list in this book. If the jeweler's regular price is more than double the wholesale price, you're not getting any bargain.

For example: Joe's Jewelry Store has a one-carat VS1, G(1) on sale for $19,152, marked down from $38,304. You look at my price list and see that a one-carat VS1, G(1) wholesales for $11,154. Therefore, full retail should be $23,308. Joe has artificially inflated the "regular" price to trick you into believing you're getting a bargain.

Bait and Switch

This is a term that's been around for a long time, and it's not limited to the diamond business. Bait and switch refers to anyone who runs an advertising special on a particular item just to get you into the store. When you go to the store, however, you're told that the advertised item is sold out. Then they try to sell you something else—invariably, something more expensive. The jeweler hopes that since you've already made the trip to the store, you won't want to go home empty-handed.

Don't be impatient! Many people arrive at the store determined to buy something and get talked into something they don't really want. Take control! Grade the jeweler using your Jeweler Questionnaire Sheet, and if he or she passes that test, stick around and look at some diamonds, using a scratch sheet to check each one. Compare the prices to the wholesale prices in this book, to see what kind of deal you're being offered. And for an exact updated price on a particular stone, call my HelpLine, 1-800-275-4047.

Is White Really White?

Jewelers love diamonds that fluoresce blue, and will sometimes install special lighting to enhance the fluorescence of their diamonds. The blue masks the yellow color that might be in the diamond and make it appear to be a higher color grade than it really is. Always take the loose diamond you're looking at and place it on a white background to check the color, and make sure there are no spotlights shining on it. Always ask the jeweler if the stone has fluorescence. If he says no, ask him to prove it by placing it under an ultraviolet lamp so you can see if it glows a particular color. If you decide to buy the diamond, get it in writing whether or not the stone has fluorescence.

Grade Bumping

The Federal Trade Commission requires that a diamond be within one clarity and color grade of what it is originally sold as. Because of this, jewelers tend to "bump" the grade. For example, if a jeweler buys a stone as a VS1(G) he'll bump it up and sell it as a VVS2(F). If you buy it as a VVS2(F) and have it appraised as a VS1(G), the dealer is legally covered, because he sold it within one grade of what it really is.

The Fraction Scam

Some jewelers will list the weights of their diamonds only in fractions, such as 3/4 of a carat. Your next question should be, "Well, is it seventy-five points or not?" Many jewelers will call anything from sixty-five to seventy-five points a 3/4 carat diamond. These same jewelers will call anything from ninety points to one hundred points a full carat. *This is illegal.* A diamond must weigh within *half a point* of its stated weight. You'll notice a jeweler will never round a diamond down—they'd never call an eighty-five-pointer a 3/4 carat stone. Ask the jeweler to weigh the stone, in front of you, on an electronic scale.

If he says he can't because it's in a setting, you shouldn't be looking at it anyway. Only buy loose diamonds.

The Old Switcheroo

You've shopped around, rated the jewelers, graded the diamonds, and finally found the stone you want. You lay your money down and order a setting. When you get the ring, you have it independently appraised—only to discover that the diamond in the ring isn't the same stone you purchased! The jeweler has pulled a switcheroo. You go back and confront him, and he accuses *you* of switching stones.

What now? There's really nothing you can do, no way to prove a switch was made. You must prevent the switcheroo before it happens.

When you decide on a diamond, get the jeweler to put in writing the exact weight and the clarity and color grades of the stone. Before the diamond is mounted, have the jeweler show you where the blemishes and inclusions are, and plot them on a drawing. Keep this drawing with you, and when you return to pick up the mounted diamond, check it again, looking for the same flaws that are on your drawing. If they match, you have the right diamond.

The Sandbagger

If you've purchased a diamond by following all my instructions, you shouldn't feel the need to go to an independent appraiser to double-check your purchase. But if you do, watch out for the sandbagger! The sandbagger is someone who lies to you and tells you that you've been taken, that your diamond isn't worth what you paid for it. Why would he do that? So that he can recommend where you should buy your diamonds—no doubt at a place which gives him a kickback! Or he may tell you, "You should have bought from me."

The Vanishing Act

Now you see it—now you don't! Carbon, that is. There is a laser beam process for removing carbon from inside a diamond. It's called *laser drilling*. A diamond that contains black carbon, visible with a 10X loupe, is zapped with a fine laser beam which vaporizes the carbon, removing the black spot.

The problem is that the laser beam creates a *tunnel* from the surface of the diamond to where the carbon used to be. You might not be able to see this tunnel with the naked eye, but you'll see it under a loupe. And if a stone has been drilled several times, it can be weakened.

Laser drilling can make a diamond more attractive to the eye, but it can also lower the resale value. The Federal Trade Commission requires jewelers to disclose to consumers whether a diamond has been laser-drilled.

So, you think it's easy to get a good engagement ring? Or do you think you've already got a good one? Better think again, the cards are stacked against you...

The Dirty Dozen

Twelve Little Facts You Probably Didn't Know

1. The average person in the United States pays twice what they should for their engagement ring.

2. One out of every three diamonds sold in the United States is laser-drilled.

3. One out of every twenty diamonds sold in the United States is fracture-filled.

4. One out of every three diamonds sold in the United States has been treated to some degree, including doublets, coating, and irradiation.

5. Seventy-five percent of all round diamonds are cut poorly to salvage weight, resulting in diamonds that lose two-thirds of their potential sparkle.

6. Eighty-eight percent of all fancy diamonds (pear, marquise, emerald cut, etc.) are poorly cut to salvage weight, resulting in diamonds that lose two-thirds of their potential sparkle.

7. The average diamond sold in the United States has been over-graded in quality by two grades to enhance its salability.

8. Two out of every three diamonds have fluorescence (a diamond's reaction to ultraviolet light) that causes the diamond to look oily and milky in sunlight.

9. Three out of every five diamonds are weighed incorrectly to increase the profit margin of the jeweler.

10. The average diamond sold in the United States is tinted yellow and will probably never appreciate in value.

11. The average diamond sold in the United States has cracks, breaks, or contains carbon that you can see with your own eyes.

12. If we define a good diamond in general terms as a diamond that is big, white, clean, sparkly, and will appreciate in value over time, less than twenty out of every one thousand diamonds sold in the United States would classify as good.

Torquing

Webster defines torque as something that produces or tends to produce rotation or torsion and whose effectiveness is measured by the product of the force and the perpendicular distance from the line of action of the force to the axis of rotation. Boy like that helps…Sorry. To "torque" however, is a slang term in the business for over-tightening with the intent of trying to damage the rock. Torquing is kind of like spiking a punch bowl or a disgruntled chef adding a little something to your entrée that doesn't pass the health code. Torquing is usually done by someone you may have purchased the setting from but not the diamond or a jeweler you stopped by for ring cleaning that didn't sell you the diamond. Torquing is the destruction of your property just like vandalism with you as the victim.

The scenario usually goes like this:
Jeweler (The Torquer): Good morning, may I help you?
Happy Couple (You & Fiancée): Nope, already have our ring, just killing some time.
Jeweler: Grrr… (under his breath) Killing my time!
Happy Couple: Excuse me?
Jeweler: Umm. I was just admiring your ring. Would you like a free ring cleaning?
Happy Couple: Oh my, that would be delightful!
(All right maybe nobody says "delightful" these days, but it's my story.)

Jeweler takes the ring to the back and hands it off to the henchman,
I mean bench man.

Jeweler: Give it the "They should have bought it here special!"

Bench Man: No problem boss, one torque job coming up.

He pulls out a pair of tightening pliers and crunches the prongs till
he hears a high-pitched ping (high-pitched ping is the diamond
cracking under prongs).

Jeweler: Good as new!

Unaware Couple: Thank you; it looks lovely.

End of scenario

The mean bad jeweler has now accomplished two things: one, he's
vented his anger out on your ring, and two he's set up the poor jeweler who sold you the diamond to take the fall when the pieces of
the girdle fall off. When that happens, the M.B.J. (Mean Bad
Jeweler) will hope that you are mad at the old jeweler and maybe
you'll remember the nice guy who cleaned your ring for free for
your replacement diamond.

What's the lesson here? Whoever you buy your diamond from sets
it, cleans it, tightens it, and does all annual checkups. We want to
keep all M.B.J.s out of our lives.

Inscription Deception

One of the latest crazes is to have your diamond laser inscribed.
What I'm talking about is the placement of serial numbers by a
laser on the girdle of diamonds for identification purposes.

Perception:

By placing a serial number on the girdle of a diamond that matches a lab grading report an independent appraiser can verify if the diamond matches the lab grading report. Also, if the diamond is ever stolen and recovered the serial number can be put into a database so the diamond can be returned to you. The inscription is permanent like a tattoo, and cannot be removed or altered without a major weight loss or potential damage to the diamond.

Reality:

The only way to be 100 percent sure a diamond matches a lab grading report is to check its measurements and match up its plotting of inclusions and blemishes. Anybody can take an extra lab grading report and laser inscribe its number on a diamond that doesn't match it. If some common thug stole your diamond, having a serial number that matches your lab grading report might bring it back to you, but it is unlikely. All sophisticated jewel thieves have the girdles repolished to remove the laser inscription so the diamond cannot be traced. This of course dispels the notion that an inscription is permanent and cannot be removed.

I have to hand it to all those companies that keep trying to come up with some new gimmick to hook us on. But come on; let's put this in the simplest of terms. If we already have the fingerprint (the plotting) of the diamond, we don't need to carve our initials into it to prove it's ours.

The "True Weight" of Diamonds

One carat diamonds offered for sale rarely truly weigh one carat if cut correctly.

Let me explain. Diamonds are a lot like people. They come in all shapes and sizes and just like people, they can carry a little extra weight. In fact, in the community of diamonds, more diamonds are "overweight" than in the community of people: Up to 88 percent of all diamonds. The sad part is that it's the diamond industry that is purposely producing all of these chubby diamonds! In 1919, over eighty years ago, a gentleman by the name of Marcel Tolkowsky determined that the diamond industry as a whole was cutting diamonds incorrectly and adversely affecting the diamond's sparkle. Mr. Tolkowsky released a paper on the correct way to cut a diamond so it would have maximum sparkle (light return); no excess body fat. The Tolkowsky cut ended up becoming the American ideal. Subsequently, in the 1950s, a gentleman by the name of R.W. Ditchburn applied the same mathematics in order to trim the fat off the other shapes (marquise, pear, oval, etc.). For decades, if you asked for a well-cut "Ideal" diamond of a particular size, you got it. Then the marketers convinced the public that a one carat diamond or more was the dream size. That's where the problems crept in. Diamond cutters all over the world started inventing their own criteria for "a well-proportioned stone" so they could fatten up the diamond. Clearly we have a problem when 75 to 88 percent of all one carat diamonds are overweight! Just like in the old commercial where there was a whole lot of bun and very little meat, we are running into the same problem today with diamonds that should be one carat but are cut fat so that they will tip the scales over one carat.

The only way the problem is going to be solved is for the diamond buying public to start asking for the diamond's "True Weight." True Weight is a diamond in which the crown height plus max girdle thickness plus pavilion depth equals the total depth percentage and whose proportions meet class I or class II criteria. I've never met a jeweler who will volunteer to the consumer that the device used to measure the diamond's vitals (sarin or megascope machine) also has a fat content measuring button! It's called the re-cut feature. Once a diamond has been analyzed, all the grader has to do is enter the recorded data into the re-cut program, enter the desired results (like a plastic surgeon showing you what your nose will look like after the surgery), and click the mouse. In seconds, the re-cut program will announce what the diamond should have weighed if it had been cut correctly vs. its current weight. Practically every diamond I see is overweight by 20 to 30 percent!

It is the diamond's "True Weight" we should be paying for, not extra love handles left on by the cutter. If enough of us demand to only pay for a diamond's "True Weight" versus its "over-weight" then maybe someday the cutters will get the message.

Diamond Mysteries
Things Aren't Always What They Seem

Story 1—Mistaken Identity
It was a crisp February morning when Sarah finally got around to going through Gram's jewelry box. She opened the box of memories filled with charm bracelets, add-a-bead necklaces, sterling silver from her turquoise phase, and of course, "The Ring." As the only granddaughter, the ring had been promised to her when she had barely learned to walk. She could still hear Gram's words echoing in her head, "Little Sarah, this ring used to belong to my grandmother. Bought on a rail man's salary and some day it will belong to you."

With all the sparkling baubles and beads, was a neatly organized stack of papers. In that stack of receipts and appraisals she found the original sales ticket of $629 (a king's ransom in those days) for the ring. It was over one hundred years old. With that were a few appraisals that had been done on the ring, the last one dated Nov. 14, 1929. It valued the ring at over $3,100!

As Sarah slipped the ring on to her finger for the first time, it didn't make its way past her knuckle. Gram had lost a lot of weight over the years and it had been sized down repeatedly. Gramps always took care of that before he past away almost a decade ago. The ring would need to be sized again for her to wear it.

Later that afternoon she went by a popular jeweler she had heard her friends talk about, had her finger sized and left her heirloom. It would be ready by the end of the week. The next day, Sarah received a phone call that would change her life.

"Mrs. Allen, this is John Stevens. I'm the manager at McKay's jewelry shop. I don't know how to tell you this, but the center stone in your grandmother's ring isn't real. It's a diamond simulant. Something that looks like a diamond but isn't." Sarah practically passed out.

What happened? Was the jeweler telling the truth and if so how could that be since she had the original sales ticket and appraisals on the diamond? Also, if the jeweler was innocent, why did it take him a day to discover the stone was imitation and not when she brought it in? Is the jeweler the thief or an accidental pawn in a game of the vanishing diamond?

Keep reading to learn the answer to this and the following mysteries.

Story 2—Change of Heart

Michael had been dating Mary Katherine off and on for almost three years. It seemed every time they would get close to a commitment, some monkey wrench would send them back to square one. After a lot of soul searching, it finally dawned on Mike that even though he had told M.K. he loved her, he had never "put his money where his mouth was." So when it came time to clock out on Friday, he headed straight for the mall to buy an engagement ring. This would finally settle once and for all to Mary Katherine and the rest of the world that he wanted to spend the rest of his life with her.

Michael planned to pop the question on the following Friday, but by Saturday it just slipped out, "Mary ah, M.K., Mary Katherine, will you marry me?" Mike stumbled for the ring that had been in his pocket since yesterday. "Well, just don't sit there, what do you say?"

"Um, ah, sure, wow, how big is it? You betcha."

During the next month things seemed to go the same between Mary Katherine and Michael, but there was something he couldn't quite put his finger on. Something was wrong. And exactly six weeks to the day Mike had popped the question, he found out what: "Mike look," Mary Katherine started, "I've had some time to think about it and well, I don't think I'm ready." She promptly handed the ring back. Before Michael could say another word, the woman of his dreams walked out of his life with a hug, a kiss on the cheek, and "Let's still be friends."

It took Michael two weeks before he could bear to look at the ring he had tossed in his sock drawer since the break up. But with the sixty-day return policy looming, he didn't want to own the ring and not have the girl. So he headed off to get his refund. He felt sure the jeweler would understand.

"Hi Mike, how's that new fiancée of yours doing? When's the wedding day?" asked Stan, the jeweler.

"Well, the thing is, Stan, it didn't work out, I'm going to need to get my money back."

"Geez, sorry to hear that, can I see the ring?"

With that Michael handed over the little ring box of broken promises when... "Hey Mikey, I don't know what you're up to but this ain't no diamond! What are you trying to pull?"

"What am I trying to pull? That's the same stone you sold me! If something's amiss, it's by your doing!" The battle lines were drawn and out came the sabers! What happened?

Story 3—Double Take
"So how much is the diamond?" asked Allen to the attractive sales girl at Clark's Department Store. "The tag says it's $850. Got anything more expensive?"

"I believe so but they're in the vault and only the store manager, Mr. Peters, can handle that." As much as Allen enjoyed talking and flirting with the curvaceous blonde, he relented.

"Well I guess I need to meet with Mr. Peters, but you have a fine day with your fine self!" The clerk excused herself.

Within a few minutes Mr. Peters stepped out of one of the corporate offices. "May I help you?"

"Yes," replied Allen, "I'm looking for an expensive diamond, preferably loose."

"So," Mr. Peters said with a smile, "Someone getting engaged?"

"Something like that," Allen replied.

"You said expensive but how big do you think your future fiancée would like?"

"Let's not worry about her, what do you have in a loose diamond, must be round, 2.11ct?"

"Hmm, let's see, around 2ct, here's a lovely 2.02 VS1, E in a four prong platinum tiffany setting."

"No, no thank you," replied Allen. "Loose, I want to buy it loose."
"Okay, that's fine, but what kind of setting are you eventually going to put it in?"

"I'll worry about that later," Allen snapped back. "Can I please see some stones now? I'm kinda in a hurry."

"No problem, let's see what I've got. How about a 2.05; its clarity is…"

"No, no bigger!"

"Alright how about a 2.20?"

"Okay." This piqued Allen's interest. "How much?"

"$19,000 flat," replied Mr. Peters. "It's an SI1 with an H color, ideal cut."

"Wow, that looks pretty good, I'll take it."

"Well, okay sir." Mr. Peters was surprised; he'd thought this guy was wasting his time. "How would you like to pay for it?"

"Charge it, the American way."

Within fifteen minutes Allen was on his way with his new diamond. When he got home it only took Allen a few minutes to retrieve the yellow pages he had perused earlier. "Here we go," Allen thought to himself. "While You Wait Appraisals." He called and made an appointment.
"Mr. Richmond will see you now," said the small, quiet-spoken receptionist at the appraiser's office.

"Thank you," replied Allen. Mr. Richmond sat behind a small metallic desk surrounded by microscopes, scales, monitors and things with blinking lights.

"Mr. Allen Ball? How can I help you today?"

"Well, I just bought this diamond a 2.11ct, Round, I mean a 2.20 Round SI1(H) and I just want to make sure everything is on the up and up." Allen handed Mr. Richmond the small, neatly folded parcel paper that held the loose stone. Mr. Richmond took it, opened it, and let the rock slide out of the paper into an awaiting polishing cloth, where it was quickly covered up and rubbed.

"I'm giving it a good cleaning before we take a look." Within seconds he opened up the cloth and gently dropped the stone on to a white pad that laid in front of him. There he picked it up with a pair of tweezers and viewed it under a 10X magnifying lens. "Hmm, oh my, Mr. Ball, I don't know how to tell you this, but this isn't a diamond. It's a cubic zirconia."

"What? That's impossible! I know it's a diamond. All I need for you to tell me is that's not the quality I paid for!"

What happened?

Story 4—Now You See it, Now You Don't
Every day Margaret started her day with the same ritual: shower, breakfast, and a dip. Not a dip in the pool but a dip in the ultrasonic cleaner for her beautiful 2ct VS2(G) round diamond anniversary ring. The ring was mounted in 18K yellow gold and meant the world to her. Four children, twenty-five years of love and devotion, six relocations and one grandchild later, this ring was her gold medal.

Today, like all other Thursdays, she met with her gal pals for a roaring game of cutthroat bridge. True to her schedule, right after breakfast she pulled down the ultrasonic cleaner from the bay window above her sink.

Upon looking inside, she realized that she had allowed her ammonia and water solution to evaporate, so she would need to mix up a fresh batch. "Hmm, let's see, where's that Parsons sudsy ammonia?" she said to herself as she looked under the cabinet. "Ah, here it is! Darn! Empty!" She glanced down at her ring to break the bad news that it might have to skip today's bath when it hit her. "Clorox! I bet Clorox will work. I've got plenty of that!" She ran to her laundry room, grabbed the Clorox, poured it in the ultrasonic cleaner, dropped in her ring, placed the ultrasonic cleaner back onto the bay window and ran upstairs to get ready.

"Mrs. Williams," called out Maria, the housekeeper. "Mrs. Lawrence is here to take you to bridge."

"Now Maria," Margaret said, "lock up and set the alarm. After that string of robberies in the neighborhood, I want you to be safe." Maria locked the front door behind Margaret and pressed the four-digit code to the alarm of the house.

As Margaret sat down to shuffle the cards to start the game, she realized she had forgotten to retrieve her ring from the ultrasonic cleaner. "A few hours of extra cleaning will do the ring some good," she thought. "Anyway the house is secure and Maria is there for safe keeping."

The ninety-second warning signal for the alarm beeped when Margaret opened the front door to her home. Within seconds the alarm was disabled and Margaret headed straight to her kitchen. She could still hear the ultrasonic cleaner running when she pulled it down, only to discover her ring was gone! "Maria, has anyone besides yourself been in this house today?" she asked.
"No, Mrs. Williams, nobody, just me."

"Then where's my ring?"

"I don't know." At that moment, Margaret's husband Roy was returning from his day at the golf course and was soaking wet with perspiration; it had been almost one hundred and two degrees that day.

"What's all the commotion Marg?" What happened?

Story 1 Answer

There could be a lot of finger pointing here. For starters, the jeweler should have looked at the ring under a microscope and determined its authenticity before Sarah had left the store. Sarah should have insisted on a plotting (a mapping of what the interior of the stone looks like under magnification) of the stone to make sure she would get the same thing back. Both Sarah and the jeweler did a poor job of protecting themselves. Also, what about all the ring sizing that Gramps had done? Was it possible some other jeweler along the way had done the switching? Things aren't always what they seem. There was a very interesting clue that was right under Sarah's nose from the beginning. It was the date on the last appraisal: November 14, 1929. During the previous two weeks, the stock market had crashed, losing over thirty billion dollars in its assets. Was it a coincidence that as the United States entered the Great Depression, Gramps suddenly decided to get the ring appraised? No, it was no coincidence. During the court case against the jeweler, Sarah found a pawn ticket dated November 14, 1929 in her grandfather's chest! Apparently times had gotten tough and he had to sell Gram's diamond. I'm sure he always planned to switch it back before anyone found out but he died before he had a chance. Jeweler innocent.

Story 2 Answer

In this little mystery, you've got three potential suspects, maybe more. For starters, the jeweler could have certainly sold a fake versus the real thing, but if he were smart he would have plotted the diamond to prove he had sold the real McCoy. Also, if the customer had immediately appraised the diamond after the purchase, he would have known instantly if the jeweler was up to no good. Also, what happened to the ring while his good little girlfriend had it? Could she have been devilish enough to have made the switch herself? Or is the culprit Mike himself? Finally, let's not forget the ring was in an insecure sock drawer that many people had access to. In the end, the jeweler had made the mistake of not plotting the stone to prove or disprove the jeweler's innocence or guilt and the case went off to court.

Jeweler sued by customer, customer countersued by the jeweler. It wasn't until almost a year later and thousands of dollars in legal fees that old Mary Katherine confessed under threat of a subpoena she had actually switched out the stone. I repeat again, things aren't always what they seem. All the litigation would have been avoided if the jeweler and the client had done a better job of protecting their own self-interests.

Story 3 Answer

Believe it or not, this one isn't as easy as it might seem. Sure the jeweler himself may have switched the stone when he sold it (not likely; if a jeweler gets even a hint of scandal of selling fakes, he's out of business), or we might quickly blame the appraiser for switching the stone when he had it hidden in his cleaning cloth. Or how tough would it be to accuse the customer of setting the whole thing up himself? These should have been your clues; for starters the customer purchased the diamond quickly, no negotiating, and no asking for documentation. Allen was also obsessed with talking about a 2.11ct diamond, once when buying the 2.20, and again a Freudian slip with the appraiser. During the sale, Allen didn't want to discuss either the setting or the girlfriend, which should have made the jeweler nervous rather than anxious to sell. Everything here, from Allen flirting with the first sales girl to his reaction at the appraiser points to Allen being up to no good. How else could his final statement to the appraiser be, "I know it's a diamond, I just want you to prove it's not the right quality?"

Here's what really happened. Allen had bought, using cash, a 2.11ct from another jeweler, a very poor quality but real diamond valued at $4,000. His plan was to buy a good one for $19,000, get the poor one appraised representing it as the one he had just bought, then act surprised when it wasn't the SI1, H 2.20 he had paid for. Then he'd call his credit card company, act shocked that the diamond was misrepresented, stop payment, and leave the poor honest jeweler with a 2.11ct piece of junk. A perfect plan but with one hitch. When he took the 2.11 to get appraised, he never thought the appraiser would switch it for a fake! In this instance two people had their hand in the cookie jar.

Story 4 Answer

Surprisingly or not, the maid was arrested for the theft of Mrs. Williams's ring. However, in the end she would be proven innocent. The ring had disappeared of its own accord, and as it turned out, Mrs. Williams would be shown to be the unwitting accomplice.

Here's what happened: As we already know, Margaret kept her ultrasonic cleaner in a glass bay window. We also know that it had been a very hot day. Combined with a Clorox solution, which should never be substituted for ammonia, all the elements were there. The sun through the bay window heated the Clorox, boiling the solution until the 18K yellow gold setting did the only thing it could do, and that was dissolve. When Margaret looked into the ultrasonic cleaner, her ring wasn't gone, it had just been destroyed. The only things that were left were her three diamonds that appeared transparent in the cleaning solution. Where Margaret became an accomplice to the disappearance of her own ring is when she poured the solution with her diamonds down the drain.

As unbelievable as this all sounds, it's all true. I was the expert that was brought in at trial to testify to the value of the ring. When I heard about the Clorox, I put two and two together and got the maid off. Oh, if you're wondering how I proved my theory, it was when the plumber came in and removed the elbow of the drain under the sink and found Mrs. Williams' three little sparklers!

In Conclusion

For practically two decades, I've done my utmost to be the best consumer advocate in the purchase of a diamond. I've told consumers about the tricks of the trade, fracture-filled diamonds, baking, and every dishonest thing a bad jeweler could do to take your money and leave you holding the bag. But with these handful of true stories, I wanted to show you how easily it is for the shoe to be on the other foot.

Every time a customer walks into a jewelry store, the jeweler is not only concerned with the hopes of making a sale but the fears his wish will come true and it winds up being the first step in a scam against him! Even as we saw in the first story, an honest jeweler got pulled into court because he had his guard down while trying to do someone a favor by sizing a ring he never sold in the first place.

The lesson here is, "I do believe that in the heart of man is goodness," to quote a great man and innovator in the retail industry, L.L. Bean. And we shouldn't be too quick to judge and cast the first stone. Even on the darkest days, there's always at least one light that shines in the distance, and it's the light of truth. Sometimes difficult to find, sometimes difficult to see, but it's always there. All we have to do is look for it. And please remember, things aren't always what they seem.

Chapter 6

Common Myths About Diamonds

1. A diamond is forever

A diamond will only be forever if you take care of it. If you don't, a diamond can chip, fracture, or break. Even a diamond should come with a care instruction tag.

2. Diamonds are very rare

Nope! There is more of a man-made shortage than a natural shortage. The distribution of the number of diamonds put on the market each year is highly regulated. There are really enough diamonds to give each man, woman, and child in the United States a whole cupful.

3. Women are more size-conscious than quality-conscious

This one is almost true, but not quite. Even though most women believe that bigger is better, there are still quite a few women out there that will sacrifice size to get a better quality diamond.

4. A diamond is the most expensive gemstone

The truth is there are quite a few more expensive gemstones on the market. For example, a top-quality ruby can be worth over thirty thousand dollars a carat.

5. A large diamond is always worth more than a small diamond

Size is only one criterion by which a diamond can be judged. A small, high-clarity, high-color diamond can cost more than a large, low-clarity, low-color diamond.

6. After a diamond has been cut, little diamonds can be cut from the shavings

Usually there are no shavings, only dust. Most diamonds are ground down and there aren't any little pieces left over to cut anything else. Most people believe a diamond is whittled, not ground down. This is another myth.

7. A fancy-shaped diamond is more difficult to cut than a round diamond

All diamonds, to a certain degree, are difficult to cut, and some very large diamonds take more time and effort to cut than smaller diamonds do. But one diamond is not harder to cut than another just because of the shape.

8. Diamonds are a good investment

Webster's dictionary defines investment as "an outlay of money for income or profit." Since most people purchase diamonds to be worn and not to be resold, diamonds are not a good investment. Only through proper education and training could diamonds become a good investment. For the average Joe, I would recommend buying a diamond for the enjoyment and prestige it brings and don't be too concerned about making a buck.

9. A diamond should be bought strictly on its visual appearance: "If it looks good, buy it"

A lot of people believe "what I can't see can't hurt me!" Well, we all know that blind ignorance will only lead to disaster. Practically any diamond looks good in a jewelry store. The jeweler spends quite a bit on spotlights to make any quality diamond sparkle. But unless you plan on carrying a spotlight with you everywhere you go, you'd better check the four Cs or you might purchase a diamond that only looks good in a jewelry store and is lifeless everywhere else.

10. An emerald-cut diamond is the most expensive shape diamond

I don't know why some people believe this. I constantly have clients tell me that they like emerald cut diamonds but know that they are the most expensive and can't afford them. This is crazy! The emerald cut diamond is the *least* expensive of all the shapes. You see, it is the shape that is most like the natural shape of the rough, so there is a little bit less waste during the cutting process. If you like emerald cut diamonds, enjoy them, don't avoid them; they are not any more expensive.

11. Diamonds are a bad investment

Diamonds may not be a good investment for the average person, but they certainly aren't a bad investment. If a diamond is purchased at the right price, it will most certainly hold its value. Since the diamond crash of 1979, when D flawless diamonds fell in value from $75,000 to under $15,000, the price of diamonds has been increasing constantly.

12. No diamond is perfect

The definition of a perfect diamond would be a diamond free from inclusions and blemishes when viewed under 10X loupe (flawless), with no trace of color (D-color), and perfectly proportioned. Even though they are rare, there are such diamonds around.

13. It is difficult to tell the difference between a diamond and a cubic zirconia

Any good jeweler can tell the difference immediately. A cubic zirconia has more of a plastic look. There seems to be a light-blue cast throughout the entire stone. One sure way to determine the difference is by weighing the cubic zirconia. A cubic zirconia will weigh 55 percent more!

14. Diamonds are expensive

Some are, some aren't. It depends on their quality. Believe it or not, it's possible to get a one-carat diamond for as low as three hundred dollars if it's junky enough.

15. Diamonds are a girl's best friend

This one would have stumped me, too. I've always believed that all women like diamonds. It wasn't until recently that I learned there are some women out there that very much dislike diamonds and think they are a waste of money. I guess for them maybe a dog is their best friend.

16. A diamond with a lab grading report must be a good diamond

I can't even count how many jewelry stores I've gone in to and asked a jewelry salesperson if a particular diamond is good, only to hear,

"Sir, it must be good. It has been graded by Laboratory XYZ! And only the best diamonds in the world can come with this lab grading report!" Give me a break; any lab anywhere in the world will grade any diamond sent to them. Purebred or rabid dog, it doesn't make a difference to them. The labs just want their fee.

17. An ideal cut diamond is ideal

In the 1960s jewelers would toss around the term "perfect" like they were passing out candy. "Sir, this is a perfect diamond," "Ma'am, this is a perfectly fine diamond," or "Heck, this diamond is just plain perfect!" The FTC eventually stepped in and said the term was just plain misleading. Jewelers argued that they should have the right to call anything perfect that in their opinion was perfect to them.

They were overruled; the FTC passed a guideline that said only a D flawless well-cut diamond could brandish the label of "Perfect." The jewelers changed their pitch. Forty years later we are hearing the same thing. "Sir, this is an ideal cut diamond," "Ma'am, this is an ideally fine diamond," and finally, "This diamond is exactly cut; it is ideal!" Only one problem, FTC hasn't stepped in yet. And until they do there will be over one hundred interpretations of ideal. But don't be fooled, it's easy to identify the scammers. They are the ones that insist that total depths can exceed 61 percent for rounds and non-rectangular fancies. They are the ones that insist on tiny tables for rounds and giant tables for emerald cuts. They insist that these measurements are ideal, and I guess in some respects they are ideal in increasing the weight of the diamond so their bottom line goes up. Want ideal? Be more specific and ask what class of cut a diamond is. In that arena there are hard and fast rules.

18. Great symmetry equals great proportions

For the most part, symmetry refers to the arrangement of the facets on the diamond, length to width ratios, out of roundness, and inline cutlets. Symmetry, excellent or otherwise, does not infer great proportions or the relationship between crown and pavilion angles. If any salesman tries to imply that just because the symmetry on the lab grading report is good or better means it must be a well-proportioned stone, it's time to leave.

19. Only diamonds can cut glass

There are a number of things that can cut glass. From synthetic diamonds to glass itself. Anyone who suggests that the best way to prove a diamond is real is to rub it against glass should have their head examined. This wives' tale should stay just that.

20. A jeweler will tend to mount his best diamonds in ready to go settings

On the contrary, a jeweler will always premount his worst diamonds in settings. That way he can hide any chips under prongs and make it impossible for you to get an exact color and weight measurement. Always remember a jeweler's best diamonds are in his safe, and the only way to see them is to ask for them to be brought out.

Exposé

The Rock Talks

He's been described as a girl's best friend, socialite, movie star, tough guy, and

he's been the subject of over six hundred books. He has been known to hang

around royalty from Queen Elizabeth to as far back as Henry VIII. His list

of friends past and present are the who's who of not only Hollywood (Marilyn

Monroe, Elizabeth Taylor, Julia Roberts, to name a few) but of professional

athletes like Ruth, DiMaggio, Jeter, and Chamberlain. His movie credits

include The Pink Panther, Gentlemen Prefer Blondes, Diamonds

are Forever, Marathon Man, *and hundreds more. He's been described as*

the silent type, but insiders have told this reporter that he loves to talk to

women. We've finally been able to corral Mr. Diamond in this once-in-a-life-

time exclusive interview where he talks with such clarity and honesty, this

reporter had to dry his eyes more than once.

Reporter: *Mr. Diamond thank you for taking time from your busy schedule to* *talk to me today.*

Mr. Diamond: Please call me "Ice." My friends call me Ice.

Reporter: Thank you, Ice it is. Tell me, what was your first big break?

Mr. Diamond: Break is probably a poor choice of words, but I dig where you're coming from. But nevertheless let's call them opportunities. Without question there isn't a success story that would happen without people who stuck their neck out for you. Friends that support and believe in you, like Agnes, Charles VIII, Mary of Burgundy, the Duke of Burgundy, Oppenheimer, DeBeers, Gerald, and so many others, too many to name in this interview.

Reporter: Ice, I'm familiar with a few of the people and organizations you mentioned. Perhaps you could give our listeners a rundown of how these select few deserve a mention.

Mr. Diamond: I'd be glad to. Agnes Sorel was the first person ever to believe in me. In the fifteenth century when she hung around Charles VIII she became the first woman to wear diamonds in public. I had been a shut-in until then.

I wasn't very good with people, a little shy.

Reporter: *Shy? You? I don't believe it!*

Mr. Diamond: *Yes, it's true. Agnes believed in me enough to push me out of my nest and into the public's eye.*

Reporter: *What about Mary of Burgundy, daughter of Charles the Bold, Duke of Burgundy. What's your connection here?*

Mr. Diamond: *Agnes taught me to believe in myself, face the world, and not be afraid to be me. Mary, oh sweet Mary, taught me about love. Nothing in this world matters if you have love. She was the first person to wear a diamond engagement ring.*

Reporter: *And Oppenheimer, DeBeers, and Gerald. I'm assuming you're referring to Gerald M. Lauck, past president of N.W. Ayer Advertising agency in New York?*

Mr. Diamond: *Of course I am, but let's start with Oppenheimer, chairman and CEO of DeBeers. Oppie, even though not my first agent, was my best. He represented me like my father. He knows everybody and put me in the right circles. It was through Oppie's effort in 1939 that led to the introduction to Gerald Lauck. It was Oppie and G that hatched the plan to introduce me to movie stars and literally put me in the movies.*

Reporter: *Were you nervous?*

Mr. Diamond: *Maybe a little, but when Marilyn Monroe sang, "Diamonds are a Girl's Best Friend," any butterflies I had went away.*

Reporter: *How do you account for the fact that in the 1920s less than 10 percent of women in the U.S. wore diamonds compared to the almost 70 percent today?*

Mr. Diamond: *Because they didn't know me then, not the real me. Before Oppie and G started their publicity campaign people thought I was aloof. I* guess I deserved that since I only hung out with royalty, but I wanted the world to know that there was something more to me. That I had something to offer everybody.

Reporter: And what is that?

Mr. Diamond: If something grown from carbon can make something of himself then the dream is alive in all of us. Nothing is impossible. We are all capable of grand things. If a rock can make it, so can you.

Reporter: Nice message.

Chapter 7

After the Purchase

Once you own the ring, you have to take care of it as you would take care of any major investment.

Insurance

As soon as you get home with the ring, take steps to get it insured. If you don't already have an insurance company, start shopping for one. Many insurance companies will only insure personal jewelry if you have a homeowner's or renter's policy with them. If you have to shop for an insurance company, use this questionnaire.

1. Name of company: _____

2. Will they insure jewelry?   Yes ❑   No ❑

3. If yes, under what conditions will they insure jewelry?

_____

4. What is the cost of the insurance, per year, per $100 of value?

_____

5. Do they need an appraisal, or will the sales receipt do?

_____

6. Do they need a photograph of the jewelry? _____

7. Does the policy cover loss, theft and damage? _____

8. Does the policy cover replacement value at the time of the loss?

_____

9. Following a loss, does the insurance company pay the insured amount, or replace the lost article with a new one? _____

Do's and Don'ts

• *Don't* let people touch your diamonds. People seem to have an overwhelming desire to touch a pretty ring. Politely tell them look but don't touch. Oil from their fingers will quickly dim the brilliance of the stone, and the oil makes it easier for airborne dirt to stick to the diamond.

• *Do* clean the ring *daily!* Diamonds just don't look good when they're dirty.

• *Don't* wear the ring in the bath or shower. Soap scum gets trapped under the prongs and can make the diamond look dull. Also, it's too easy to whack the ring against the tub or shower stall, possibly damaging the ring or loosening the diamond.

• *Don't* be tempted by jewelry store window offers of "Free Jewelry Cleaning." Never leave your jewelry with a jeweler you don't know and trust. Unfortunately, there are jewelers who would use this opportunity to switch your diamond for a fake. Or they might not know what they're doing and damage your jewelry accidentally while cleaning it.

Some Final Suggestions

1. Don't make an engagement ring a birthday or Christmas gift. First, if on the off chance she were to break up with you and the engagement ring was a birthday or Christmas gift, then she would be able to keep the ring. Second, the giving of an engagement ring should be on a special day all by itself—for example, on the one year anniversary of your first date. The more thought and preparation you put into this, the more it will be appreciated.

2. Once you've purchased the ring, as tempting as it might be to want to show off your purchase to your friends and family, don't. The showing off is for your girlfriend to do once she gets the ring. What you don't want happening is for everyone to say, "Oh, yes, that's pretty; we've seen it before!" One of the most exciting parts about receiving an engagement ring is showing it off and watching your friends and family's reaction to seeing it for the first time. Don't take that away from her. Once you purchase the diamond, don't show it to anyone. That will be her job.

3. If you can't follow rule two and break down and show the ring to someone and it happens to be a lady, don't—I mean don't—let her try it on. Some women are very superstitious about being the first and sometimes the only one to wear the ring. You don't want your wife-to-be to run into this person and have her say, "Oh, yes, I saw it last week and tried it on and told your fiancée that if it looks good on me it will look good on you!" You're a dead man if this happens, and all the money you spent on the ring will go down the drain!

Cleaning Your Diamond
And Other Jewels

You can keep your jewelry sparkling clean at home with a little time and effort, but you should also take your jewelry to your jeweler twice a year for a professional cleaning and to have the stones checked to make sure the setting is tight.

The easiest method of home cleaning is ultrasonic. An ultrasonic cleaner sends sonic waves through a cleaning solution to literally vibrate the dirt off your jewelry. Every morning you can place your jewelry into the cleaner and in ten minutes the jewelry is ready to wear. You can buy an ultrasonic cleaner for under $50 in specialty stores. If you have a hard time finding one, write to me c/o Sourcebooks and I'll have one shipped to you.

Jewelry Cleaning Discovery

Ronald Lockhart from Downingtown, Pennsylvania, has invented an ingenious product called the "Powerescent Tablet." Here's how it works: you place the jewelry to be cleaned in a bowl or glass, add hot water, then drop in the Alka-Seltzer-like tablet. Ten minutes later, ba-boom. Jewelry is clean! I really love this product. Since it is not an ammonia-based solution, it's safe and easy to use on all jewelry including pearls and emeralds. It's also great for travel. An ultrasonic cleaner can be difficult to take on the road, but these tablets are a piece of cake!

Not all ultrasonic cleaners are safe for all gemstones. Read the directions to be sure yours is safe for your jewelry.

You can also clean your jewelry by hand. Purchase a plastic container with a lid (24 oz.), a bottle of Parson's Sudsy Ammonia, and a medium toothbrush. Fill the container with two parts water, one part ammonia. (Keep the lid on this solution—the fumes are pretty strong!) Each day, place the jewelry in this solution and let it soak for at least ten minutes. Take the jewelry out of the solution and scrub it with the toothbrush, making sure you scrub *underneath* as well as on top. Rinse with warm water, shake off the excess water, then dry with a lint-free cloth.

Jewelry Care Guide

Gemstone	*Recommended*	*What to Avoid*
Amethyst	Any ultrasonic; bristle brush*	Nothing
Aquamarine	Some ultrasonics**; bristle brush	Some ultrasonics
Citrine	Any ultrasonic; bristle brush	Nothing
Diamond	Any ultrasonic; bristle brush	Sharp blows
Emerald	Warm soapy water; bristle brush	Jewelry cleaner; household chemicals; treated cloth; sharp blows; extreme temperature changes; some ultrasonics

Gemstone	Recommended	What to Avoid
Garnet	Some ultrasonics; bristle brush	Jewelry cleaner; household chemicals; treated cloth; sharp blows; extreme temperature changes; some ultrasonics
Onyx	Any ultrasonic; bristle brush	Sharp blows
Peridot	Some ultrasonics; bristle brush	Jewelry cleaner; household chemicals; treated cloth; sharp blows; extreme temperature changes; some ultrasonics
Ruby	Any ultrasonic; bristle brush	Nothing
Sapphire	Any ultrasonic; bristle brush	Nothing
Tanzanite	Some ultrasonics; bristle brush	Jewelry cleaner; household chemicals; treated cloth; sharp blows; extreme temperature changes; some ultrasonics
Topaz	Some ultrasonics; bristle brush	Jewelry cleaner; household chemicals; treated cloth; sharp blows; extreme temperature changes; some ultrasonics
Tourmaline	Some ultrasonics; bristle brush	Some ultrasonics

Gemstone	Recommended	What to Avoid
Tsavorite	Some ultrasonics; bristle brush	Jewelry cleaner; household chemicals; treated cloth; sharp blows; extreme temperature changes; some ultrasonics
Zircon	Some ultrasonics; bristle brush	Sharp blows; some ultrasonics
24K Gold	Any ultrasonic	Treated cloth; sharp blows; scratching

* *I recommend a medium toothbrush.*

** *Some ultrasonic cleaners may damage certain stones. Check the directions that come with your cleaner.*

Chapter 8

"Will You Marry Me?"

Those four little words form what may well be the most important question you'll ever ask. The rest of your life flows from that question. It joins two families and begins a new family, and determines everything from what you'll eat for dinner, to where you'll spend your holidays, to what your children will be like.

In other words, this question is a BIG DEAL! Too big to treat casually. You don't want to just pull out the ring box while you're watching TV and say, "Oh, yeah, I thought you might like to, uh, y'know...would you?"

Make it a moment you'll both remember forever!

She will remember it, every tiny detail of it—the weather, what she was wearing, what you were wearing, the time, the place, *everything*. She'll remember who she told first, and what they said, and how her parents reacted, and how your parents reacted—everything. So take the time and make the effort to plan it, and make the details come out right. Why spend a lot of time and money getting the perfect diamond only to have the Big Moment turn out to be a flop? The diamond is just one part of the Perfect Proposal. It takes thought, planning, loving attention to detail, and occasionally teamwork to create the kind of fireworks that will leave a lasting glow on your lives together.

Planning the Perfect Proposal: A Worksheet

Attire Will you wear a tux? Maybe a gorilla suit to say that you're not monkeying around? Make a statement with your wardrobe.

Budget Do you rent a plane or a limo? Take her to the most romantic restaurant? Feed her champagne and caviar? Determine what you can afford to spend on a once-in-a-lifetime occasion.

Location *Very important!* The observation deck of the tallest building in town? A hilltop under the stars? On the deck of a sailboat? On a moonlit beach? Don't forget, it can be a "combo": first a restaurant, then the beach, for example.

Day & Time Pick a day that's special to you, such as the anniversary of your first date. Or evening, when a full moon rises over the lake.

Food Taking her to the first restaurant you went to together can be fun. Cooking her a meal is a sure winner!

Flowers Absolutely! Whether it's great bouquets of flowers or a single red rose, flowers are a must for romantic moments.

Candy　　　Find out what her favorite is, and present it as a treasure, wrapped in gold paper and tied with a bow, even if it's a Snickers bar.

Accessories　　　Take along a cellular phone so she can call her mother or her sister. She'll be bursting to tell everyone! If you can, set up a video camera to record the moment.

Scrapbook　　　Write down all the details of the moment—details that you (and your children) will savor in years to come. Include newspaper headlines from the day you got engaged.

Engagement Facts

- *Approximately 2,400,000 couples wed in the U.S. each year.*

- *One-third of all couples that get engaged do so during the last quarter of the year, October through December.*

- *The average age of a man getting engaged is 26.5 years; the woman's average engagement age is 24.4.*

- *The average price of a diamond engagement ring is $1,597. If the engagement ring is purchased as part of a bridal set, the average price is $880.*

Five Proposal Styles

Over the years, I've come across five basic styles of proposals. Which best describes your situation?

The Total Surprise

She doesn't know it's coming—not a clue, not a hint. You've never even discussed it. This is gutsy! It reminds me of the school dances of my youth, where all the girls were on one side of the gym and all the boys stood on the other. You'd finally get up the nerve to make that long walk across the floor to ask a girl to dance. If she said, "No," and they often did, the walk back across the floor was very, very long.

I figure fewer than 10 percent of all proposals are in this category. It's like doing a high-wire act without a net. Most guys drop hints first, or get hints from her that indicate which way the wind is blowing. But there are the big risk-takers, the guys who live on the edge, who just go out and buy the ring and make the dinner reservations and GO FOR IT! Hurrah for them, but—*I have to tell you I don't recommend popping the question "cold."*

She Knows

You've talked about getting married; you know you both want to get married and spend your lives together; you've talked about having kids; you've pledged your undying love. The only thing she *doesn't* know is when it's coming.

Men, the time between when she knows you'll give her a ring and the moment when you actually give it to her can be one of the greatest times of your life. Have some fun! Keep her guessing, plan

the moment well, and when she least expects it, spring your wonderful surprise.

Let's Elope!
"Will you marry me? Right now? Tonight?"

Wow! This one makes no sense to me unless:
- The Early Pregnancy Test came up positive
- *America's Most Wanted* is profiling you tonight
- It's her fifth marriage, your seventh
- You don't want to give her a chance to change her mind
- World War III has broken out and you've been called up
- You love her so much you just can't wait

It's Now or Never
Way to go—you've waited so long she's resorting to threats: "We're
getting married or I'll find someone who'll appreciate me!" Fish or
cut bait, guy. If you love her, get off the fence and show her you
can't live without her. If it's come to the threatening stage, you have
to be extra, extra romantic to make up for her long wait. Use my
proposal planning guide on page 208 and make it a great one!

Ringless
You and your True Love are in each other's arms, caught up in a
rising tide of passion. The dialogue goes like this:
"*Honey, I love you!*"
"*I love you, too, sweetheart.*"
(*Kiss kiss smooch kiss*)
"*I can't live without you!*"
"*Oh, baby, you're the only one I'll ever love!*"

(Smooch kiss smooch kiss)
"Will you marry me?"
"Yes! Oh, yes yes yes!"

But does Romeo have a ring in his pocket? Nooooooo. So where do we go from here?

Don't think this lets you out of getting her a ring! Get that thought out of your head right now!

A lot of Ringless Proposals lead to a couple shopping together for the ring. Or, you could revert to the "She Knows" proposal and keep her guessing. *Either way, the Ringless Proposal shouldn't be ringless for long.*

Soul Mate or Cell Mate?
Miss Right
She looks like an angel, she walks like an angel, she talks like an angel, but she's a devil in disguise! Oh yes, she is a devil in disguise! If these words sound familiar, it's because they're from an old Elvis Presley song, but they still ring true today. How can a fella know when he's got a catch or needs to throw her back? Sometimes it's difficult to tell, but the rejects will always tip their hand before the dealing is done. Let me share a few of my favorite stories about when some women dropped their guard to reveal their true intentions.

Story I: Woody Allen & the Playboy Bunny
"Mr. Cuellar, your next clients are here. Shall I bring them back?" asked my assistant.

"Bring away," I replied, as I quickly made an attempt to clean up my perennially messy desk. When I looked up, I saw one of the most striking, intriguing couples I had ever seen. She was a bomb-shell, a Marilyn Monroe type with an hourglass figure, tight black leather pants, and a purple tube top that defied gravity. He, on the other hand, was ten years her senior and about five feet, six inches tall with a comb-over and Woody Allen glasses. He probably weighed about ninety-eight pounds dripping wet and was wearing a short-sleeved baby-blue shirt with a pocket protector and char-coal gray, shiny polyester pants hiked up so high that they were looking for a flood. She was attached to his arm like an extra appendage and kept repeating, "Oh baby, oh baby, I love you, I love you so much."

As I asked them to be seated, I couldn't stop wondering what this guy's secret was. Genius? Wealth? Was he a lover extraordinaire? Who cares! This looked like the real thing. She hung on his every word and laughed at every corny joke. I was impressed. Love is blind! It conquers all boundaries. Good for Woody! Good for all men who aren't tall enough, buff enough, or handsome enough! This was a victory for geeks and freaks everywhere. Until...

"Mr. Cuellar," he said.

"Call me Fred."

"Can you point me to the restroom?"

"Sure. Go out of my office and take your second left."

"I'll be right back, honey!"

"Hurry back, love muffin; I'll be here," she replied.

As I returned to my seat after letting my new hero out, Marilyn's demeanor changed instantly. "So how long you been in this diamond biz?"

"Most of my life," I replied.

"Must be raking it in, huh?"

"I do okay," I replied.

"Look, I can break free from the doofus in a heartbeat. Let's hook up."
"What? You're here getting an engagement ring. What the hell are you talking about?"

"Ah, I'm just here getting the ring, then I'm splittin'!"

"Mr. Cuellar, can I let your client back in?" Lesa rang in on the intercom. Within seconds, the couple was reunited, and the game began again.

"Oh baby, you was gone so long! You know better than to leave honey bunny so long," she said as she gave me a wink and a smile. How your woman acts when she's not around you is probably more important that how she does when she's with you. Always look at both sides of the coin.

Story II: Big Rock or I Walk

When I returned from lunch, my next clients were already seated in my office waiting for me. "Hi guys, how's everything going? I'm Fred Cuellar."

"I'm looking for a three-carat, round, VVS1, D diamond and not a bit less," she snapped back.

"Well," I said. "The lady knows her diamonds! How does that sound to you, sir?"

"It doesn't make a difference to him. He's just here to write the check!"

"Sounds like the rough part," I replied. He smiled; she didn't.

"Well, I guess we better get down to it. Let's pull out some diamonds." I reached into my drawer, pulled out a lovely two-carat diamond, placed it in a mounting and handed it over. "Here you go, a beautiful three-carat, round, VVS1, D diamond, just like the lady ordered!"

She smiled, but it would be the last time. "You see, now that's a rock. That's what I'm talking about!" she said.

"Really?" I asked. "Do you think you could be happy with that?"

"Oh, yes," she replied. "It fits my hand like a glove."

"Well, that's wonderful, because you'll be glad to know it's really a two-carat, not a three-carat, and that should save you over $10,000!"

Again, he smiled, she didn't. "What!" she bellowed. "You said it was a three-carat!"

"I lied. I just wanted to see if you could tell the difference and since you can't, you might as well save the money."

"Look, I don't know what you're up to, but either I get a three-carat, or I walk."

It was probably wrong of me to stick my nose where it didn't belong. Maybe I should have pulled out a three-carat from the get-go and let this couple be on their way. But she angered me. Since I had spoken with the man on the phone previously, I knew going in that this wasn't a man of great wealth. He was thirty-nine, never married before, and was going to have to get a loan to purchase the ring. So when she started spouting demands, I guess I lost my cool. What's the lesson here? Love doesn't come with a price tag.

Story III: A Class Act
"Miss Ward is on the phone," chimed my assistant.

"Any idea who she is?" I asked.

"Says her fiancé bought a diamond from you and she would like to talk to you."

"Put her through...Fred Cuellar here!"

"Hi, Mr. Cuellar. I...I...don't know where to start," Miss Ward said, and began to cry.

"Calm down, calm down. Whatever the problem is, I'm sure we can fix it. Just start at the beginning."

"Well, you see, last night my boyfriend proposed to me and it was so wonderful. Dinner, dancing, and your beautiful ring!"

"Sounds pretty good so far. What's the problem?" I said.

"He can't afford it. I know he can't. He's between jobs and he just went overboard."

"Well," I said, "have you told this to him?"

"Oh, no. He's so proud of my diamond; how he researched it, shopped around—it would just crush him!"

"Well, what can I do?"

"I'd like to give you some money, then have you call him and tell him you overcharged him and need to return some of his money. You see," she said, "he has a job interview coming up and he needs a new suit. With the money he gets back, he can get the suit and hopefully get the job. The diamond is pretty, but I have to take care of my man."

The good ones always pick you up when you fall; the great ones don't let you fall at all.

Mr. Right

Tall, dark, and handsome? Knight in shining armor? Or is the dude a dud? Ladies, now it's your turn. For every woman playing games, there are probably ten men who have mastered the art of deception. Here are my stories.

Story I: The List

One late Friday afternoon I sat down with a man I affectionately call the List Maker. Not really different from most of the anal retentive men you've ever met, with the exception that this man had gone too far. His life had become a list—a list of pros and cons, check and balances, pluses and minuses. Every action had been carefully scripted according to a plan that must have been meticulously thought out over and over.

"Mr. Cuellar, it appears it's time for me to get married, so I'm going to need a diamond."

"Congratulations. Who's the lucky lady?"

"Don't have one," he replied, "but I will."

"Wait a minute. Don't you have this backwards—first you find the girl, then you get the diamond?"

"Nope, the girl will be the easy part. There are plenty of women looking to be a homemaker. But to get her, I'm going to need a diamond."

"Do you mind if I ask you a question?"

"Shoot!" he said.
"Where does love fall into all of this?"

"Haven't you heard?" he replied.

"Heard what?" I said.

"Only fools fall in love! Marriage is a partnership, a legal agreement to share responsibilities. You know; two heads are better than one. Love is nothing more than a fancy word for convenience."

Don't want to be lonely? Get a pet. Need a homemaker? Hire a maid. Love is not convenience. Love is magic.

Story II: What She Doesn't Know Won't Hurt Her
"Good morning. What can I do for you two today?"

"Well, my name is Max and this is my fiancée. We're getting married at the end of the year and whatever kind of diamond my lady wants, she gets."

"What size would you like to start with?" I asked.

"We want a big one because the best deserves the best. Let's try five carats."

"Oh, honey!" she exclaimed. "I don't need a big diamond! In fact, any size will do."

"Nope," he said. "The best deserves the best! Price is no object."

Within thirty minutes, they had chosen a lovely six-carat platinum and diamond ring for $82,000. He pulled out his platinum American Express card for the deposit and they were on their way. I don't think I had ever seen a smile as wide as hers was when she left. About an hour later came the phone call.

"Fred?"

"Yes?"

"This is Max."

"Oh, hi, Max. Any questions that need answering that I didn't cover?"

"Nope, just one adjustment."

"What's that?" I said.

"Please exchange the diamonds out for cubic zirconias. What she doesn't know won't hurt her."

Not everything we see should be believed and not everything we believe can be seen. It's okay to trust people, but be sure to cut the deck.

Story III: The Shoe Box
Mr. Schwartz stood all of five feet, four inches tall. By the age of sixty-four he had been married forty-two years, had two daughters, and four grandchildren. He had been an industrial engineer

(garbage collector) since he dropped out of high school to marry his childhood sweetheart who would soon be having their first child. I still remember the first day I met him. I commented on his Members Only jacket that had been all the rage in the '70s. "Oh, this old thing? You'd be surprised what people throw away. Sylvia, that's my wife, just sewed up a torn pocket and bada bing, bada boom; good as new."

The second thing I noticed was an old tan shoe box under his arm. When he laid it down on my desk, I saw that the words "Rainbow's End" were scribbled on the top in pencil. "You're wondering what's inside, aren't ya, son?" he asked me.

"Maybe a little bit," I replied.

"Well, let me tell you. It's the vacation we never took, the fancy meals we passed up, and a lifetime of bottles and cans that these two hands dragged home. That there is the one-carat-diamond ring I told her she would get someday," he said, pointing to a ring in the case. "Go ahead—count it up and be quick about it. My wife's waited long enough for her diamond rainbow."

A new, good quality, one-carat diamond was going for over $6,000 those days. I thought that this box must be filled with thousands of dollars—more than enough for Sylvia's dream diamond. But as I started counting the cash, there were more tens than twenties and more ones than fives. At the end of my count there was exactly $2,231.55. He was short—there would be no one-carat diamond, not with what was in the box. Maybe in the late 1950s this would be more than enough for the diamond of their dreams, but not in today's market. The best they could get would be a half carat.

"Well, son, do I have enough? When can I pick up my one-carat-diamond ring?"

"Let's see. $2,231.55. That will just cover it. You can pick up the ring tomorrow."

A good man keeps his promises even if it takes a lifetime; if you're ever in the position to save a dream, do it.

Note: All the stories here are true with the exception of name changes.

For Men Only

Many a man in a fit of rage has blurted out, "What in the name of God does my woman want?!" "I give and I give and I give and she's still not happy!" I can relate. I've been trying to figure women out my whole adult life. Heck, even the better part of my adolescence was spent on the question. And it was always the minute I got close to the answer that I'd be sent blindly into a black hole of confusion. Women are a lot like a golf swing: just when you think you have mastered it, your next ball slices off the fairway. Women by definition equal confusion or that which lacks explanation. So, hand in hand with the search for the meaning of life, I ventured out on this crusade to answer the one question that seems to defy logic. What do women want?

At the beginning of my search I had to accept the possibility that the question may not even have an answer. I mean certainly not all women think the same, so how in heaven can they all want the same thing? A single gal can't possibly have the same needs as a married gal. A career woman can't possibly relate to a homemaker. A teenager can't crave what a thirty-year-old might, or for that matter what a senior citizen desires. Women are different, so they must want different things. Right? Well, kind of yes, and kind of no. There are, if you look carefully, some common things all women want. How do I know? I asked them. Here are my results.

Women want it all or none of it. They want to be understood, but not typecast; they want to be happy, but allowed to be sad; they want companionship, but don't need someone to be happy; they want honesty, but seldom the truth; they want equality, while being placed on a pedestal; and most of all they want respect. Respect for who they are, where they've come from, and where they are going. Don't pity them or coddle them. Today's woman is a woman of diversity and contradictions. What she wants today is not what she will want tomorrow because she is setting new goals. Men can't figure women out because they are a masterpiece in progress. A woman doesn't grow old; she just gets better. Wonder why you can't put lightning in a bottle? Because it just moves too quickly. Just like women. Ask your average man what 2 + 2 equals and he'll say 4 every time. Ask a woman and she'll say "looks like a little get-together." Women are always one step ahead and always will be. If we are to keep up, there are a few key ideas we need to survive.

1) Listen. 2) Listen. 3) Listen. See a pattern here? Men do a lot of hearing and not enough listening. Want to stay out of trouble? Listen. Want to be the man of the house? Listen. Want to have a long, loving relationship? Listen. My God, listen till the blood drips from your ears; listen until you want to scream out a solution; listen until she has nothing left to say; and when she's done, shut

up and listen some more. Most women are the caregivers, and if you want her to give, you'd better do some caring.

4) Hug her. Hug her in the morning; hug her before you leave for work; email her a hug; and hug her ten times when you get home. A woman is a fire. Want to keep her burning? You have to fan the flames. You do that with hugs.

5) Don't lie. Don't white lie, and don't sugar coat the truth. Tell it like it is. A woman can forgive a lot of things, but she won't put up with a snake in the grass liar. If you screw up, lose your Christmas bonus at the track, forget to take out the trash, stare at another woman—give it up. Take your licks and move on. I repeat, a woman can forgive anything, but she will not allow herself to be disrespected. Lie to a woman and you are dissing her. Tell the truth, you live to play another day.

6) Every woman I talked to listed structure in their top three needs. A woman wants stability, balance, and a sense of order. She wants someone she can rely on. You say you're going to be home at 6:00, you be home at 6:00. Running late, call. The hardest thing for us guys is to differentiate between support and total control. Creating a foundation and stability doesn't mean trying to solve all the problems to the point that you disempower the one you love. Your love is not a crutch, but a bond. A bond where dependability is synonymous with trust.

7) Love them. Love them most of all. Let it all out. Let it all out every day, every minute of every second of every day. Be love. Crawl up inside of it and approach every problem with the question, what

would love do now? If you do this, fear will never enter your life.

What do women want? They just want to be happy like us. They just have a different way of showing it. Learn their language; listen when you'd rather speak; hug instead of walk away; tell the truth until it hurts; be a man she can depend on; and love her like you love yourself. You'll no longer ask what women want, they'll be asking you what you want, and giving it to you.

When Is It Time to Get Married?
When I was a teenager growing up there was a rock group I listened to called Three Dog Night. For those of you who haven't heard of them they had over a dozen top ten hits like, "Joy to the World," "One," "Old Fashioned Love Song," "Black & White," and "Never Been To Spain." One of my favorites was "One." The opening lyrics are:

> *One is the loneliest number that you'll ever do*
> *Two can be as bad as one*
> *It's the loneliest number since the number one*

I used to love that song and believed its message; nothing can be lonelier than being by yourself. Two can be as bad as one or being with someone else can be as bad as being by yourself, but clearly there is no hope for being alone. So when I ask the question, "When is it time to get married?" it almost implies a rite of passage we must undertake if we are to be happy. I mean, who would ask the question, "When is it time to stay single?" Naw, that makes no sense since the song clearly states two is the only number that has a chance. But is the song right?

After a lot of reflection I realized that we live in a society where "one" gets a bad rap. Think about it, if a male or female friend of yours is single and getting up in age, nobody says, "Good for him, Mr. Independent!" No, everybody says, "What's wrong with him?" "Doesn't anybody love him?" "At least he has his friends." Or, God forbid a woman! Turn thirty and she should be sent to a nunnery or off to spinster preschool. We are brought up believing in soul mates and not being completed till Mr. Right or Miss Right comes along. And you know what? We are wrong! Two may be less lonely, but two doesn't equal joy.

For example, have you ever been with someone so long that you want to pull out your hair and if pushed hard enough you'd scream out, "Look I just have to have my own space?!!" I bet you have. Look at the Buddhists. Inner peace and happiness comes from within when we find our center, our purpose, our reason to get out of bed in the morning. Look, I'll repeat the question, "When is it time to get married?" Or put a much better way, "When is it time to share your life with someone?" That answer is simple. When you know who you are, know where you're going, and have some idea of how to get there. Then you can figure out if someone is headed in the same direction and wants to share the ride of a lifetime.

Thirty-four Percent

A recent survey of women ages eighteen to fifty-four asked, "What was the single most important factor in choosing a marriage partner?" Thirty-four percent responded personal wealth. Personal wealth? What in God's name does money have to do with love, soul mates, and forever? As males, should we be mortified that one in three aren't looking for a sparkling personality, or a winning smile?

Or on the contrary, should we be happy that at least the numbers are in our favor? We have a two out of three chance that who we are matters more than our purchasing power!

When I first read this statistic in a magazine I couldn't help but take notice, 34 percent! To me it seemed high. In an age when Destiny's Child has a number one hit with "Independent Women," and Jennifer Lopez belts out "My love don't cost a thing," who the hell are these 34 percent, and how can single guys stay away from them? Now I guess if you see yourself as a nerd or a wanna-be Sugar Daddy in training you might not care. But it seems to me that the rest of us want to know who this 34 percent is. Maybe we could get them to wear buttons. You know, something catchy like "You can't have this ass without some cash!" No, they'd never go for that! Maybe "With some money you'll get lucky!" That's a little better.

On second thought, it just hit me that they don't want us to know because if we did we'd pack up our gear and head upstream. Nope, sadly the 34 percent are destined to be secret agents. Only when it's too late will their true identities come out.

Is the secret to act poor and then reveal we're loaded when they fall for us? Or try to borrow money for a month from them and see how they react? Nah, I doubt it. I think man's only ally is time. Don't rush it, take it slow, and be yourself. I imagine these 34 percent aren't very patient ladies (and I say that loosely). Yup, that's it. Take your time and see if your relationship turns to wine, or dies and withers away on the vine. Yeah, that should be our motto.

Comatopia

More than a few decades ago I was born in Kittery, Maine, the second child, the first and only son. My dad, a pilot in the U.S. Air Force (later a wing commander) brought me up with a code of ethics that I still use today. "If a job is worth doing, do it right the first time." "Be a man of your word." "Be a gentleman." There are a lot of life's lessons he taught me, but he never told me about "comatopia." True, it's a made up word, but it does have its origin. It comes from the word, "coma" (unconscious, can't wake up) and "utopia" (a country of perfection). The irony is that "comatopia" is a perfect place to live but you can't appreciate it because you're out like a light.

"Comatopia" is a land that every man, young man, or schoolboy will visit, is visiting, or is stuck in right now. We were not forced there against our will. We volunteered gladly. Let me explain: when a man/boy meets a woman/girl, his brain goes through an almost instantaneous checklist:

Face:

Breasts:

Booty:

Legs:

Then a quick addition followed by a question that if answered, "yes" is a weekend pass into "comatopia."

"Would I do her?"

The minute a man asks and answers this question to himself, he not only has entered "comatopia" but will be stuck there till he gets kicked out, takes a cold shower, or rounds third base.

"Comatopia" is a state of mind where a man says and does things purely for the possibility of a booty call. Is she smart? Who cares! Is she kind? Who cares! Are you compatible? Who cares! Who cares! Who cares! I'm in combat mode: get the booty, get the booty. Women, most of them, are more evolved. They have the capability of not just evaluating the book by its cover; they'll even skim a few chapters. Women make educated decisions. Men make "comatopia" decisions. There are very few women who will sleep with a man they don't like, but ask any man from "comatopia" the same question and he'll snap right back, "What do liking somebody and sex have to do with each other?" I'm not proud that "comatopia" exists or that I've even visited there more than once. What I'm trying to do is make all men aware of it so they will stop making fools of themselves for superficial reasons.

1) You don't go out with a girl just because she passes the extremely low, low bar of "I'd do her."

2) Realize that big breasts do not compensate for character flaws.

3) Ask yourself if this new person in your life meets the standards of going from an unknown to an acquaintance to being your friend before you even consider how hot she is or isn't or whether you should do the horizontal shuffle.

4) I know trying to act like 007 may be fun, but women can see through a phony in a heartbeat. Be yourself; at least if you're shot down you won't spend the rest of your life wondering if she hated the real you or your poor James Bond impression. It's true that the truth can hurt sometimes and it may be brutal but without it we can't make adjustments at halftime to be a better person.

The key for men in finding "Miss Right" versus "Miss Right Now" is to fall for who she is, and what she believes in, not how she fills out a swimsuit. If on top of all that she's beautiful too, you truly are a lucky man. But you know what? If you do allow yourself to get to know and fall in love with the person inside first, I guarantee the book cover won't matter. Just look at us, how many Robert Redfords and Brad Pitts are among us? Not many, but we're loved anyway. We can learn a lot from women and very little from "comatopia."

For Women Only

The following articles are targeted at explaining, understanding, breaking down, and excusing what might be one of the toughest nuts to crack—the Male Species. Why he does what he does, why he doesn't do what he should, why he says one thing and then another, why some are scoundrels and some saints. We'll dive into the male psyche to hopefully shed a little light on what makes a guy tick.

Having been a guy my entire life and played the game, it's now time for someone to call a time-out and share with you gals the locker rooms secrets most men would take to their grave. Enjoy!

Secondhand Men

I went to an antique store to browse the other day. As I walked in, I saw a line of beautiful mahogany curio cabinets, a chest of drawers, and a rolltop desk that would have taken anyone's breath away. As I continued my stroll, I saw an eighteenth-century, four-poster canopy bed, hand carved and meticulously taken care of, shining under a chandelier. "Looking for a bed, mister?" the spunky old saleswoman asked.

"Nope," I said, "Just looking around."

"You know that bed has quite a history behind it," she replied.

"Oh really?" I said. "Fill me in."

She was delighted that she had piqued my interest. "Rumor has it Roosevelt himself slept on it!"

"No kidding? How do you know that?" I asked.
"His initials are carved into the headboard," was the quick reply. Sure enough, once she pointed it out, you could easily pick out the T.R. amongst the scrolled pattern. "Also take a look at this. You see the slight cracks in the wooden support slats that held the mattress?"
"Yeah, I sure do," I said.

"Well, that about cinches it, don't you think?"

"Why is that?" I asked.

"Hell, sonny, everyone knows he was a rough rider!"

I fought hard against breaking out into laughter, but lost the battle. "No, no, that's OK, maybe if you just let me look around."

"The bed goes for $25,000," she whipped back, "but I'm willin' to deal."

"No, ma'am, that's OK, just let me…Excuse me, what's all that stuff under the must go sign?"

"That's junk nobody wants. Can't give that stuff away," she sniffed.

"Mind if I take a look?"

"Go ahead, it's all 75 percent off."

As I stumbled through the broken rockers and silver-plated candleholders, I saw something that caught my attention. "Whatcha want for the lamp?"
"It's broke, don't work, fifty bucks and I'll wrap it up myself."

"Seems like a lot for a broken lamp."

"OK, OK, $35, but you wrap it yourself."

The lamp was probably a knockoff and would need rewiring, but I figured, what the heck, the leaded glass dragonfly pattern was pretty. "OK, I'll take it." As it was being rung up, I noticed a curious, rusted old stamp underneath the base of the lamp: Tiffany Studios. The lamp was later appraised for $80,000.

I tell this story for a reason. Most assuredly Teddy Roosevelt didn't sleep in that bed, and a broken-down lamp in a junk pile can shine again and be worth a fortune. Men are no different. To some degree, we are all secondhand men. We have pasts, futures, and stories to tell. None of us comes to the antique store new. The question for the woman is, which of our stories are false and which ones are true?

The Scarecrow, The Cowardly Lion, & The Tin Man

All men—not some men—are either one, two, or all of the above. Knowing which one you have and how to deal with him will either make or break your relationship.

Let's start with the scarecrow. Unlike his title, the scarecrow is brave, loyal, and trustworthy. He would fall on a brush fire if it meant saving a life. Scarecrows are so kindhearted that their mates always take top priority. Scarecrows remember birthdays, anniversaries, and special occasions. Their downfall lies in self-maintenance. Their stuffing is always falling out. Their organizational skills are poor at best and matching the right tie, sports coat, and slacks can sometimes be disastrous. Scarecrows are generally considered loners that avoid large crowds and will stay introverts unless forced out of the nest. Most scarecrows think they lack the brain power for success, but they're generally geniuses. If you don't mind a man with maintenance problems, who is probably a little sloppy, scarecrows make great husbands and can be molded with little or no extra effort. Don't get me wrong, scarecrows aren't wimps, they're just guys that are too smart to know how smart they are.

Cowardly lions are direct opposites of scarecrows. They are boisterous, loud, sometimes obnoxious, and very macho. They are extroverts to the third power. They are the athletes, the lawyers, and the salesmen. You see, to a cowardly lion, the "cowardly" is silent. To them they are just lions—kings of the jungle. But the sad part is that it's just an act—partly for their benefit, partly for others—but it is still just an act. You see, ladies, men are a nation of opposites. If he acts macho, he's really shy; if he's shy, he's a conqueror; and hidden inside of every cowardly lion is a man that thinks if he acts tough enough and talks tough enough, maybe he can convince himself he's tough enough. Cowardly lions can make great husbands, but they are tougher to tame. If you don't get through the macho man act, you're doomed. Until the cowardly lion realizes he doesn't have to act tough to be a man, you'll never get anywhere. By the way, some cowardly lions are smart, but very few. Unfortunately, they spend much more time thinking about themselves than they do others. A cowardly lion's favorite saying is, "What's in it for me?"

The Tin Man, if you recall, was looking for a heart. That's probably the best way to describe a tin man—a man in search of emotion. Tin men can be accountants, engineers, even architects. Usually they are great men—overachievers, men of logic, cause-and-effect fellows. The biggest problem with tin men is that they overanalyze everything and can be extremely anal. They have a sense of perfection that must be a standard for all others to live up to. Quite frankly, most tin men end up living very empty lives. They get left behind because they can never learn the art of compassion and the voice of the soul. Want to be a wealthy wife? Find a tin man, he'll be a great provider. Want to live a glorious life? Teach a tin man how to feel, how to touch, how to love. Give the tin man a heart and you'll have a love affair that will never die.

Now don't get me wrong, not all men are just one of these characters, some are combinations—heck, there's even a Dorothy or two out there. But what you should get from this article is that there is no one definition of a man. We are all different and if you're going to want to get to know your man better, it might be a good idea to know whom you are talking to.

Superman Syndrome

Big boys don't cry. If you want a job done right, you have to do it yourself. Survival of the fittest. The boy with the most toys wins. A real man solves his own problems. Behind every good man is a good woman. Young boys are told a lot of things growing up. Stereotypes are created at a whim to please society and the world around us. Superman Syndrome is the fallacy that a man ain't worth two cents if he's not a good provider and problem solver. Ever hear the expression, "I wonder who wears the pants in that family?" It stems from ignorance bred by the idea that a real man is head of his family and makes all the final decisions. It's that ignorance that turns young boys into men who think every time their family or their wife has a problem, they're expected to be supermen and solve the problem.

Real men solve problems—that's what we're told our entire lives. That's why I think men get confused when our mates tell us about their day and, instead of listening to understand and sympathize, the superman in us listens to fix, solve, and save. Most men don't understand that women don't need saving anymore. I don't know if they ever did. Women just want to be heard. Not solved or fixed, just heard and understood. Nothing has meaning until we give it meaning. A problem is not a problem until we label it one.

I don't know what women do when they sit around and share ideas. But I do know what men do when they group together. They tell war stories: battles won, problems solved, questions answered. We puff ourselves up, I think not so much out of ego, but to help each other garner a little more confidence to take on another day.

You see, deep down we know we aren't supermen and we can't solve all the problems, but that doesn't stop us from trying. Maybe this article should be targeted to men, telling them to stop labeling everything out of a woman's mouth as a problem and trying to fix it. But there is also a message here for women: try to understand that when we don't have something to fix we feel useless. I don't know how to make men better listeners, but if I could make one request, maybe once in a while when you do have a problem to solve, even though you can probably solve it yourself, you could be Lois Lane and let your guy be Superman. Because even if we can't save the world, we still want to be heroes.

Sophomore Jinx

In baseball when a pitcher is doing well (striking everyone out) they say he is in a zone. His fastball, curve ball, split finger, and slider are all probably working for him! He can do no wrong. He's got the right stuff. When a pitcher is getting lit up (hit on) they say he's lost his stuff, no zone, throwing up junk. He typically gets pulled for a relief pitcher. But if a pitcher does get lucky enough to stay in a zone for 9 innings, 27 batters, 27 outs, and no walks, they say that pitcher has pitched a perfect game. In the history of baseball few pitchers have ever thrown a no-hitter, even fewer have ever pitched a perfect game, and no pitcher has ever pitched two consecutive perfect games in a row. Never. Ever.

For some men perfection can be a curse. A ghost they end up chasing for the rest of their lives. Others just quit rather than face the certainty of constant disappointment. Without question the quest to the top of the pyramid is certainly much more enjoyable than defending the crown. Consistency in achievement on or off the field can be paralyzing to men. The bedroom is no different.

236

At the beginning of every relationship a man is attempting to throw his good stuff. He goes all out. He stands up on the mound, winds up, and tries to put one over home plate. Right in the pocket. Flowers, dinner, massage, foreplay, doubles, triples, home runs. Sometimes, and I mean rarely, it's magic, euphoria, time stops, and even the gods give a standing ovation. For that moment the man is perfect. The perfect lover! Now keep in mind the male is proud of himself but somewhere deep inside regardless of how happy he is with his performance anxiety quickly sets in. "Oh my God!!" "What if she thinks I can pull this off every time?!" "What if she thinks this is just my run-of-the-mill, day-to-day stuff?" "I'd kill myself if I had to try and pull this off again!" Panic has taken over. He has become his own worse enemy. "Why in God's name did I have to set the sexual bar so high?!" "Should I run or confess?" "No, better that she think I'm a sex god than admit I'm human." "I'll run."

You know what happens next? Nothing. The phone doesn't ring; the man doesn't call. If it's the beginning of the relationship it becomes the end. The confused gal whose world was rocked thinks she was just played when in reality the man just has sophomore jitters or is afraid of a "Sophomore Jinx." All men know that no pitcher has ever thrown two perfect games and the likelihood he's going to be the first is slim and none. The sad part to this story is that this couple actually did have magic, did make time stop, but now it's lost because most men who care about a woman's feelings at some level are insecure. It's that insecurity that allows boys to be heroes, fight wars, become scholars, become dads, become men. Men do great things to squelch insecurity, and as we get older it gets smaller but it never goes away entirely. If as a woman you can see through our bravado there might be a few relationships you can save before it's too late.

If you're dating and perfection shines on you in the bedroom, make a point to let him know as a reward next time he gets to sit it out while you take charge. Men, whether they admit it or not, love to be made love to. We don't always need or want to be in control.

If you're in a relationship already and you sense signs of performance anxiety, take the bull by the horns (literally) and relieve a little tension. Men don't get headaches in the bedroom, it's just sometimes they don't feel like going nine innings. It's your job to be the relief pitcher every now and then.

Snugglers' Blues
I'll be the first one to admit my wife has snugglers' blues. Snugglers' blues is when a snuggler marries a nonsnuggler and feels deprived. You see, there are a lot of us men that are two-pillow men. When we go to sleep at night, we have one pillow to hold and one under our head. Snugglers want us to nix the snuggle pillow and snuggle them instead. Here's the problem:

1) The dead arm: When we enter into an official snuggle (spooning position), inevitably a man's arm gets pinned under his mate's body, where it quickly falls asleep, becomes numb, and goes into shock.

2) The inferno: A man is generally carrying around a few extra pounds of insulation, and when his body comes into contact with another body, he heats up. Look, bears go into hibernation because they're cold, which then allows them to get a good

night's sleep. Heat up a bear and he won't be able to sleep.

A man is no different. Some of the biggest fights my wife and I have are over what temperature to keep the thermostat in the house at.

3) Incapacitation: Men need to alter between three positions during a good night's sleep (side to side, belly flop, and flat on the back). If a snuggler ambushes a nonsnuggler during one of these positions, he feels trapped—trapped in a position that at any moment he may decide needs to be changed, and will find himself unable to escape. Trapped position equals no sleep.

Now, it may appear to the average observer that, being a nonsnuggler myself, I'm trying to defend my position (no pun intended), which is true. But I am not unsympathetic to the snuggler who equates snuggling with intimacy and nonsnuggling with being a jerk. Look, we nonsnugglers are just trying to get a good night's sleep. Obviously there needs to be a compromise, so I think I've concocted a plan: fifteen to thirty minutes of snuggle time prior to lights out, then break to separate corners. Or, set your alarm thirty minutes early in the morning and snuggle then.

I want to live in a world where snugglers and nonsnugglers can come together as one and live as happy people. I want to live in a world where a man is not judged by the color of his skin. Oh, wait a minute, I'm getting carried away. How do you solve snugglers' blues? Compromise.

Will I Marry a Cheater?

If you're married, you'll probably remember the words, "I (fill in your name) do take (fill in his name) to love, honor, and cherish through sickness and health; through good times and bad; forsaking all others; 'til death do us part." Or, maybe you were more creative and wrote your own vows. Either way, I'll bet my bottom dollar monogamy and 'til death do us part were part of your vows. If your man said these words, or is going to say these words, you can stop reading this article right now. You have married or are going to marry a cheater. I don't know whose idea it was to put boundaries on love and death in the same sentence, but the person was an idiot. The quickest way to drive a man to cheat is by putting boundaries on him or bringing up his own mortality. That's why so many middle-aged men run off with another woman—because 'til death do us part pops up in their head and they feel they have to leave their current relationship because it's only heading one place: Deathville.

Statistically, 99 percent of all men will cheat on their spouse during their marriage. The other 1 percent doesn't exist, it's just there because no statistical average is 100 percent accurate and the survey has a + 1 percent error ratio. That's right, that's what I'm saying, all men cheat, are cheating, or will cheat. Now, don't get me wrong, not all men's mistresses are women. In some cases, it's football, golf, sports in general, work, money, or possessions. Heck, men can cheat on a woman with a television set. Cheating can be anything that makes a woman feel lonely, depressed, taken advantage of, or replaced. Ever feel jealous of something your boyfriend or husband is doing or has done? Then you've allowed yourself to be cheated on.

Want to know what I believe are the two reasons most responsible for divorce in this country? Jealousy and boundaries. Tell a kid he can't have a cookie and I promise you will catch him with his hand in the cookie jar. Even Adam and Eve, who had everything, blew it the minute someone (who will remain nameless) said you can eat everything, but don't touch the apples. Come on, the nameless one was practically begging them to take a nibble. Men as well as women tend to want what they are told they can't have. Want a forever-lasting relationship? Loosen the reins. The tightest relationships are the ones with the loosest reins. Remove jealousy, remove boundaries, and you'll remove cheating.

I think if I could write the perfect vows, they would be, "I'll always try to do my best but if there are times when I am weak, you'll allow me to speak and not judge me for my thoughts." Want to blow a man's mind? Tell him, "Honey, just because we are getting married, you don't have to give up your other interests. Just always be honest with me. Tell me the truth. Loving me doesn't mean letting go of others or the things you love." Do you know the No. 1 reason women give for leaving a man if he cheats on her? It isn't the other women—it's the deception.

So if you're a man reading this article (and you really are a man) and you're thinking of letting something else come between you and your spouse, be at least big enough to be honest with your woman and tell her. And if you're a woman reading this, make your man understand that you can be loving and understanding of just about anything, unless he disrespects you or is dishonest.

Why Won't the Question Pop?
Someone once said that the only two things that are certain in life are death and taxes. I think either of these absolutes could be argued, but that's for another discussion. If, however, I could add one more absolute, it would be the search for happiness. I think it's

fair to say that we all want to be happy. In fact, I'd even say that some people spend their entire lives trying to achieve that state. Some people believe money, friends, or family will make them happy. Some believe that when they find the perfect mate, happiness will blossom. Then, when that perfect mate pops the question, they'll have someone to share their life with forever and ever. That sounds good, doesn't it? No loneliness, just sharing, loving, and joy. But I'm getting too far away from the title of this article.

Why won't the question pop? If you're in a relationship and have exchanged I love yous, why won't he jump over the broom and pop the question? Does time have something to do with it? Maybe a lack of commitment? Maybe he hasn't cut the apron string from his mother. Maybe he was in a bad relationship and needs time to heal. Maybe he's never been in a relationship and doesn't understand the rules. Maybe he's saving up for a big rock and doesn't have the last payment yet. Or maybe the question was never supposed to pop in the first place. Ever hear the saying, "A watched pot will never boil"? Love doesn't come with a rule book. In fact, if it did, I probably wouldn't play. Love doesn't wait for anything or anybody. Love just is. Love isn't a question, an answer, an agreement, or a proposition. Love just is. Are you wondering when your man is going to pop the question? Well, maybe you should stop worrying. If your man has to think about whether he wants to spend the rest of his life with you, he's not the one. And if you think a ring on your finger is going to somehow magically change your love for each other, you're wrong. The question you should be asking yourself is, "Am I happy when I'm with him? Does he build me up when I'm feeling down? Does he help me smile when I'd rather frown?" Love isn't a question. Love just is.

Now, I'll be the first to admit that life equals change, and relationships must change as well. We must reinvent ourselves every day to show the world who we are and what we represent. But does a woman need a man? I hope not. If you ask the rich, the famous, and the philosophers, they will probably tell you happiness is not found in possessions or even a person. Happiness is found in sharing, not needing! Let me repeat that again, happiness is found in sharing, not needing. If you need a man, you'll push him away. If you need a job, you'll lose it. If you need money, you won't have it. The act of needing admits to the world you are without. Instead, try sharing yourself, sharing your love, sharing your happiness. You cannot share something you do not possess.

Why won't the question pop? If you need it to, it won't. Strong relationships are built on sharing, not dependency. Show your man you can stand on your own two feet, then you can ask the real important question, "Why should he be asking the question anyway?"

Necessities

I think we can all agree that there are some basic necessities we all must have to survive: food, water, clothing, and shelter. Now, whether your food of choice is caviar or a burger, and your beverage, a beer or Don Pérignon, has a lot to do with your value system and personal taste. Personally, I'm a blue jeans kind of guy, but I have enough Giorgio Armani suits hanging in my closet to keep my wife happy. It's so easy to get caught up in a race of one-upmanship— keeping up with the Joneses. I've seen men motivated by a lot of things. Fear of loss certainly is a big motivator in our society. As a couple creates a union, there are some things I think had better be ironed out before the knot is tied, and that's necessities.

Before I ever got serious with a woman, my list of necessities was actually quite small. An apartment seemed just as good as a house and a couple pounds of bologna, a few loaves of bread, and Kraft macaroni and cheese could sustain me for weeks. I remember that at one time I ate nothing but Taco Bell tacos for dinner for six months straight. (My God, do you know that to this day you can still get two tacos for 99¢?) What to wear, how to look, what to eat seemed like decisions low on the totem pole of life compared to striving after my real passion: work. Success consumed me, not the trappings, the winning. There are many men that are no different. Einstein wore the same slacks and shirt practically every day of his life. Now, he had many pairs of the same pants, but he'd made a conscious decision that certain choices weren't worth worrying about day after day. What's for dinner? What am I going to wear? If it weren't for women, there would be a lot of men living very happy lives in huts.

Women change all that for a man. For the most part, women raise our necessity bar to a new level. Women add humanity to men. Women create necessity. I think most women by nature have an appreciation for beauty that most times has to be taught to us (cave)men. When a man loves a woman, he'll want to lasso the moon for her. That's a task I've tried many times, only to fail. I think it's important that when a woman makes her lists of needs and wants, preferences and wishes, she does so very carefully. Preferences can turn into needs and needs into necessities, so that a man can become overwhelmed very quickly. And when possessions take priority over your relationship, you've lost the war. Necessities are necessary, but please don't make the list too long, or you may get what you desire, but lose us in the shuffle.

"Possessions usually mean less once possessed," a famous man once said. So don't stray too far from the truth. It's one thing to have a house as a home, but does a palace have to be your roof? If a couple can't see eye to eye on what are priorities and what are preferences, they're in for a rocky marriage. Not every man wants to be a multimillionaire, and not every woman would sacrifice time with her husband to live in a mansion. The road map to a successful marriage lies in two people wanting to end up in the same place. So you'd better make sure you're on the same page, and for that matter, reading the same book.

Newlyweds' Prayer

Lord, watch over us as we venture into uncharted seas.

Protect and guide us to live in your glory and be an example of your love.

Watch over our families that have become one through our union.

Give us patience and understanding to weather the storms that test every alliance.

Be our shelter when we are homeless and our compass when we have lost our way.

Lord, let us be always be forever grateful for the gifts you have bestowed upon

us so that never a day goes by that we take for granted the love we share now.

And let the everlasting love we will share together always fill our hearts.

Chapter 9

Buying Your 2nd, 3rd, or 4th Diamond

There's a very good chance that the diamond engagement ring won't be the last diamond you buy! Perhaps you're already looking for your second diamond. In my experience, there are five main reasons people shop for another diamond: Remarriage, Replacement, Upgrade, Trade-in, and Special Occasion.

New Marriage

Marriages end, sad to say, by death or divorce, but love can bloom again! New love, at any age, brings springtime back into your heart and pretty soon you find yourself gazing into jewelry store windows. Now I'm going to give you one piece of advice which will spare you a lot of grief.

Love is beautiful the second time around—but a ring isn't! Never recycle or even duplicate the ring from your previous marriage.

God forbid you should ever recycle a ring that you gave to a former fiancée or an ex-wife. Never!

Diamond Factoid

The country which produces the most diamonds, both by weight and by number: Australia! (40 million plus carats)

Your new love wants to feel special, wants to know that there's never been a love such as her. You'll shatter that feeling if you give her a ring from a previous relationship.

Of course, the exception is a family heirloom, perhaps your mother's or grandmother's ring—but not if it was also worn by your former wife. If you do give your beloved an heirloom ring, she's entitled to a new setting if she wants one. It's only the diamond that's forever. If your family has a problem with a setting change, it might be best to leave the heirloom in safe deposit and purchase a new ring.

Replacement Diamond

If her first diamond is lost, stolen, or damaged, you'll be shopping for a replacement. Don't assume she'll want an exact replica! Some women love the original so much they will want exactly the same thing if the original is gone, but other women will be ready for a change. Tastes do change over time, after all, so talk this over. Be diplomatic, and give her the option of change. Say to her, "Honey, I know your old ring meant a lot to you, and it meant a lot to me, and I'd do anything to bring it back, but it's gone. And since we're doing (a little)(a lot)(tons!) better than we were then, I want this ring to be all you want it to be. So I'll be happy to get you a duplicate of the old ring, or a new one that's bigger, better, or just different. The choice is yours—I just want you to be happy." You'll be a hero!

If the old diamond was damaged so that the clarity grade has dropped by two grades or more, the insurance company should cover the cost of replacement. If your damaged diamond was not insured, maybe you can still use it as a trade-in.

Diamond Upgrades

This can be an upgrade in size, quality, or both. Many women are happy with their original ring but would still like to have a bigger one. An anniversary is an ideal time to make this upgrade. This is another time to be practical and talk things over together. Does she want to trade in the original, or want to keep the original and get a new one? Many women treasure their original engagement ring, and even if they get a bigger diamond later, they want to keep the original and wear it as a pendant or save it for a child's future engagement. Or, some women will take a more practical approach and use the trade-in value of the original to get an even larger new diamond.

Fred's advice: Never trade in her existing engagement ring without her knowledge!

Trade-ins

Diamonds for trade-in can come from a lot of places. Your wife's old engagement ring, a ring from a failed engagement or former marriage, or a family heirloom. The keys to getting the most for your trade-in are as follows:

1. Get an independent appraisal of the trade-in diamond and ask the appraiser for the Rapaport value of the stone. "Rapaport" is a price sheet all appraisers use to determine a diamond's wholesale value. The Rapaport value=wholesale price; retail is 2X Rapaport. You should always be able to buy a diamond at its Rapaport price, and receive credit on a trade-in at Rapaport.

2. After you get the appraisal, you can visit your jeweler knowing what you should get for the trade-in. Don't be lazy and let the

jeweler appraise the diamond. A lot of jewelers might undervalue your trade-in.

3. Jewelers hate trade-ins, so always negotiate your new purchase *before* indicating you have a trade-in. If you tell the jeweler up front you have a trade, he'll just jack up the retail price.

- Determine what type and grade of diamond you want.

- Negotiate the price, using the guidelines in this book.

- Show your trade-in, telling the jeweler you've already gotten an independent appraisal.

- Make sure the trade-in amount equals the appraised wholesale value.

- Subtract the trade-in value from the price you negotiated for the new diamond, and that's your bottom line.

> *Example:*
> You're buying a .90ct SI1-1, Class 2, no fluorescence.
> Price: $5,534
> Your trade-in is a .50ct VS1-J1
> Appraised value: $1,395
> You pay: $4,139

Special Occasions and Gifts

As time goes by, you'll want to add to her diamond collection with gifts for a birthday, Christmas or Chanukah, an anniversary, or some other special day. This might mean diamond stud earrings, a diamond tennis bracelet, a pendant, or an anniversary ring. The number one question I'm asked about these purchases is, "Do I get the same quality as the engagement diamond?" Well, my friend, how important is the purchase to you? Most people see the engagement ring as something they'll treasure for a lifetime. Is that how you view this new purchase? If so, don't waste your money on second-class merchandise. If not, get a cubic zirconia or costume jewelry.

The decision is yours.

Trunk Shows

Many jewelers offer what are known as "remount trunk shows." These are basically marketing events at which they offer hundreds of settings, and where jewelers try to entice you to replace or trade in your old diamond. The problem with a trunk show is that all the diamonds have been mounted in settings, so it's impossible to check their weight, clarity, and color. And don't ever trade in your old diamond at these shows—they'll probably undervalue it.

Fred's Advice: Never buy a diamond in a prefabricated setting for more than $2,000 unless the jeweler will let you view the diamonds loose.

Chapter 10

How to Sell a Diamond

I know this book is called *How to Buy a Diamond*, but let's face it: not all diamonds are forever. There may come a time in your life when you want to sell a diamond or two, for one reason or another. It may be an engagement ring from a previous marriage, or a pair of diamond studs from an ex-boyfriend. It may be a family heirloom, or just a diamond you don't wear anymore. Rather than let it gather dust in your safe deposit box, you'd like to convert it to cold cash. Here's what you need to do. And remember: patience is a virtue! If you rush into a sale without doing your homework, you'll get burned. Follow these steps:

Step 1: Appraisal

Have the diamond appraised. You need to know what you have, and a qualified appraiser can tell you. Find one by calling the Appraisers Association of America, 386 Park Avenue South, 20th floor, New York City, NY 10016, at (212) 889-5404. Tell them where you live, and ask for a list of appraisers in your area. They won't tell you over the phone, but they'll send you a few recommendations—it'll take about a week. If you can't wait, look in the Yellow Pages under Appraisers. Check the appraiser's affiliations. The top three groups are:

Appraisers Association of America, www.appraisersassoc.org
American Society of Appraisers, www.appraisers.org
International Society of Appraisers, www.isa-appraisers.org

Membership in any of these is a good indication the appraiser is okay.

Step 2: Rapaport Value

Ask the appraiser for the Rapaport value. Rapaport is a wholesale price sheet published in New York that tells jewelry stores all over the country the prices they should pay for diamonds. The Rapaport prices are wholesale, based on Class III cut diamonds. *The price the appraiser gives you will be the highest price you can get for your diamond.* For example, if your diamond is a 1-carat, round, VS1-G, Class III cut with no fluorescence, the Rapaport value would be $7,800 (Note: Class IIIs are discounted 25–50 percent from Class IIs). That's the most you'll get for it. That same diamond would sell for more in a jewelry store, but you're not a jewelry store! Anyone who buys a diamond from an individual, who gives no guarantees or warranties, is simply looking for a good deal.

Step 3: Buyers

Find a buyer. There are a number of possibilities here, but I'm going to firmly guide you away from most of them. In my mind, the two best choices are: 1) family or friend, and 2) a jeweler.

A. Family or friend:
This is my top recommendation hands down. I've seen people try every which way to sell a diamond or piece of jewelry, then finally discover that a family member or friend would love to buy it. Before you go to strangers, look close to home for a buyer. You'll always make your best deal with someone who knows you, loves your jewelry, and wants to own it, while a liquidator just wants to resell it for a quick buck.

B. Jewelry store:

Yes, but be careful! Never let the jewelry out of your sight—you don't want someone pulling a "switcheroo" on you. Before the jeweler starts a spiel about how poor your diamond is, show him the appraisal. At that point, the jeweler will probably make you an offer that is below "dump value." Dump value is a trade expression—it means 60 percent to 80 percent of the diamond's Rapaport value, and it's the lowest price a diamond should ever sell for. If the jeweler offers you *below* 60 percent, don't take it. He's going for a fast buck, because he knows he can resell the stone overnight to a dealer at regular dump value. But if the jeweler offers you 60 percent to 80 percent of the Rapaport value, he's actually being fair. Remember, to make any money from the deal he'll have to find a new buyer for the diamond, and who knows what expenses he'll incur to do that.

Let's take our one-carat VS1-G, Class III cut diamond from Step 2, which has a Rapaport (wholesale) value of $7,800. Dump value would be 60 percent to 80 percent of that, or between $4,680 and $6,240. Try to negotiate the best price, of course, but don't feel insulted if the jeweler's offer is 5 percent below the low dump price. He's just trying to make a little money for handling the deal. But if he offers you only 40 percent or even 50 percent of wholesale, tell him NO DEAL!

Now let's talk about some options that I do NOT recommend.

C. Newspapers:

The premise is simple: you take out an ad, a buyer calls you and gives you money for your diamond. But it's never that simple. I have seen the classified ads work, but not often. In fact, I did a little survey on my own and found only an 11 percent success rate. You can do better than that in Las Vegas! Furthermore, placing an ad exposes you to all sorts of people including crooks who want to steal your jewelry. You'll make appointment after appointment with "buyers" who don't show up. Even if you attract a legitimate buyer, he'll drag you back to the appraiser and then make a ridiculous offer. I would avoid the classifieds. It's not worth putting yourself in danger.

Diamond Mystique at Work

The diamond weighed forty carats. It was discovered in Lesotho, South Africa, and had been cut into a Marquise shape and mounted as a spectacular ring. The clarity grade was high—VVS—but the color was only M or N, and at wholesale the diamond would fetch perhaps $260,000. But when the ring sold at auction in April 1996, the winning bid was $2.58 million—ten times the wholesale value! Why? Because this was the ring Aristotle Onassis gave to the widow of President John F. Kennedy as an engagement ring, and bidding at the Sotheby's auction of the Jacqueline Kennedy Onassis estate was a feeding frenzy by the well-heeled who wanted to touch and own a piece of Camelot. For *the high bidder, Anthony J.F. O'Reilly, the ring had a special appeal. His wife*

Chryss was a Goulandris, a member of a powerful Greek family that had been

an archrival of the Onassis family in the shipping business.

D. On consignment:
A jeweler might say, "Hey, why not leave your diamond with me and I'll sell it on consignment and make big money for you." DON'T DO IT!! NEVER leave your jewelry with anyone unless you're paid up front. He can promise you the moon, switch your good diamond for a piece of junk or a cubic zirconia, then call you in a couple of weeks to tell you to pick up your jewelry because he couldn't sell it!

E. Pawn shops:
They should be called "Prawn Shops," because they'll dip you in cocktail sauce and eat you alive. On average, pawnbrokers will offer you only 10 percent of wholesale. STAY AWAY!!

You may have heard of *Diamond Dealer Clubs,* but these are only for the trade, and unless you're in the trade you won't get within ten feet of these places.

Another option, for high-end jewelry only, is an auction house. Two to consider in the U.S. are:

Christie's
502 Park Avenue at 59th Street
New York City, NY 10022
(212) 492-5485

Sotheby's
1334 York Avenue
New York City, NY 10021
(212) 606-7000

Antique or "Estate" Jewelry

Many people love to shop for antique jewelry, in hopes of finding a beautiful and unique piece of jewelry, softly glowing with the patina of time and enhanced by the mystique of history. Fine, but remember that buying previously owned jewelry is a lot like buying a used car. Be smart enough to get a trained mechanic to look under the hood—that is, get an independent appraisal, and follow the guidelines in this book just as if you were buying a new piece of jewelry.

There are two things to be careful of. One, a lot of antique diamonds are Old Mine or Old European cuts. These styles, popular in the late 1800s and early 1900s, are cut very high and deep and allow a lot of light to leak out the bottom. They really are nothing better than a Class III or Class IV cut diamond. If you're buying an antique diamond with one of these cuts, expect a 35 percent to 40 percent discount off the prices listed in this book.

The second caution is, watch out for fairy tales! Dealers know that a diamond with a fascinating history is going to sell faster and for a higher price than one without a history. Don't be mesmerized by tales of Russian princesses or Arab sultans. Listen politely and smile, but then say, "That's great, but it's still a VS1-G, Class III cut!"

Chapter 11

Anniversaries and Occasions

If there's any man out there who believes that his jewelry-buying days are over after he purchases the bridal set— let me dispel that notion here and now! The fire in that first diamond always ignites a burning desire for more. "My engagement ring is lonely," she'll say. "It needs diamond earrings to keep it company." Or a tennis bracelet, or a pendant—the list goes on.

Anniversaries are perfect times for gifts of jewelry, gifts that say "you'd marry her all over again," to quote from the advertisement. Never make the mistake of getting your spouse a practical anniversary gift, like a new toaster or a vacuum cleaner. Anniversaries are occasions to celebrate and renew your love for each other, and only a personal gift such as jewelry is right for the moment.

Here's a traditional anniversary gift list.

Anniversary	Gift
1	Clocks
2	China
3	Crystal, glass
4	Electrical appliances (Yuck!)
5	Silverware

6	Wood
7	Pen & pencil set
8	Linen, lace
9	Leather
10	Diamond jewelry
11	Fashion jewelry
12	Pearls or colored stones
13	Textiles, furs
14	Gold jewelry
15	Watches
16	Silver hollowware
17	Furniture
18	Porcelain
19	Bronze
20	Platinum
25	Sterling Silver Jubilee
30	Diamond
35	Jade
40	Ruby
45	Sapphire
50	Golden Jubilee
55	Emerald
60	Diamond Jubilee

Here's a Gem Anniversary List, developed by several trade associations.

Anniversary	Gift
1	Gold jewelry
2	Garnet (all colors)
3	Pearls
4	Blue Topaz

5	Sapphire (all colors)
6	Amethyst
7	Onyx
8	Tourmaline
9	Lapis
10	Diamond jewelry
11	Turquoise
12	Jade
13	Citrine
14	Opal
15	Ruby
16	Peridot
17	Watches
18	Cat's Eye
19	Aquamarine
20	Emerald
21	Iolite
22	Spinel (all colors)
23	Imperial Topaz
24	Tanzanite
25	Sterling Silver Jubilee
30	Pearl Jubilee
35	Emerald
40	Ruby
45	Sapphire
50	Golden Jubilee
55	Alexandrite
60	Diamond Jubilee

Natural Birthstones

January	Garnet	A red lustrous stone which occurs mainly as crystals.
February	Amethyst	A clear purple or bluish violet variety of quartz crystal.
March	Aquamarine	A transparent beryl that may be blue, blue-green or green in color.
April	Diamond	Need we say more?
May	Emerald	A rich green variety of beryl, highly prized.
June	Pearl	Dense, lustrous layers of nacre formed around a foreign object within the shell of oysters and some other mollusks.

July	Ruby	A rare red corundum, sometimes worth $30,000 per carat.
August	Peridot	A deep yellowish-green olivine stone.
September	Sapphire	A rich blue transparent corundum gemstone.
October	Opal	A hydrated silica gemstone noted for its iridescent play of colors.
November	Topaz	A silicate of aluminum, usually a transparent yellow to brownish-yellow.
December	Turquoise	A sky-blue copper aluminum phosphate, highly prized.

Conclusion

Congratulations! You have finished *How to Buy a Diamond.* You've learned about the Four Cs, how to grade diamonds, how to select a jeweler and how to get the best diamond for your dollar. You have your questionnaire sheets to guide you. Now, I want you to ask yourself two more questions:

Do I really want to marry her?

Does she really want to marry me?

If you don't answer these questions immediately and emphatically "YES!!" then maybe you should think this over before you make a serious investment in a ring that says "Forever." Marriage is a magnificent institution for two people in love who have no doubts about wholehearted commitment to one another. Please be sure you're in that category before visiting the jeweler.

Also, I believe there are good reasons to buy a diamond and also reasons you should avoid taking the plunge. I'd like to share them with you now. They're called Diamond Values: What Giving a Diamond Should and Shouldn't Represent.

I. Give from the heart; not out of fear

II. Give through knowledge; not out of ignorance

III. Give to create joy; not because of intimidation

IV. Give to celebrate commitment and success; not to impress others

V. Give what you can afford to give; don't overextend yourself

And please remember one more thing: any diamond can make a good first impression, but only a good diamond will keep your attention.

I hope you've had as much fun reading this book as I have had writing it. I know that buying a diamond can be one of the most expensive and nerve-wracking purchases you'll ever make, but it can also be one of the most exciting and rewarding—if you apply the lessons you've learned in this book. Follow my advice, and you should be able to get the right diamond at the right price. And isn't that what it's all about?

Happy diamond shopping!

Post Script

Latest Industry News

My goal was to cover all you need to know in one medium sized book but at best, I've covered the highlights. All the press from a GIA bribery scandal, rough diamond shortages, fake lab grading reports, doomsday predictions on availability, and DeBeers' offer to pay $250 million to settle a majority of class action suits filed against DeBeers in the US, would fill another book. Instead, all up to the minute news that couldn't make the book is up on my website at www.TheDiamondGuy.com. My final words of advice are:

• If a deal seems too good to be true, it probably is.

• Truly good diamonds are more expensive or just not available and are not being discounted.

• The "labs" experiment failed when we decided to trust the fox guarding the hen house

• A diamond is only worth what somebody else is willing to pay for it.

• If it's not fully bonded it's probably full of baloney.

Appendix A
The Alphabet Rules

L-M-N-O-P

Recently I appeared on a PBS special about diamonds, and the producer asked me if I could come up with four or five easy-to-remember rules for diamond shopping. So I came up with the Alphabet Rules, a quick and simple consumer protection guide that will help even a novice avoid getting ripped off.

L = Loose   Always look at loose, not mounted, diamonds. The setting may hide flaws.

M = Magnify   Always look at your diamond through a jeweler's loupe or a microscope, which will reveal imperfections invisible to the naked eye.

N = Negotiate   Most retailers dramatically increase prices. Never pay the sticker price unless you've shopped around and you know they're already giving you a wholesale price.

O = Opinion   Always insist that the final sale be contingent upon the opinion of an independent appraiser. If the appraiser agrees you've done well, the sale will be final.

P = Plot   Always have the diamond's flaws plotted on a drawing of the stone. That way you'll be able to identify your diamond by the location of its blemishes and inclusions.

Appendix B

Carat Size Charts

Carat Weight	Shapes		
.50			
.75			
1.00			
1.25			
1.50			
2.00			
2.50			
3.00			

Carat Weight	Shapes
4.00	
5.00	

Carat Weight	Round	Carat Weight	Round
1/150	○	.03	○
1/100	○	.05	○
1/70	○	.07	○
1/50	○	.10	○
1/40	○	.15	○
1/33	○	.20	○
1/25	○		

Carat Weight	Round
.25	◯
.33	◯
.40	◯
.50	◯
.65	◯
.75	◯
.85	◯
1.00	◯
1.25	◯
1.50	◯

Appendix C
Glossary of Terms

Speaking the Jeweler's Language

Annealing The process of treating a diamond with high temperature and high pressure (HTHP) to remove nitrogen, boron, and other impurities that discolor a diamond. Also known as baking or heating.

Blemish A flaw on the exterior of a diamond, such as a scratch, abrasion, nick, or chip.

Blue-white Refers to a diamond that glows (flouresces) blue under ultraviolet light.

Bonded A bonded diamond is a natural diamond that is fully warranted by the jeweler and covers breakage, buy back, and exchange.

Brilliance White light reflected back from a diamond.

Brilliant A round diamond with fifty-eight facets.

Carat A unit of weight, equal to two hundred milligrams. In ancient times one carat was equal to one carob bean or four grains of rice.

Carbon The raw material of which diamonds are made. Occasionally a diamond will contain tiny pockets of carbon which can be seen as black spots within the stone.

Cloud A cluster of small inclusions, or internal flaws, within a diamond.

Color Matched™	The process of taking fancy-colored diamonds and intensifying and equalizing the color through neutron bombardment in order to match neighboring diamonds.
Crown	The top of a diamond. Everything above the girdle.
Culet	The bottom facet of a diamond, usually very small.
Dispersion	Colored light reflected from within a diamond; also called "fire."
Eye-clean	Refers to a diamond that has no inclusions or blemishes visible to the naked eye.
Facet	A polished surface on a diamond. A round, full-cut diamond usually has fifty-eight facets.
Flagship	Standard and box radiants that abide by the 65/65
Fluorescence	A diamond's reaction to ultraviolet (UV) light, causing the stone to glow in various colors.
Full-cut	A diamond with fifty-eight or more facets.
Gemologist	A person who has been trained and accredited in diamonds and colored stones.
GIA	Gemological Institute of America, an independent, non-profit organization which sets and upholds standards for grading diamonds and other precious stones.
Girdle	The narrow, unpolished or faceted band around the widest part of the diamond; the girdle separates the crown and the pavilion of the stone.
Head	The prongs which hold a diamond in its setting.
Inclusion	A flaw within a diamond, such as carbon spots or fractures.

Karat	The measure of the purity of gold; 24-karat being pure gold. Jewelry is usually made from 18K and 14K gold, which contain other metals for strength.
Laser-drilled	A diamond that has been treated with a laser to remove carbon spots or other inclusions.
Loupe	A small magnifying glass used to view gemstones.
Off-make	A poorly proportioned diamond.
Pavé	A method of setting diamonds very closely together, giving the illusion of one or more larger diamonds.
Pavilion	The bottom of a diamond; everything below the diamond's girdle.
Point	One-hundredth of a carat. A diamond weighing one-and-a-half carats weighs one hundred fifty points.
Semi-mount	A setting which is complete except for the main stone, which will be selected separately.
Single-cut	A diamond with only sixteen or seventeen facets.
Sparkle	The liveliness of the light reflecting from a diamond; the sum of the brilliance and the fire (dispersion).
Tiffany	A simple, elegant 2–3mm ring setting with a head that holds a single diamond.

Rock Slang Dictionary

In the jewelry industry we throw around a lot of slang terms like, "chubbies," "four grainers," "off-makes," and "glow worms," to name a few. Some of this slang terminology is derived from decades of usage and other terms are technically correct definitions to describe a diamond like the "65/65 Rule." Here, I've tried to give definitions of the most popular slang terms that jewelers, dealers, and cutters have been using for years. Hopefully, it will make it a little easier for the consumer to understand the secret language we jewelers use on a day to day basis.

65/65 Rule	A square or rectangular diamond whose table and total depth percentage does not exceed 65 percent of the diamond's width.
As Is	A diamond that comes with no bonding or warranties. Its sale is final, no exceptions after the buyer takes possession from the vendor.
Back Alley	A diamond that has had at least one previous owner and is being purchased on the secondary market. Example: Joe has purchased a back alley diamond. Translation: Joe has bought a used diamond.
Bananas	A marquise shaped diamond whose length to width ratio exceeds 2.25 to 1. The diamond appears to have been stretched to look like a banana.
Big Brother	Diamond Trading Company, a.k.a. DeBeers.
Bling Bling	A sparkly, valuable diamond or diamond jewelry.
Blue Booked	The dollar value placed on a diamond at time of purchase that the seller agrees to purchase the diamond back at some time in the future.
Bonded	Synonymous with warranty. All diamonds are either fully bonded, partially bonded, or not bonded. A new subcategory that has been popularized of late is the fully-bonded diamond with an expiration date (i.e. a limited lifetime warranty). The diamond is warranted not for the life of the diamond or person, but for the life of the

warranty itself. Most of these bogus warranty packages (breakage guarantee, buyback, exchange) run ninety days. A true fully bonded diamond has no expiration date or restocking fee.

Canaries

A canary diamond is yellow in color due to the fact it is saturated with nitrogen. The four main categories of canaries are light fancy, fancy, intense fancy, and vivid.

Chubbies

Diamonds that are poorly proportioned. Typically, diamonds that have oversized girdles or deep pavilions that cause the diamonds to appear smaller than they should when viewed from the top for any given weight.

Cognac

A brown diamond dramatized as attractive and valuable with an appealing title.

Commercial Grade

Non-gem quality diamonds that are recovered in bulk form and distributed for the masses. These goods are typically poor quality with little or no warranties.

Consolidator

A clearing house for commercial grade, off makes, or poor quality diamonds. These seconds are sold both online and in brick-and-mortar locations.

Decorate the Tree

How the facets are arranged on a diamond.

Doublet

A diamond or gemstone that is made of two pieces. Example: The crown is diamond but it is epoxied to a pavilion made out of cubic zirconia.

Duping	The con of selling a diamond with a Lab Grading Report that does not match the diamond being sold but rather matches a diamond that was shown loose to make the initial sale and later switched for the understudy.
Estate	A diamond or piece of jewelry that has been previously owned and is up for sale.
Fancies	Has two meanings. 1.) Any shape other than a round diamond or 2.) Any diamond of any particular color of the rainbow but white. These would include blues, pinks, violets, and yellows. The most famous fancy in the world is the Hope Diamond, which is steel blue.
Fisheye	The circular, centrally dark light pattern that appears in the table of a round diamond when it is cut shallow. It derives its nickname due to the fact that the light leakage through the pavilion creates the look from the crown of that of a fish's eye.
Footballs	The opposite of a banana shape marquise. A football is a marquise that closely resembles the shape of a football. A marquise could be described as a football if its length to width ratio is less than 1.75 to 1.
Fully Warranted	Can be synonymous with fully bonded. A diamond that has a breakage, buyback, exchange, and market crash guarantee. When it comes with no expiration dates, it is considered fully bonded, otherwise it is a limited lifetime warranty.
Glow Worms	A diamond that exhibits fluorescence in the

presence of ultraviolet light. Fluorescent diamonds are 20 percent less valuable than non-fluorescent diamonds.

Grade Bumping   A diamond whose clarity or color grade has been raised by one or more grades by a lab, appraiser, or salesman to enhance the value of the diamond.

Grainers   In the orient, diamonds were weighed using grains of rice. (4 grains = 1/5 of a gram which = a 1ct diamond on a counter balance) Example: a 6 grainer = 1 1/2ct diamond

Grandfather   An old diamond (Old Miners, Old European) or a diamond whose paperwork is outdated. A Lab Grading Report is considered a grandfather when it is over six months old and an appraisal is considered a grandfather at two years old.

Guild Store   A Guild Store is slang for a premium jewelry store. For example, Tiffany's, Fred's Joalliers, VanCleef & Arpels, Harry Winston, or Cartier and other top tier retailers.

Hot Rocks   Diamonds whose country of origin (South Africa, Sierra Leon, etc.) is linked to wars and oppression fueled with the funds acquired from the sale or barter of diamonds.

Illusion Setting   The placement of a diamond into a mirrored high polished plate of metal to give the illusion that the diamond is larger than it appears from a distance.

Laser Drilled   A diamond whose inclusions have been drilled out with a laser.

Melee	Small diamonds, usually used to describe diamonds under 1/4ct in size.
Non-Commercial Grade	Gem quality diamonds that are extremely scarce.
Off-makes	Generally speaking, a poorly proportioned diamond that is either cut too shallow, too deep, or warped. All Class III and Class IV cut diamonds are considered off-makes.
Old European	A round diamond popularly cut in the early 1900s for the public from European cutting houses. These diamonds had the same characteristics as an Old Miners (small table, high crown, open culet) with the exception that they were not squarish round but round in diameter.
Old Miners	A squarish round diamond typically seventy-five or more years old, whose facet arrangement is highlighted by a small table, high crown, and open culet. Old Miners are also referred to as heavy makes.
Orphan	A diamond that is being sold at an auction and has no current owner that is wearing it. Orphan can also be used to describe a diamond that does have an owner but the owner no longer wears it. Example: Mary owns a beautiful 2ct orphaned diamond. She should rescue it from her safety deposit box.
Padded	See spreads and chubbies. The cutter kept extra weight on the stone that does not optimize the optics of the diamond. The goal is to increase revenue.

P.B.'s	Not peanut butter, but "Partially Bonded." A diamond with some warranties.
Pegasus, Monarch, or Bellataire	Brand names for annealed (heated, baked) diamonds introduced into the market by General Electric and Lazare Kaplan in 1998.
Pick Pocketing	A salesman has been said to be "pick pocketing" a customer when he uses the two month salary guideline in order to make a larger sale.
Plot	The mapping of inclusions and blemishes on a paper diagram of the facet arrangement of any given diamond for identification purposes. Similar to a fingerprint.
River Rock	A diamond that is so heavily included (I2 and I3s) that they deserve to be thrown in the river. River rock is synonymous with a bad diamond of little or no value.
Rovals	A poorly proportioned oval diamond that has a length to width ratio under 1.2 to 1 causing the diamond to look not quite round and not quite oval. Hence "Roval."
Sandbagger	An appraiser who misgrades an appraisal to sabotage a sale in order to recommend that the client purchase somewhere else.
Single Cuts	Round diamonds that have sixteen or seventeen facets.
Spreads	A diamond that is purposely cut wide to give the impression that the diamond is larger than its corresponding weight when viewed from the top. All spreads are also shallow with less than 38 percent light return.

Warped   A diamond whose crown height percentage
                        plus maximum girdle thickness percentage plus
                        pavilion depth percentage doesn't equal the
                        total depth percentage within .5 percent.

Appendix D

Diamond Guy™ Q & A

I have picked a few of my favorite questions and thought I would share them with you here. If you have any questions of your own, I can be reached at www.thediamondguy.com or through my HelpLine, 1-800-275-4047.

Subject: Cleaning a diamond

What is the proper way to clean a diamond? I use alcohol sometimes and other times I use Efferdent denture cleaner. Can either of these damage my diamonds?

Answer

I recommend cleaning your ring daily. There is no better home care system than sudsing ammonia and a good ultrasonic cleaner. Let the ring soak, then use a brush to get to any hard-to-reach crevices. Ultrasonic machines cost between $25–$50 and are available in most major department stores.

Subject: Tiffany setting

What is a Tiffany setting?

Answer

A Tiffany setting is generally a 2–2 1/2 mm band with a 4- or 6-prong head. No side diamonds.

Subject: Is it really a diamond?

I heard from someone in a chat room of a laboratory that "creates its own diamonds" by "speeding up" the coal-to-diamond process. I heard of someone purchasing a 2.5 carat stone for $500 from this place. The stones are called diamond essence, I believe. Is this too good to be true, or are these legitimate diamonds?

Answer

If it were true, I'd be out of business! The cost for a good quality 2 1/2 ct diamond is around $31,460. This "diamond essence" is a simulant. Translation: not a man-made diamond, just cubic zirconia that kind of looks like a diamond! The correct price for a 2.5 ct "diamond essence" should be $1.00 per carat or $2.50, not $500. Wow, what a mark up!

Subject: Diamond cuts

What is meant by a miner's cut?

Answer

The miner's cut or old miner's cut was the first predecessor to what is now called the American Ideal cut or the round diamond. Its shape was a cross between a round and a square. It was more like a square with rounded corners, a high crown, and a deep pavilion, with the traditionally chopped off culet (the culet is the facet on the bottom of the stone). Diamond cutting has come a long way since the old miner's cuts of the early 1900s, and it is a good thing too. Old miner's cuts were nothing more than an athlete fifty pounds overweight. The modern day cuts are more durable, beautiful, and valuable.

Subject: Inclusions

My diamond has a small visible (with the naked eye) inclusion towards the base. You can see it only from looking up through the bottom. How does this affect the value?

Answer

There are two ways to describe any diamond: commercial or non-commercial. Commercial represents the average, low-quality diamonds that are generally sold. They are diamonds with one or more of the following faults: not eye-clean, tinted yellow, poorly proportioned, treated, or fluorescent. Non-commercial grades are eye-clean, white, well-proportioned, non-treated, and non-fluorescent. The diamond you're describing, due to the fact that the inclusion can be seen without magnification, would in most cases classify the diamond in the commercial category. Unfortunately, this is a bad thing. With approximately 97.5 percent of all diamonds sold being commercial, you're probably holding onto a diamond that is not extremely rare. And with that lack of uniqueness comes the following problems:

1. It will appreciate in value little or not at all
2. It probably has no trade-in value
3. Its cash liquidation value is approximately ten cents on the dollar

A non-commercial grade, natural diamond with SI1, I color, Class II, no fluorescence, at a minimum will:

1. Appreciate in value by at least 6 percent per year
2. Have trade-in capabilities
3. Have a cash liquidation value (or dump value) of sixty to eighty cents on the dollar

If it's possible to trade in or get a new diamond, I would recommend it.

Subject: Natural/Treated Diamonds

In your responses, you occasionally refer to a diamond as being "natural" as opposed to being "treated." I am not familiar with what that means. My assumption is of some type of bleaching process to aid the color of a diamond. Could you please explain the meanings of those terms and what the effect of "treating" a diamond has on its quality and value.

Answer

Approximately one out of every three diamonds is treated after the faceting process. By treated I'm referring to laser-drilled, fracture-filled, heat-treated, coated, and irradiated. Treated diamonds have very poor to no secondary market value and in many cases are not structurally sound. A non-commercial grade diamond that is natural could expect to appreciate 6 percent to 8 percent per year. Treated diamonds do not appreciate.

Subject: Natural/Treated Diamonds

How can one ensure that a diamond one is looking at has not been treated?

Answer

With the exception of baked diamonds (e.g. Pegasus), the only way to be sure that you are getting a natural diamond is to get it in writing at the point of purchase. Then have it verified by an independent appraiser. The only way to ensure against a baked diamond is with a bonding document.

Subject: Basic Question

1) How much does it cost to get a GIA lab grading report?
2) How long does it take?
3) What is the best way to ship and insure a diamond in the mail?

4) Will they also point out any sort of treatment, if any, that's been done to the stone?

Answer

1) The price of a GIA lab grading report is based on the size of the diamond. The average cost for a GIA lab grading report is around $177.
2) They say four to five business days, but it is more like two weeks.
3) Registered mail is your best choice.
4) If the diamond is treated, GIA should catch it.

Subject: Diamond Color Grades

I read somewhere about diamonds being referred to as white but still having further divisions: Blue White, Fine White, White, Commercial White, Top Silver Cape, and Silver Cape. It said that any of these diamonds could all be referred to as "white" by a jeweler. Is this true? What is the difference in these diamonds?

Answer

The terms you've listed are called "old school terminology." No one who is trying to be straight with you should use these terms. Only some places in Europe still use them.

Blue White refers to D, E, F colors. Fine White refers to G, H. White refers to I, J. Commercial white and lower are slightly tinted yellow diamonds. Blue White can also refer to a fluorescent diamond.

Subject: Tiffany's

I wandered into Tiffany's in Chicago the other day and was surprised to find that they don't sell loose stones—only the finished product! I took a look at their little booklet that describes everything, and I can't believe people are buying these expensive rings already set! Is it because of the name and that they are historically known for quality?

I've been really learning a lot about diamonds and have been doing a lot of research—I should be able to get a fine diamond and setting just as good as the Tiffany's on my own, right?

Also, I never asked my jeweler about the polish—should I? What should I be looking for? Is there a way to check it against what the jeweler's telling me? Is this going to hugely devalue the ring if it's not right?

Answer

When buying a diamond, everyone generally has two main concerns: Getting the right diamond and getting it at the right price. While satisfying any one of these isn't difficult, getting both takes a lot of time, patience, and work. The high-end stores like Tiffany's, Cartier, Harry Winston, etc., cater to one type of client—a person who wants quality but does not have the time to shop around to get it. Tiffany's customers feel that their time is extremely valuable. They feel that the price difference between buying at Tiffany's quickly and spending hours to find the same thing at a lower price are equal since they can take the time they would have spent shopping and use it to make money.

Tiffany's is practically beyond reproach. They represent quality with a capital "Q." But is it possible to get the same quality for as much as 1/2 to 1/3 the price? Absolutely! It just takes work!

In regards to polish, I can't recall ever seeing a well-proportioned diamond with bad polish. Don't worry about it.

Subject: *Place of Purchase*

I want to purchase an upgrade diamond for my wife. I'm on a budget. However, I still want to buy the biggest, clearest diamond for my buck. Can you recommend a vendor that doesn't mark up extremely high?

Answer

Look in your Yellow Pages under Diamonds; Wholesale. Their average markup is 10 percent to 15 percent above their cost. They should be cheaper than retail outlets.

Subject: Lab grading report/appraisal or both?

I have a trusted diamond dealer whom other members of my family have bought from before. He told me that he can get a diamond with an appraisal, but it won't have a lab grading report. Is it OK to not have a lab grading report? What is it REALLY for? Is it necessary?

Answer

A lab grading report is nothing more than an opinion. When you consider that for every one thousand diamonds that are sold in the United States, less than twenty-five would classify as good or noncommercial, do you think your jeweler is getting you one of those elusive gems? If so, I guess, don't worry about it. But even if you don't get a lab grading report, you need to get an independent appraisal. Lab grading reports are definitely required with investment grade diamonds or fancy colored diamonds.

Subject: Lab grading report/appraisal or both?

If a diamond comes with a lab grading report, should it be more expensive than a diamond that is of the same quality and grading but does not come with a lab grading report?

Answer

Diamonds with a lab grading report should not cost more than diamonds without one. If the jeweler is working very tightly on the price of the stone, there is an argument (small) that the diamond would cost approximately $177 more since that is the average cost of the typical lab grading report.

Subject: Basic Questions

1. How can you tell for sure that a diamond has been laser-drilled? In a diamond we recently purchased can be seen a straight line that I've been told is a laser drill mark. Two jewelers told me this, and I saw it myself. Then, just to complicate things, another jeweler told me he didn't think that's what it was but that it was a natural inclusion. How can I be sure? I've heard everything from looking for "orange light" to putting it under high heat. Can one be sure?

2. Is it required by law that it be disclosed if a diamond has been "laser-drilled?"

3. Why would a diamond lose its sparkle over the years?

4. Will I get the same general appraisal from several qualified appraisers? In other words, is one appraisal enough?

Answer

1. Your best shot is to go to one of the labs.

2. Yes, it is now required by law that it be disclosed if a diamond has been laser-drilled.

3. Improper cleaning or a poorly cut diamond that becomes abraded will cause a diamond to lose its sparkle.

4. One independent appraisal is enough.

Subject: Is the price set?

Are prices on rings from those chain jewelry stores at the mall always set? Is there any room to bargain or bring the price down? I wasn't sure if shopping for engagement rings was anything like buying a new car.

Answer

The average jewelry store in the United States charges twice what they should. No one pays sticker price. Generally, the price listed in the average store can be cut in half. Go negotiate!

Subject: Lab grading report

Does a lab grading report ever become dated?

Answer

Yes. A lab grading report must be recent (within six months) and the diamond must not have been worn since it was graded.

Subject: Jeweler Questionnaire from Book

While shopping for a diamond, one jeweler told me that they use their own scale that has been in existence since the 1940s, which they say is longer than GIA's scale. They said they would provide a chart that shows how their grading scale correlates with GIA's scale. You said to disqualify any jeweler who does not use GIA grading scale; would this be okay, or should I still disqualify the store? They were the most friendly and helpful of all that I contacted.

Also, a store told me that they specialize in "Lazare Diamonds" and they mailed me some info on them. The information says that they have higher standards for these diamonds, and they have a logo and an individual identification number specially inscribed on its circumference. It says that the inscription is visible under a 10X microscope and does not affect the clarity grade of the diamond. Is that true? Are these diamonds really better than any others? Can any jewelry store get them, or are they rare?

Answer

To question #1, disqualify the store or make all sales contingent on a lab grading report or independent appraisal. That way you will be able to see if you are getting what you really want.

Some Lazare Kaplan diamonds can be equivalent to Class I or Class II diamonds. They are very well cut. As long as the price is in line, Lazare Kaplan stones can be a good choice. Only stores that have an account with Lazare Kaplan can get their diamonds.

Subject: Four elements

On a recent interview on MSNBC, you referred to the four elements to any purchase. Can you go over those again?

Answer

In any purchase, not just diamonds, there are four factors that must be taken into consideration before purchase:

P–Price Q–Quality

S–Service W–Warranties

So, mind your Ps and Qs, but don't forget your SWs.

Let's start with price first. Everyone in this world, including jewelers, has a right to make a living and a profit. But a living and price gouging are not the same thing, which is why you have to be educated and know what a fair price is. Otherwise, you'll leave yourself open to the wolves.

In quality, it is true that beauty lies in the eyes of the beholder. But with 99 percent of the public unable to tell the difference between a cubic zirconia and a diamond, appraisals, lab grading reports, and independent evaluations can sometimes be the only things that can keep you from making a big mistake beyond knowing what to ask for. Thirdly, service. Most people don't realize that even diamonds need to have checkups every now and then, as do their settings. An annual polishing, cleaning, and tightening of your jewelry is a must. Top-notch jewelers will provide the annual checkups free of charge.

Last, but not least, are warranties. It is my honest opinion that bonded diamonds are going to be prerequisites to any serious diamond buyer from now on. The president of GIA, William Boyajian, recently said in an interview that baked diamonds are the biggest threat to hit the diamond industry in the twenty-three years he's been with GIA. As long as laboratories can no longer guarantee a diamond is 100 percent natural and untreated, a diamond without at least a buy-back policy and breakage guarantee isn't worth the setting it's in.

Subject: Round

What do you think of the following: round, one carat, 6.44 x 6.49 x 3.89, depth: 60.2 percent, table: 55 percent, girdle: medium to slightly thick, culet: none, polish: VG, symmetry: G, clarity: VS1, color: D, fluorescence: none. It also has in the comments: "Additional pinpoints, internal graining, and surface graining are not shown." What does this mean?

Answer

At this point, the diamond looks "Report Pretty"—meaning that with all the data present the diamond looks good. But please remember that, just like beauty can be only skin deep, so too can a diamond be only "Report Pretty." You need to find out the crown angle, pavilion angle, crown height, and pavilion depth to make a total evaluation. As far as the extra comments, pinpoints are just inclusions the size of the head of a pin that the grader was too lazy to plot. Graining, whether it be internal or surface, is just like graining you might see in a piece of wood. It is nothing to worry about.

Subject: Total depth does not equal crown + pavilion + girdle

I have done quite of bit of diamond shopping, and I have found that when I add up the pavilion depth plus crown height plus girdle (produced from a megascope report), the total is about 1–2 percent off of the total depth listed on the lab grading report for diamonds from what seem to be reputable jewelers. For example, a (EGL lab graded) G, VS1, 1.02-carat, total depth: 59.8, crown height: 14.5, pavilion: 42.6, girdle: 1.1. When I add the last three numbers, the total is 58.2, a 1.6 percent difference from what is listed on the total depth. When I brought this up, the dealer seemed just as perplexed as I because those were the printed numbers from his megascope report too. Is there any reason the total depth would not be exactly equal to the sum of those three measurements?

Answer

Boy, you are a sharp cookie! You are absolutely correct that they must add up! So why in God's name are they off on so many stones? There are three possible reasons. (1) The sarin or megascope machines have been calibrated to choose just the perfect crown or pavilion angle instead of a large multiple average. Then, taking the tangent of the angles, the machine calculates the crown height or pavilion depth. Now, if the crown angle and the pavilion angle that were chosen were warped angles, the rest of the data will be wrong! (2) Some graders "guesstimate" instead of actually measuring correctly. (3) Some sarin and megascope reports are scanned into a computer, altered, and reprinted. The most the totals should ever be off is one-half of 1 percent.

Subject: Bonded dealers on the Internet

Are their any fully bonded diamond dealers on the Internet?

Answer

Yes. FullyBondedDiamonds.com™ (our sister company) is up and running. They are the first online retailer to follow, to the exact letter, all the guidelines outlined in *How to Buy a Diamond*. Come on, which would you rather have, a cheesy thirty-day return policy or the security of a lifetime return? What does it say about a company that it will not buy back their own merchandise after thirty days? I'll tell you what it says. They don't believe in their product. Go ahead and get a fully bonded diamond. Give Keith Owen (CEO of FullyBondedDiamonds.com) a call and tell them The Diamond Guy® sent you!

Appendix E
Getting Into Shape

A palm reader supposedly can tell you your future and numerologists say they can do the same thing by adding and subtracting the numbers of the day, month, and year you were born. Astrologers go so far as to say they can tell you who you are, where your future lies, and what you're going to have for lunch by what phase the moon was in when you were born!

According to all these mystics, who we are and why we do what we do is all predetermined by fate. All we have to do is know how to read the signs to tell us what path our lives will follow and what our final destination will be. "Yeah, right!" you're probably saying, "I am the captain of my own ship and the creator of my own destiny." Well maybe so, but how can you explain the fact that every time you check your daily astrology guide, it seems to be pretty accurate? Lucky guess? Maybe. So vague it could apply to anyone? Maybe. Or maybe it's just as simple as thought creating reality. If you are told something and you believe it, I guess it doesn't make a difference whether it's true or not. If it's true for you, even if it's just a perception, it's your reality, your truth.

Now, probably at this point (if you're still reading) you're thinking, "What the heck does this have to do with diamonds and 'Getting into Shape'?" which I know you have figured out doesn't mean doing push-ups or jumping jacks. What we are delving into here is why women like and/or choose one shape of diamond over another. Believe it or not, what shape a woman chooses for an engagement ring tells a lot about the woman doing the wearing. After almost two decades of watching women choose different shapes and sizes, I found that certain personality types tend to gravitate toward one particular shape or another. I've also found that certain shapes tend to have a higher divorce rate than other shapes! Oh, I've got your interest now, have I? Yes, I've actually been able to graph which shapes tend to have the highest divorce rates, which ones result in the best marriages, and which ones are more likely to fool around! Am I crazy? Probably. But if you're interested in one guy's observations, here it goes. Astrologers, numerologists, palm readers, and tarot card readers step aside. (Drum roll please.) I'd like to introduce for the audience's enjoyment the wonderful world of Dia-shape-ology!

Fill out the following questionnaire and answer honestly to determine what your diamond says about you.

1. Do you have a diamond? (Circle One)

      Yes No

      (If no please stop taking this test.)

2. What shape diamond do you have?

3. What size diamond do you have? (Circle One)

      A. Microscopic

      B. Nice Size

      C. A Boulder

      D. I can't lift my hand from the weight.

4. How long have you had your diamond? (Circle One)
    A. Less than 2 years
    B. 2–5 years
    C. 5–7 years
    D. I can't remember it's been so long.

5. Are you still with the person who gave you the diamond? (Circle One)
    Yes No
    (If you bought it yourself, the answer will always be yes.)

6. How often do you clean your diamond? (Circle One)
    A. Once a day
    B. Once a week
    C. When it gets dirty
    D. I'm supposed to clean my diamond?

7. Pick the statement that best describes your relationship with your diamond. (Circle One)
    A. I will keep my diamond till the day I die, we are inseparable.
    B. I will keep my diamond till the day I die unless something better comes along.

Check the following answer guide to see how you've done and determine what your diamond means to you and what it says to the world about the person you are.

Question #1: Obviously, for the purpose of this exercise, having a diamond is a prerequisite. Not to say that if you are not the owner of a diamond you are any less loved and appreciated. It just seems that way.

Question #2: Here's the meat and potatoes; the meaning of the top shapes:

Round—Congratulations! Round is the most popular, faithful, traditional, and religious. Most round-wearers chose a round for its clean lines and symmetry. The idea that a circle has no beginning and no end adds to the romance of a round. Round-wearers tend to be old-fashioned and honest with values and beliefs they would fight for. The only downside to some that choose a round is their lack of spontaneity and leadership abilities. Round-wearers tend to be more team players than team leaders. If a round-wearer is married, her main goal in keeping a long, loving relationship is to not be afraid of change.

Oval—Look, you would have gotten a round if everyone in your family, including your aunt Gertrude, didn't have one. You have all the same values of a round but there is something inside you that cries out to be different and not go with the crowd. Oval-wearers make great wives! On one side they are predictable, stable, and dependable, but every now and then they have wild hair and let loose! If not for the poor brilliancy of an oval, I believe a lot more women would be in this camp.

Pear—Where round-wearers tend to go with the crowd, pear-wearers want to create the crowd. Pear-wearers want to be different, pure and simple. If also being better comes along with the package, so be it. Pear-wearers tend to be more demanding and higher maintenance. Everything has to be just right or don't do it at all is their battle call. Pear-wearers are the third most likely to get a divorce. (Top two coming up.) Due to, in many cases, forgetting that happiness isn't always asking, "What's in it for me?" The happily married pear-wearer never forgets that there is no I in team and applies the same standards of excellence to herself as to her partner.

Emerald Cut—Here's a tough nut to crack. Emerald-cut-wearers are old-fashioned like round-wearers, but being in the crowd or following the crowd are not the drum beats they follow. In fact, the interesting thing about emerald-cut-wearers is their lack of ambition to do anything to impress others. Not that other people's opinions don't count, it's just that they don't see themselves through the eyes of others. Emerald-cut-wearers are leaders. They are attracted to an emerald cut for its quiet elegance, its regal temperament, and bold strokes. The emerald-cut-wearer doesn't need pop to sell her diamond—that's what she's there for.

Princess & Radiants—Princess- and radiant-wearers are electric. They are fun, exciting, cutting edge, and not afraid to take chances. They live life to the fullest. Since princess and radiant are the most sparkly shapes, wearers of these rocks don't mind bringing attention to themselves. They love the spotlight. Whitney Houston, for example, is a proud wearer of a radiant. The only time princess and radiant wearers split up with their mates is if the guy can't keep up.

Heart Shape—The heart shape, a.k.a. "Black Widow" and "Three Strikes," holds the title of the least sparkly, second-highest divorce rate, and most-cheated-upon diamond in the group. (Hence the alias "Three Strikes.") A lot of analysis has gone into why this diamond and its wearer have so much trouble, but I think it can best be explained by what type of woman and couple gravitate toward the heart—pure romantics. And when I say pure romantics, I'm not just saying soul mates, I'm talking maple syrup, knight in shining armor, Romeo and Juliet kind of romantic. Heart-shape people tend to live in fantasyland. Their motto is love conquers all, love has no restrictions, love has no boundaries. Then they get married and quickly find out that even though love, in its own little world, is perfect, life isn't. Life isn't fair or just or even-handed. Life equals change. The heart-shape-wearer tends to have a problem with this. If love is perfect, there is no need for change, and certainly no need for reality. So, when they come to the conclusion that their mate isn't perfect (he never was, nobody is) and discover pure love doesn't seem to pay the bills, they flee—into the arms of another, into another job, into another life—constantly searching for the equation of pure love equals perfect life, which doesn't exist.

Marquise—The marquise, in all its grandeur and magnificence (one of the largest looking shapes), is the crown jewel for divorce—even more so than the heart. Heck, at least the heart had good intentions. Marquise-wearers tend to be very concerned with first impressions, second impressions, all impressions. They are very goal-oriented and certainly believe that size matters. Marquise-wearers believe in division and being "better than." There is the wrong side of the tracks and it's never the side they are on. A lot of socialites and wannabe socialites choose marquise because, when cut correctly, they look bigger than they really are. And that's where the problem is. Marquise-wearers, not all, but quite a few, spend the better part of their lives trying to be something or someone they are not. Success never lies in not being and loving who you are. For a marquise-wearer to survive, she must realize that regardless of how nice a package is, it always fades away—inner beauty doesn't.

Question #3: What actual carat size you have is irrelevant to how you perceive it. To some people, the one-carat diamond they have is puny. For others, it's the rock of Gibraltar. But that's the key here: not what you have, but how you perceive it. Is the glass half full or half empty? It appears that the happiest marriages tend to be those in which the engagement diamond is viewed as magnificent and substantial. The minute a woman finds fault in the rock, it's not long before she finds fault in the giver. Want to appreciate your diamond? Just think of the one out of three women who got married and didn't get one.

Question #4: If you had to write a list of all the things you want, how long a list would it be? Long? Short? How about a list of all the things you need? Long? Short? The three steps for creation are thought, word, and action. To get anything done, you have to think it, verbalize it, then take action. When you announce to the world that there are things you need, want, or expect, you cannot be whole till you get them. And if your brain perceives that it is without or not whole, it won't be happy. The key to any long-term happiness is not getting everything you want, but wanting everything you have. The longer you've had your diamond and the longer you appreciate it, the better your life and marriage will be. The diamond is a symbol of where you were and where you are going. To always embrace your past as you do your present will empower you to learn from your experiences and not repeat those events that no longer define who you are today.

Question #5: Well, I think this one is pretty self-explanatory. If the diamond is a symbol of two that have joined to become one, and one of you is not on the scene any more, chances are your rock means very little to you today.

Question #6: "To have and to hold" doesn't necessarily equal "to love and to cherish." I've lined up a hundred couples and asked them the condition of their marriage and relationship, and I found a direct correlation between clean rings and great marriages and filthy rings and relationships that are no longer connected or were drifting apart. Just a coincidence? Could be. Or maybe it's that any good marriage takes work, care, and effort. Marriage isn't easy. When a problem arises, a lot of people just let it go, thinking it will fix itself. It won't. A clean ring will always get dirty unless you don't allow it. A good marriage will do the same unless you work at it and keep the dust off.

Question #7: Fifty-four percent of women who receive an engagement ring say they would never get rid of their original engagement ring. They would keep it until they die. Forty-six percent, however, say that even though they have fond memories of their original engagement ring, they wouldn't keep the first car they ever had, or first home they ever had! If something better comes along they will snatch it! That being said, here's how the divorce bug attacks each group. Seventy-five percent in group one—"The I'll keep it forever" folks—tend to stay married, while 80 percent in group two are splitsville.

Appendix F
One Guy's Opinion

My job is to talk about diamonds. How to get a good one, how not to get ripped off, how to get the most for your money. But I'm seeing a society where the "truth" belongs to the one who can tell the best story, not the one based on the facts.

For example, every year five thousand people are indicted, convicted, and sentenced for a whole list of horrific crimes. From petty theft, to rape, assault, and even murder. What is even more horrific is that all these crimes hold three special things in common; the men and women that are convicted were primarily incarcerated on eyewitness testimony, spend an average of ten years in prison, and all of these criminals are eventually set free because they are later proven to be innocent. How must it feel to spend a decade of your life telling the whole world you didn't do it, to lose your family, friends, and livelihood all based on what someone else believes they see. As it turns out magicians knew it a long time ago. The hand is quicker than the eye. The eye can be fooled! It happens every day. In our streets, and in automobile showrooms with tires we're told are safe enough to drive our families around on. Now, I'm not here to talk about how our justice system is broken or about slick car salesman who try to sell us the virtues of undercoating and who roll back odometers to give us the perception of more value. For me, it's still about diamonds.

"Seeing is believing," you might say. But does believing constitute the truth? Does it constitute a fact? Well, try this on for size. For the last few years the diamond industry has been fighting the Federal Trade Commission (FTC) so they will not have to disclose laser-drilled diamonds. The industry felt it was an insult. For starters, to require disclosure of a treatment that alters the value or durability by changing the FTC guidelines would be paramount to announcing to the world that jewelers are dishonest. Jewelers can't be trusted to tell the truth. For God's sake, the industry can police itself. But, every year over five thousand complaints are registered at the Better Business Bureau, the FTC, and Jewelers Vigilante Committees. People were and are buying diamonds every day based on who has the best story to tell, and a constant reminder "See for yourself, isn't it a beautiful diamond?" Even in the casinos with no clocks and free liquor you know what your odds are. But in a jewelry store with its hundred canned spotlights, lab grading documents, and very good stories, we lay our money down. Is it worth it? It must be, it's an AGS000. Is it worth it? It must be, it's GIA graded. Is it worth it? It must be, it's 100 percent natural. Is it worth it? It must be, just look how pretty it is. And that is where they get you. That is where they set the hook. Then to reel you in, the jeweler says, "How can you put a price on something that lasts forever?" The love card. So you forget about the months or years it took you to save your money or the loan you have to take out or even the VISA you're going to max out at a 22 percent interest rate, because how can you put a price on love? The illusion is complete. Like the frog that turns into the handsome prince. The rock becomes the magical diamond. Seeing is believing, or maybe better said, believing is seeing. That's where any good salesman will get you. Recently, the FTC changed their guidelines and made it mandatory to disclose laser-drilled diamonds, or for that matter any form of treatment that would give you the impression that something is better or more valuable than what it is. Let me ask you this: if five thousand men and women are convicted for crimes they didn't commit, and if there are over five thousand complaints each year about non-disclosure in treatments, how many people are still in jail that are innocent, and how many worthless diamonds are on the fingers of our loved ones?

Here's one more thing to chew on. It has just been announced (to the jewelry industry, not the public of course) that a company by the name of 3-Beams Technology (a separate division of Norsam) has created a process called Focus Ion Beam Technology (FIB for short). Apparently taking ideas from Los Alamos National Laboratory, FIB instruments can focus a beam of ions down to a diameter of 7 nanometers (that's .000007 millimeters, or .00000028 inches). Using this technology they can drill a diamond to remove carbon leaving a drill hole 1/1000th the size of the current technology. According to 3-Beams's CEO, Jayant Neogi, with a special modification a gas can be injected into the void which will solidify, making the drill hole practically invisible.

FTC makes a law that treatments must be disclosed, then the industry we were supposed to trust announces a new way not to get caught.

What's the moral of this story? Seeing is not believing. Take everything with a grain of salt, and please cut the deck before you're dealt a hand.

Index

A

B

C

Cubic Zirconia, 160, 298, 306
Culet, 39, 63, 289, 298
Cut, 1, 2, 28-33, 44, 298-299, 306

D
Depth, 305
Diamond, 12, 160, 209; care, 209-210; cleaning, 208-211; rough, 33; synthetic, 160, toughness of, 11-12
Diamond weddings rings, 117-118
Dispersion, 289, 290

E
Eye clean, 8, 289, 299

F
Facet, 36, 289, 299
Federal Trade Commission, 7, 163, 171, 173
Fire, 289, 290
Fluoresence, 26, 299
FTC see Federal Trade Commission

G
GIA, 12, 38, 50, 53, 63, 85,123, 138, 285-287
Girdle, 36, 39, 62, 289, 290
Gold, 119, 298
Grade bumping, 171

I

K

L

M

N

O

W

Y

About the Author

F red Cuellar, the founder and president of Diamond Cutters International, is one of the world's top diamond experts. Diamond Cutters International (DCI) is one of America's few diamond houses open to the public by appointment only. He is an importer and creative designer of jewelry. His clients include the Saudi royal family and hundreds of professional athletes. Mr. Cuellar is accredited in diamonds and colored stones by the Gemological Institute of America and is ranked as one of the top diamond experts in America by *National Jeweler*. He is also the author of the number one bestselling book on diamonds in the country, *How to Buy a Diamond*.

Some Highlights of Fred's Career:
- Diamond advisor to the *Wall Street Journal*, the *Washington Post*, and *UsWeekly*, *Fine Living*, *Cosmopolitan*, and *InStyle* magazines.
- Diamond advisor to MSNBC.
- Diamond advisor to *Newsweek*.
- Writer and diamond advisor for *Icon* magazine.
- Has been featured and discussed on *The Tonight Show with Jay Leno*, *The Today Show*, *CBS Morning News*, *The Phil Donahue Show*, *Crook & Chase*, CNN, ESPN, as well as over one hundred other news and talk shows.
- Created the players' championship rings for the 1994 NBA Champion Houston Rockets.
- Created the International Hockey League Championship rings for the back-to-back champion Utah Grizzlies and was the first

American chosen to create the Canadian Football League Championship rings for the 1995 champion Baltimore Stallions.

- Created the Stanley Cup Championship rings for the New Jersey Devils in 1995 and the Colorado Avalanche in 1996.
- Created the 1996 Super Bowl Championship rings for the Dallas Cowboys.
- Created the 1997 Super Bowl Championship rings for the Denver Broncos.
- Created the 1997 & 1998 NHL Stanley Cup Championship rings for the Detroit Redwings.
- Created the 1999 Stanley Cup Championship rings for the Dallas Stars.
- Created the 1999 New York Yankees Players Championship Rings.
- Created the 2000 NHL Stanley Cup Championship Rings for the New Jersey Devils.
- Created the World's Greatest Athlete Ring for Olympic Gold Medalist Dan O'Brien.
- Created the "Million Dollar Puck" for the Houston Aeros, made of platinum, diamonds, and emeralds.
- Created Cal Ripken's commemorative ring for breaking Lou Gehrig's record of consecutive Major League Baseball games (2,131).
- Created the first ever baseball bracelet for the Houston Astros, made of mini ruby and diamond baseballs.
- Inventor of the interlocking diamond bezel, interlocking diamond logo, interlocking logo trophy, and gem-sculptured logo.
- Created the $2 million "Super Pizza" consisting of over six hundred carats of diamonds and colored stones in five pounds of gold for Little Caesars Pizza.
- Creator of the $200,000 "Gem Prowler" in conjunction with Chrysler Plymouth.

- Created the "world's most expensive toy," The Rubik's Cube Masterpiece—a full-size, fully working Rubik's Cube, covered with 185 carats of precious gems.
- Created the "Harley of Gold," a gold and diamond scale replica of a Harley-Davidson motorcycle.
- Created Playboy's Millennium Interlocking diamond pendants.
- Exclusive jewelry designs have been featured or discussed on *Oprah, The Tonight Show with Jay Leno, The Today Show, CBS Morning News, The Phil Donahue Show, Crook and Chase,* CNN, Telemundo, ESPN, and over one hundred other news and talk shows.

Other Books by the Author

The World's Greatest Proposals
In a recent internet contest, Fred Cuellar (a.k.a. "The Diamond Guy") offered a beautiful, sparkling diamond in return for the most hilarious, creative, or inspirational proposal story. As a result, he received thousands of wonderful engagement stories and has collected the best here in *The World's Greatest Proposals*. A perfect shower gift, this beautiful little book will bring tears of joy, love, and laughter to everyone who knows what it means to find the love of their life.
The price is $9.95.

Diamonds for Profit
Diamonds for Profit will benefit any reader who wants to sell (or buy and sell) diamonds or colored-stone jewelry—from the one-time seller to the entrepreneur. With *Diamonds for Profit* as your guide, you can make money buying and selling diamonds! It will show you how to determine the immediate cash liquidity value of your jewelry so you don't get talked into buying them for less. Also learn how to treasure-hunt for diamonds and jewelry in the classified ads, going-out-of-business sales, and national and local estate auctions in your spare time—and make money at it!
The price is $23.95.

Fredisms

Fredisms is the culmination of a personal life experience which you will be intrigued to discover as you read the Fredism on each page of this uniquely formatted book. Mr. Cuellar touches upon subjects of interest to us all, such as attitudes, health, humor, relationships, God, philosophy, and many others, in a way which will endear the book to a wide variety of readers. It will make a great gift for almost anyone and is easy to read. In fact, you will probably find yourself repeating your most favored Fredism to family and friends before long! **The price is $14.50.**

These books are available in stores or through your favorite online bookseller, or you may order through the mail by calling (800) 275-4047.